RICHARD WILSON ON RICHARD WILSON

'Victor Meldrew is what I'm known for, and what I'm good at, because of David Renwick's writing, and it has given me my rise to fame. But it might never happen again. So I do worry about that to some extent and wonder what it will be like when all the excitement stops. Part of me would be quite pleased because life would be more tranquil, but I would miss all the attention.'

James Roose-Evans is well-known on both sides of the Atlantic as a distinguished theatre director and writer. He directed Sir John Gielgud in his triumphal return to the West End in Hugh Whitemore's *The Best of Friends*, and subsequently Edwige Feuillère in the French production in Paris. His own adaptation of Helene Hanff's *84 Charing Cross Road* won him awards for Best Director and Best Play on Broadway and in the West End. He founded the Hampstead Theatre, and is also the founder of the Bleddfa Trust in Mid-Wales.

BY THE SAME AUTHOR

ONE FOOT ON THE STAGE

The Biography of Richard Wilson

James Roose-Evans

Introduction by
Richard Wilson

ORION

An Orion Paperback
First published in Great Britain by Weidenfeld & Nicolson in 1996
This paperback edition published in 1997 by
Orion Books Ltd,
Orion House, 5 Upper St Martin's Lane,
London, WC2H 9EA.

A.A. Milne 'Solitude' from *Now We Are Six* (Methuen Children's
Books, 1927). By permission of Reed Books Ltd.

Quotations from 'The Journey Back', 'Childhood', 'The Labyrinth',
'Soliloquy', and 'If I Could Know' all taken from *Collected Poems* by
Edwin Muir. By kind permission of Faber and Faber Ltd.

Extract from *William The Rebel* by Richmal Crompton, reproduced by
kind permission of Macmillan.

Quotations from 'Acquainted with the Night', and 'Desert Places' from
The Poetry of Robert Frost edited by Edward Connery Lathem
reproduced by kind permission of the author's Estate and
Jonathan Cape.

A CIP catalogue record for this book
is available from the British Library.

ISBN 0 75281 115 0

Printed and bound in Great Britain by
Guernsey Press Co Ltd,
Guernsey, C.I.

for
BARRY TURNER
friend and colleague
with gratitude

CONTENTS

ILLUSTRATIONS

The author and the publishers are grateful to Richard Wilson for his help in providing photographs. Unless otherwise credited the photographs come from his collection.

Section One
Richard with his sister, Moira.[1]
At the Lady Alice School.
Effie and John Wilson.[1]
With Effie and Moira.[1]
Toots, his first cat.
Play-acting in the back garden at 141 Dunlop Street, Greenock.
Swabbing the latrines.
As Corporal in the Royal Army Medical Corps.
In his room in Singapore, 1958.
With Tiddles in Singapore.
Laboratory technicians at Gateside Hospital, Greenock.[2]
With Margaret Dyer.[2]
With Effie.
The three inseparables: Charlie Murray, Tom Purdie and Richard.
With Charlie Murray.[3]
Role-playing.[3]
Charlie Murray.
Bring Your Own Tuba.[4]
Dark of the Moon.
Laboratory technicians, Paddington Hospital.
A press shot for *English Spoken*.[5]

Section Two
Peter Ransley's *Disabled*.[6]
In S. David Wright's *Look at them Smashing all those Lovely Windows*.
Uncle Vanya.[7]
Early television successes: *Only When I Laugh*; *Tutti Frutti*.
Passage to India.

Hot Metal.[8]
Changing Step: the cast.[9]
With Lenny Henry.[10]
Supporting the campaign for the Bridgewater Four.[11]
One Foot in the Grave.
Under the Hammer.[12]
The newly-elected Rector of Glasgow University.[13]

Sources

1   Moira McLaren
2   Beatrice McCallum
3   Charles Murray
4   Roger Booth
5   Anne Mette Andreassen (collection Maggie Ollerenshaw)
6   Peter Ransley
7   Saul Radomsky
8   © Meridian Broadcasting, 1994
9   BBC Scotland
10 Simon Walker/*The Times*
11 Clare Clifford (collection of Susan Wooldridge)
12 *Daily Star*
13 *The Herald* (Glasgow)

ACKNOWLEDGEMENTS

Because Richard is so essentially a private person, I would like to thank him first for entrusting me with the task of telling his story, and for making time when, in his overcrowded schedule, it was often far from easy.

We began with two days down at Grayshott Hall in Surrey, a house once owned by Lord Tennyson standing in forty-seven acres of ground, now a fashionable health resort to which Richard retreats when the pressure of work threatens to overwhelm him. There he has always the same suite with its hall, sitting room, handsome bedroom, marble bathroom, and balcony overlooking the gardens. *Salus Exeuntibus* – Health to those departing – are the words inscribed over the porch, where guests are asked to leave their shoes. Inside there is indeed something of the feeling of sacred ground, with people speaking in hushed tones and, like members of some religious order, moving around in white robes and bare feet. Here, in between his various treatments and massages, Richard began to talk to me about his life. Since then those conversations have continued over a meal, during a snatched hour between appointments, relaxing over a bottle of wine of an evening, or at the Garrick Club.

Next I would like to thank Richard's sister Moira McLaren, who is ever protective of him and, at our first meeting, clearly very wary of me. But her warmth of welcome, and that of her husband Jimmy, opened hearts and doors. Thanks to Moira I met Beatrice McCallum, who shared many memories of the young Richard at Gateside Hospital; Miss Mabel Irving, his former teacher; and Ed McClusky who, with his wife, now lives in the Wilsons' family home, and who had more memories of Richard's father and Scott's Yard than I have been able to use. On the Isle of Bute I was warmly welcomed by Charlie and Sheila Murray and their daughter Claire, who shared with me the beauty of the island, with its visionary glimpse of Arran at sunset. My especial thanks to my host and friend in Glasgow, Jack Notman, theatre designer and architect, for inviting me to stay in his most elegant home; and to James Convey for taking time one evening, over some beers, to talk about his experience of playing the lead in Richard's film, *Changing Step*.

Among Richard's professional colleagues and friends I am especially indebted to the following: Susan Wooldridge who, surrounded by her diaries and photograph albums, drew richly on her memories; Gordon McDougall for his detailed recollections of the early years in Edinburgh and Manchester; Jack Rosenthal for evoking Manchester in the Granada years, and Maureen Lipman for her memories of the Stables Theatre; Barbara Booth, and Roger Booth who also shared with me his journals of the years when he and Richard were amateur actors; Tom Purdie, finally traced through the fine detective work of Mabel Irving; Dr Anthony Stevens; Monty Berman, who wrote twice from South Africa; Laura and J. J. Walker for their recollections of Singapore in the 1950s; Eleanor Bron, Dinah Stabb, Rosemary Martin, Bridget Turner, Richard Howard, Mike Stott, John Fraser, Alan Rickman, Sir Denis Forman, Hugh Manning, Rima Horton, Anna Massey, Andy de la Tour, Ewan Marshall, Frank Stirling, Max Stafford-Clark, Nancy Meckler, Kevin Elyot, Peter Ransley, Dusty Hughes, Robin Hooper, William Simons, Antony Sher, Saul Radomsky, David Pugh, Billy Russo, Vernon Lawrence, Nicholas de Jongh, Sheila Hancock, Jan Francis, John Michie, Elizabeth Hamilton (mother of Laurie McCann), Susan Belbin, David Renwick, Annette Crosbie, Jenny Topper, Jennie Stoller, Maggie Ollerenshaw, Clive Francis, John Warner, Susie Figgis, Peter Barkworth, Dr John Collee, Jeremy Conway, Patrick Garland, Roy Hanlon, Sheila Wilson and Sarah from the Conway van Gelder office; Jenny Secombe, press officer for the BBC's *One Foot in the Grave*, who gave me access to all the archival material relating to the series; similarly Sue Best of Meridian for *Under the Hammer*; Enid Foster, Librarian of the Garrick Club; Sheila Rose of Hereford who tracked down certain quotations; Evelyn Hannah, Richard's secretary, and Edie, his housekeeper.

My thanks also to the following who lent photographs: Moira McLaren, Beatrice McCallum, Richard Howard, Roger Booth, Maggie Ollerenshaw, Charlie Murray, Susan Wooldridge, Elizabeth Hamilton and, of course, Richard himself. My debt is also to those critics and journalists from whom I have quoted and my apologies to any from whom I may have borrowed unconsciously. I would also like to thank Lee Donald for casting Richard's horoscope which is included in the Appendices.

My thanks to Claudia Solti and Ben Shaw; and Richard Carter who gave me a leg up at the start and so helped more than he knew; Jenny Pearson who listened when I despaired; Mark Treuthardt who tried to teach me how to use a word processor – it was not his fault that I failed – and Hywel Jones for his unfailing friendship.

Finally my thanks to my editor, Ion Trewin, for guiding me through sometimes muddied waters of my own making.

James Roose–Evans
Ballywilliam, and Stanage Park

INTRODUCTION

by Richard Wilson

No account of a life – whether one's own or that of another – can be anything other than incomplete, selective and imperfect. In my case, however, it's undoubtedly the life that's imperfect, rather than the biography! Whenever I have been approached to provide the paints that would fill in the empty pages of the Richard Wilson colouring book, I have never found it difficult to resist the temptation. I might have no hesitation if asked to pose for a photograph (the evidence here is overwhelming, I admit), or to sit for a portrait, but a permanent documentary running to several hundred pages . . . ? Whereas a picture tells a two-dimensional story capturing the outer being – the public 'face' – a work of biography is always an attempt to discover and expose the inner being, the 'soul' or the mind. The portrait becomes metaphysical, no longer merely physical. Why should anyone, except those with an insatiable vanity or incurable tendencies to expose themselves, want to put themselves to such scrutiny . . . other than from the privacy of their psychiatrist's couch?

Odd, I hear you chorus, to hear this shyness coming from a man who spends his waking hours parading in front of audiences and cameras. But the reasons for this reticence are easily explained. Firstly, I never thought I had very much to say about myself, though friends have found it difficult to stop me talking about almost everything else. Secondly, I simply cannot recall any of the necessary details that would make the account fascinating. Indeed, I am in awe of the guests of Dr Anthony Clare or Ms Sue Lawley who can remember the flavour of ice-cream cone they were licking on Camber Sands on a Sunday afternoon in 1936. Not I. Thirdly, I hold firmly to the belief, shared by a number of my professional colleagues, that the private life of an actor should remain sacrosanct, if that actor is to remain believable in any given role. If the performance is going to astonish an audience, if a human being is able to be truly metamorphic, then the less we know about the toe-nail clippings and the belching of the person behind the mask, the better. That's not to say that I haven't relished the honesty of Simon Callow or the wit of David Niven, when they have chosen to strip themselves bare before us.

Neither do I feel that my career, unlike those of, say, Shirley MacLaine or Charlton Heston, is exceptional enough to warrant its chronicling by eminent theatrical historians, or even by myself. As somebody once remarked, autobiography is now as common as adultery, and hardly less reprehensible. This is not false modesty. I am the first to acknowledge that I have had immense good fortune, and that I have achieved a level of popular recognition sadly denied to many in my profession who are far more deserving of it than I am. Perhaps I hold to the belief that if I have anything to communicate, then it isn't the minutiae of my own mundane life, but rather the ideas I want to share as a director. Certainly, I've never had any desire to keep a diary, despite frequently finding myself on location these days with twenty or thirty fellow actors who bitterly resent the moment when they're interrupted from scribbling down their detailed observations, and asked by the director to have a shot at a few lines. Even directors are not immune. I was once in a play directed by Max Stafford-Clark, who kept on the desk in front of him a notebook, which he filled in a neat, tiny hand, with his comments on everybody and everything. All of us were desperate to know what was going down on those ruled pages, and we only found satisfaction (and a few surprises) when he eventually published it.

Unlike Proust, remembrance of things past doesn't much excite or stimulate me. Although I am always impressed by anyone who can associate a piece of music with a specific day in their past, I have little interest in storing unwanted clutter in the attic of my mind. I genuinely believe in living for the day, and the future doesn't worry me that much either. I share with Cyril Connolly the notion that our memories are card-indexes consulted and then returned in disorder by authorities whom we do not control. The very idea of sitting down at a desk for days on end trying to remember incidents or research events fills me with more gloom than an English summer. It's a physical and mental torment of the ultimate kind. I'd be the last person Terry Waite would want as a travelling companion.

It may be a distinctly unfashionable or outdated belief, but I would like my private life to remain private. That's not to say I'm a reincarnation of Greta Garbo, nor am I a candidate for the next available position as an anchorite. Obviously, as a flavoursome actor, I have constantly to deal with the press, to attend public events or shows. And, even if this is more often contractual rather than convivial, I realise there is a job to be done, and I'm willing to do it. But beyond that reasonable amount of ritual unveiling, I see no need to allow my private life to become part of my public life. According to Montaigne (who, ironically, seems to have spent most of his life writing about his own life), a man must keep a little back shop where he can be himself without reserve. In solitude alone can he know true freedom.

Being constantly in the public eye and sharing so much of one's personal life, if one couldn't keep some things utterly private, one would feel denuded. So the private world will remain closed, as will my home. Neither journalists nor Loyd Grossman are allowed into 'my space'. It is not a viewing arena, and I have no wish to share it with the world at large. I used to say this even when I dwelt in a poor bedsitter (West Hampstead in those days, Hampstead these days). Now I have a home of which I am proud, and which I enjoy sharing with those I invite, but just to set the record straight, if any of my neighbours or showbusiness acquaintances are reading this: the rumours are untrue, there isn't an underground swimming-pool nor a first-floor gymnasium nor a triple water-bed.

Inevitably, as one's fame increases, so do stories like that (and some which are far less innocuous). And so I felt both touched and somewhat reassured to learn that James Roose-Evans, a close friend, was willing to write this book to satisfy the persistent demands of publishers. In early discussions, the constant refrain was 'why not an *auto*biography' (partly ghosted by Jimmy) but I found that prospect easier to resist than a three-week-old doughnut. I've since been deeply impressed by my biographer's keenness (the words dog and bone were often not far from mind), and throughout I had the good fortune to be working with a man I trusted, someone who shares a passion for theatre and an understanding of what directing is all about. We had various lengthy sessions where we would talk about childhood, about my early career, about training for the acting profession ... and I'm sure he lost count of the maddening number of times I uttered the phrase, 'I just can't remember their name ... '.

In fact, Jimmy has researched my life and the people who've passed through it with such tenacity that when I eventually forced myself to pick up the manuscript (a task I put off for as long as I was able), I came across names of people I hadn't thought about in over forty years — the faces remain a blur. There's something about reading the story of your own existence which is terribly daunting. The author's thoroughness suddenly appears a quite remarkable feat of scholarship, while of course there are opinions and facts which don't agree with one's own. The result of that research is here for you to read yourself, and it does seem to be a reasonably comprehensive account of what I'm about. But don't assume it's the full story, the whole picture. As Doctor Johnson opined, how can you expect another man to keep your secrets when you cannot keep them yourself ...

As the book goes to print, I stand back a trifle amazed at the path my career has taken, but more especially grateful for the diversity in my existence that this small measure of success has afforded me. Aside from acting, I am invited to direct for both stage and radio. I have been profoundly honoured by being elected Rector of Glasgow University by the students of that august seat of learning. This has opened my eyes to many of the problems currently besetting those involved in education, and I am both saddened and angered every time I open a letter from a drama student who has been unable to obtain funding or a grant to follow their dream. Of course, I'm not ignorant of the desperate economic difficulties within further education, but if the post of Rector offers me any opportunity to amend or even to publicise this sorry state of affairs, then I shall seize it keenly. It has also been an immensely rewarding challenge to have been appointed a roving ambassador of the Voluntary Service Overseas organisation, encouraging and supporting the work of young and older people, who themselves are having to fight funding cuts while trying to provide life-saving aid in developing countries. No less enjoyable is my task as board member of the Soho Theatre Company, trying to raise enough funds to continue their long tradition at the forefront of new writing in this country. Finally, I give the time and support I can to the Actors' Centre and to the Labour Party which, as I write, offers the brightest hope for the future of any potential government in Britain. Being in the public eye has meant a constant stream of generous invitations to attend functions from spheres which I would never normally have encountered – almost all of them enriching for me as an actor and a director. Sadly, I'm simply unable to accept as many of these as I would like.

So, there it is in summary . . . now here it is in a little more detail. My apologies if some of the colours are not as bright as you'd wished, or if the person behind Victor turns out to be not quite as grumpy as his alter ego. Arguably, at sixty, it's the account of a life which is only just beginning. Perhaps, after all, there'll be something left for me to write about some day, should the fancy take me before senility finally does. As I turn these pages, I silently ask, 'who on earth am I to warrant all these words?'

The rest, as the immortal poet averred, is silence.

Seek the beginnings, learn from whence ye came,
And know the various earth of which you are made.

Edwin Muir, *The Journey Back*

PROLOGUE

Every so often a television series turns up that becomes not only a much-loved national institution but also a barometer of the times in which we live. In the nineties it is undoubtedly *One Foot in the Grave*. Who hasn't, like Victor Meldrew, let out a heartfelt cry of 'I don't believe it!' as our society and its institutions appear increasingly to fragment and the centre falls apart? Is it any surprise that a third of the British population tunes in to the series? It is an extraordinary phenomenon. While much of the credit must go to the author, David Renwick, the series would be unimaginable, as Charles Spencer wrote in the *Daily Telegraph*, 'without the superb performance of Richard Wilson. After years of solid but not especially high profile work, he has become, at 57, one of the biggest and best known stars of the century.'

These days Richard is inextricably linked in the public mind with the character of Victor Meldrew. Everyone wants to hear him say, 'I don't believe it!' I recall going into Tandy in the Finchley Road to rescue a taped interview with Richard which had become loose on the spool. As the young technician tested the tape he said suddenly, 'That's *him*! That's Victor Meldrew's voice.' When I explained that I was writing this biography he asked, 'Have you got him to say *it*?'

People really do expect you to perform when they see you in the street, observes Richard; 'They also expect you to be witty, which I'm not. I'm an actor, not a comic.' The big danger, he says, is losing his temper. 'That's when people are going to say, "Oh, he's doing a Victor!"' He can sense people at times trying to goad him into it. Taxi-drivers will often only agree to take him, 'providing you stay civil, guv!'

If success has come late to Richard he is grateful to have it now, in his fifties. 'Young actors might think early success carries on, but I'm old enough and wise enough to know that it could stop

3

suddenly. It must be terrible to be lionised as a youngster and then lose it as you grow up. I've been lucky to break out. There are probably thousands like me in Scotland who won't.'

He has never forgotten the days when he was totally unknown. He also remembers, when they were recording the first series of *One Foot in the Grave*, being very excited, on looking out of his dressing-room window, to see huge queues forming all round the building; but when he got into the studio it was only half full. 'They weren't queuing for us at all; they were there to see Bruce Forsyth!' Today it is very different: each recording of a new series of the programme has long queues and people fight to get in. But it wasn't always so popular. It took time to catch on. The turn around in viewing figures came after the second series, when the writing became more acerbic, and the performances more finely attuned.

According to a TV Audience Report for 1994 the average audience for the series was then 17.2 million, the highest viewing figure of any sitcom series, and this shot to over 18 million for the 1995 Christmas Special 'The Wisdom of the Witch'. Over ninety per cent of the respondents said it appealed to their sense of humour and agreed that it was a high-quality, enjoyable programme, with a well-written script. A staggering ninety-seven per cent thought the characters of Victor and Margaret Meldrew, the latter played by Annette Crosbie, worked well together. Nine in every ten said they would like more. And it seems, for the time being, that there will be more of Victor Meldrew to delight a nation caught in the frustration of a recession.

Success, as Richard admits, is out of all proportion. 'Newspapers elevate you into a cult figure, the public buys it and expects you to be grumpy!' Fame, however, has made other differences. When, in 1994, he was directing a play at the Royal Exchange in Manchester, he went to Old Trafford and found he was treated like a god. Bobby Charlton said to him, 'I didn't know you were a Manchester United Supporter!'

'Since 1968,' replied Richard.

'Well, I never knew that.'

'You didn't want to then!' came the swift riposte.

Without Victor Meldrew Richard would not be able to command six-figure sums for commercials – in the British Telecom TV advertisement he played the salesman in a dress shop, struggling to accommodate the world's most impossible customer, played by Maureen Lipman. Without Victor Meldrew he would not have been able to make his debut in the West End in a leading role. When he goes to watch tennis at Wimbledon people stand up to take his photograph. Even on holiday in America he cannot escape. David Renwick describes meeting Richard for lunch in Boston when a group of English tourists, who had recognised him, started taking photographs. When Richard was in Portugal making the 1994 Christmas Special 'One Foot in the Algarve', he went shopping in the local supermarket only to find British expatriates and holiday-makers taking out their cameras and going clickety-click. Even on a remote island off the coast of Kenya, on New Year's Day 1994, resting on the sands with casting director Susie Figgis and her husband, someone came up to him and said, 'Excuse me, but are you? . . . Is it?' All of which may explain why he prefers to stay at the Ritz or Gleneagles rather than in small country hotels, where he would have less privacy and feel compelled to be polite to those guests who would, inevitably, come up to him and say, 'Are you? Is it?'

Success has not only brought fame and financial security to Richard, as well as a handsome home in Hampstead but, perhaps more importantly, the freedom to do the kind of work he really wants. He can afford to pick and choose. In addition he is able to use his fame to help those causes he believes in, from the Labour Party and the Bridgewater Four Support Group, to the Great Ormond Street Hospital for Sick Children. He is also a man who, in spite of winning two BAFTAs (British Association of Film and Television Awards) for his performance as Victor Meldrew (awards that he proudly displays on his shelves), as well as an OBE, will not yield to the more superficial blandishments of success. Recently he turned down a lucrative offer from a national travel agency, which wanted to have mobiles of Victor Meldrew hanging in every one of its shops throughout the country. He also turned down *This Is Your Life*.

Susan Belbin who, as producer and director of *One Foot in the Grave*, had first been approached by *This Is Your Life*, thought it was a good idea and even decided how to surprise Richard. He would be doing a scene in which Annette Crosbie had to make an entrance. They would film it, to make sure they had the scene in the can, when Susan Belbin would step in to say, 'Sorry, but we need to do a retake of that.' Then, instead of Annette walking in on cue, it would be Michael Aspel, the presenter of *This Is Your Life*. In the meantime, however, Richard's sister Moira had had to be consulted and she, knowing what an intensely private individual her brother is, began to get increasingly jittery about the idea. Finally, without realising it, she let the cat out of the bag (since the individual chosen should never know beforehand) by telephoning Richard and asking him if he really wanted to do the programme. He at once said no, and the programme was abandoned. He would have been deeply embarrassed to go through the public exposure of *This Is Your Life*.

Richard believes passionately that an actor should guard his creative centre from the public gaze. 'Giving away too much of yourself as a person gets in the way of what you are trying to do as an actor. Every time you see such an actor on the stage or screen you are seeing the personality that has been sold. When I am watching a performance by someone famous it takes me far longer to put them into the role they are playing, and that makes it harder for them as well. I just don't like talking about myself. Gossip about other people never interests me and I don't see why anyone should want to know about me.'

But, of course, they do; and it is not only his friends who would like to know about his early years, but also several million viewers. It is only natural that we should want to know something of each other's story.

Perhaps it is fortunate for Richard that, being so private a person, he has not had to cope with Hollywood stardom. Susie Figgis says, 'Everything about Richard is very private. I wonder if anyone really knows him?' That he should so guard his privacy (he will never allow journalists or photographers into his home) is not surprising given that his astrological sign is Cancer, the most secretive of all signs. It is almost impossible to get a Cancerian to trot out his deepest secrets or wear his heart upon his sleeve. Cancerians also have a strong urge for security, for what is known and familiar, therefore safe. For a Cancerian his home is his citadel. Once Richard enters his home the drawbridge is pulled up behind him.

These days because of the pressures of work he rarely entertains at home. Recently he remarked to his secretary Evelyn, 'I must get some chairs for the dining room.' She replied, 'What on earth for? You never entertain!' Instead of having friends to dine at his glass-topped table, with the French windows opening onto the garden, he finds it easier to meet in a restaurant.

The other most distinctive feature of Cancerians, as the astrologer and psychotherapist Liz Greene points out, is that, 'Cancer needs to be needed. He needs to love, nurture and cherish, to play the role of Mother in some form or other.' This is true of Richard, not only in his remarkable generosity, but in the way he treats everyone, from the public to the press (journalists love him, comments the theatre producer David Pugh, 'because he respects them and knows that they have also a job to do') to his fellow actors, or if he is visiting someone in hospital. The psychiatrist Monty Berman, who worked with him on the film *Changing Step*, observes, 'His care of the actors and of the whole crew was a lesson in democratic behaviour which it is a pity more do not follow.'

Though often severe and austere in his outward appearance, the depths of Richard's feelings can be glimpsed on occasions, as in a film for Comic Relief, in one of the refugee camps in Northern Uganda holding a newborn baby, its face covered with flies. But much, if not most of the time, that depth of feeling is hidden behind a carefully constructed front. As one friend remarked, 'I just feel that with Richard, especially on social occasions, you never get the chance to talk with him, or get into the real Richard, because he's socially so clever and funny and adept.'

In his sixty years he has travelled a long way from his unlikely beginnings. The actress Dinah Stabb, who has known him since the early 1960s at the old Traverse Theatre in Edinburgh, remarks,

'He seems to have made incredible voyages into himself.' There has been, on that journey, private suffering which he has always faced courageously, while he has learned to accept stoically that no partner is now likely to come his way with whom he can share his life. He remains a solitary, but of this side of his life, and of whatever disappointments he may have felt (close friends like Susie Figgis say that he regrets having had no children), he will not speak.

Often, in writing this book, I have been reminded of Hamlet's words to Rosencrantz and Guildenstern: 'You would pluck out the heart of my mystery; you would sound me from my lowest note to the top of my compass; and there is much music, excellent voice, in this little organ, yet cannot you make it speak. 'Sblood, do you think I am easier to be played on than a pipe? Call me what instrument you will, though you can fret me, you cannot play upon me.'

About each of us there is a mystery, as well as a secret immensity, which the creative artist needs to protect, and none more so than the actor who has to work through his own emotions and psychology, drawing from deep wells within himself.

Whatever other roles may yet await him there is little doubt for the present that Richard will be remembered principally for *One Foot in the Grave*, in the same way that John Cleese will always be associated with *Fawlty Towers*. Richard's performance as Victor Meldrew is not only brilliant comedic playing but is, at the same time, the most vulnerable of all his television performances. The reason for this may lie in the simple fact that he plays Victor as a Scot. For almost all his other roles, in *Only When I Laugh*, *Hot Metal*, *Whoops*, *Apocalypse*, *The Sheik of Pickersgill*, Richard has assumed an English accent; but in playing Victor he has gone back to his roots. In order, therefore, fully to appreciate his achievement as Victor we, too, need to go back to his first beginnings in the Scottish town of Greenock.

ACT I

Long time he lay upon the sunny hill,
To his father's house below securely bound,
Far off the silent, changing sound was still,
With the black islands lying thick around.
...
Over the sound a ship so slow would pass
That in the black hill's gloom it seemed to lie.
The evening sound was smooth like sunken glass,
And time seemed finished ere the ship passed by.

Great tiny rocks slept round him where he lay,
Moveless as they, more still as evening came,
The grasses threw straight shadows far away,
And from the house his mother called his name.

Edwin Muir, *Childhood*

1

Growing up in Greenock

At precisely twenty minutes to eleven on the evening of 9 July 1936, in the town of Greenock in Renfrewshire, Scotland, Iain Carmichael Wilson was born, later to be known as Richard Wilson, the actor. As the midwife opened the bedroom door of the upstairs flat in 141 Dunlop Street she saw a small seven-year-old girl in her nightdress standing outside, looking up anxiously. The nurse smiled and said, 'It's all right, Moira. You can go back to bed now. You have a little brother. You'll see him in the morning.'

Today, Greenock, a half-hour's drive from Glasgow on a new motorway, has something of the feel of a ghost town. With the closure of the shipyards, leading to massive unemployment, it is very different from the place where Richard Wilson grew up. Of the industries of Richard's childhood, only Tate and Lyle remains.

The biggest of all the shipyards, Scott's, where Richard's father worked, had been established in 1711 by John Scott. Beginning with herring 'buses' and small craft, it was to play an important role over two and a half centuries in the history of marine construction, from warships to submarines. But after 1962 shipbuilding declined, yards going at the rate of almost one a year. Although Scott's amalgamated with Lithgow's in 1970, and in 1977 became a part of British Shipbuilders, it finally closed in 1984, the last of the great Greenock shipyards. With the passing of the town's major industry, there was a sense of bereavement as though the community had suffered an amputation from which it has not recovered.

Dunlop Street, where the Wilsons lived, was part of a new housing development in the late 1920s, and because the rents were slightly higher, it was occupied by a stable, lower middle-class church-going community with a strong sense of class distinctions. Even in the 1930s it was still common for Greenock girls to go into service in the big houses on the west side of Greenock where the more affluent – the doctors and lawyers – lived in handsome houses. Nelson Street divided the west side from the poorer east. They used to say in Greenock that if you made it across Nelson Street you had 'crossed the Jordan'; in other words, you had arrived. It was this ingrained class system that was to politicise Richard and so many of his contemporaries, making them deeply committed Socialists.

Like all the other houses in the street, number 141 was divided into two flats. The Wilsons lived in the upper half, while the McCullochs lived on the ground floor. Each house had its own back garden but, being semi-detached, each pair of houses shared a lawn, with no divider down the middle. Each half of the lawn had its own clothes line, which meant that on Mondays Mrs Wilson would do her wash in the upstairs kitchen, and hang out her clothes on the line to dry, whilst Mrs McCulloch would do her washing on Tuesdays. The same pattern was followed in each house along the street. Richard remembers Mondays: their kitchen was always full of steam, while on wet Mondays it would also be festooned with damp clothes (having been squeezed out on a mangle which was brought out each week and screwed to the side of the sink) hung across the room to dry. Mondays also meant only soup and pudding for dinner as Mrs Wilson had no time to cook a proper meal.

Their parents' room was at the front, while the smaller bedroom at the back overlooking the gardens (no fences separated one garden from another), with its two single beds, its large wardrobe and ottoman, was shared by Richard and Moira. Moira was twelve when she was moved to the living room and had to make do with a sofa that opened up into a bed, while Richard was given the back bedroom to himself. Generally the family ate in the kitchen except when they had visitors; a table would then be set up in the living room, a practice that Moira still observes to this day.

The flat had few books or pictures, but because Mrs Wilson's brothers were sailors and one a tea-planter in India, it was full of brass spear carriers, vases and pieces of ornamental sculpture. One vase has a particular memory for Richard. It had been placed on the mantelpiece with a scarf wedged under it to dry in front of the fire. Richard pulled at the scarf and the brass vase fell and split open his head. Nor will he forget the large ottoman in the back bedroom which was used to store blankets and sheets; once, while still quite small, he was playing inside it, pretending he was in a motor-car, when the lid fell down and he was trapped. That's it! he thought. He can't remember who let him out but thinks it must have been Moira, whose especial responsibility he had become almost from the moment of his birth.

He and Moira used to play in their father's garden shed. Today it is still in use, but has been transferred to the house nearby, where Moira now lives with her husband Jimmy McLaren and their sons. Moira and Richard turned it into a shop, building a counter out of a plank and two uprights, and making cakes out of mud which they then decorated with flower petals. Sometimes they were joined by other children, playing various characters, and taking it in turns to 'keep shop'. Moira also invented a game in which Richard pretended he was the last baby in the world and Moira had to buy him. Half a century later this game sometimes returns to him in the form of a dream.

While Mr McCulloch looked after the front garden, Mr Wilson took care of the side and back, growing lettuces and beetroot, with tomatoes in a little greenhouse at the end. He also loved roses, several of which have since been transplanted to Moira and Jimmy's garden. 'Working in a shipyard was not what he wanted,' says Richard. 'My father was really a frustrated farmer.' He recalls after his father stayed with cousins in Leicester one of them asked him, 'Well, did you have a good time, Johnnie?'

'Aye, very good!'

'And what was the best part of the week, then?'

'I think it was in the train on the way down. There was this lovely herd of Friesians I saw.' As Richard comments: 'Show my father a herd of cows and he was a happy man. He would just stand and look at them.'

It was their mother Euphemia (*née* Colquhoun), or Effie as she was known to most people, who ran the house. Vivacious and out-going, quite the opposite of her husband, she was a natural come-dienne, and it is from her, says Moira, that Richard gets his sense of humour and comedy. But when it came to money matters their father's word was final, so that if Effie wanted to buy anything she would have to wheedle her way around him. Since he adored her, she nearly always succeeded. Although a quiet man, on occasions he loved blowing his trumpet – at local dances. This was how they had first met. He continued to play until losing his teeth when, as he said, 'You can't play the trumpet if you've got no teeth.'

At Scott's, where John Wilson was chief time-keeper, he always wore a suit and a bowler hat. Off-duty he preferred a tweed jacket and a 'bunnet' – a cloth cap, the kind that Richard himself wears nowadays. 'I've kept the last one he ever bought. We don't have any family treasures which have passed down from generation to generation; we're working-class Scots. But my father's cap is very dear to me.'

Although she was no dressmaker, Effie was a neat and tidy dresser, and used to encourage Moira to buy clothes, 'because when you're married you may not be able to!' She was a much more volatile and highly strung character than her husband. She was also a hypochondriac and suffered from a nervous stomach (which Richard has inherited), as well as a chronic throat, the latter clearly related to smoking. On one occasion she came home with a bottle of medicine which she was supposed to shake for ten minutes before taking a dose, and Richard can remember thinking: I wonder if that's psychological, that if you shake it for long enough it is bound to do some good? He shook the bottle himself, trying to imagine how it might work. 'She was always ill, my mother. She was quite frail, a thin woman, always on the go. She was always carrying bags of "messages" from the shops, either for ourselves or for neighbours. She was always looking after other people.'

Both parents loved playing cards, though only for pennies.

When Moira was old enough to be left to look after Richard, John and Effie spent one evening a week with Dougie McIntyre, a bachelor farmer, and two of his farm-hands. But Effie's favourite treat was to go off on her own on Wednesday evenings to one of Greenock's seven or eight cinemas. Whereas today Greenock has none, then West Blackhall Street, with the King's, the Regal, the Central, the Hippodrome, the BB Cinema, and the Argyll Theatre, was known as Greenock's 'West End'. The Central was referred to locally as 'the Ranch' because it showed mainly westerns; it also had a large coal fire in the foyer which, on winter evenings, was always welcome.

In those days, and up until the late fifties, there was a real sense of neighbourhood, with each street its own community. At that time very few had cars, televisions were all but unknown until the Coronation in 1953, nor did many homes have telephones, so that people were much more dependent upon one another. 'As neighbours,' says Moira, 'we were all of us there if needed, but respecting each other's privacy.'

Their father refused to have a telephone. If there was trouble at the yard and he had to be called out, someone at Scott's would telephone the McCullochs downstairs. They never minded, for this was part of being a good neighbour, like running errands for each other.

At the end of the street was Barr's Cottage, a cluster of small shops including a Co-op, a dairy and a newspaper shop where Richard used to collect his comics: *Dandy, Beano, Rover,* and *The Adventure* which contained a serial story, *Wilson, Seeker of Champions,* about a super-athlete in a black tracksuit who ran everywhere in bare feet. Richard remembers also taking *The Eagle,* and still has the very first issue. It was a revolution in comics, being better produced with superior artwork. The streets were quieter then despite the familiar sound of horses' hooves and the rumble of wheels. The baker's cart called regularly. At the sound of his handbell Moira, or Richard, looking out of their landing window, would call out to their mother, 'Baker!' and race downstairs to buy the week's supply of bread – and always some large doughnuts, still warm and oozing with blood-red jam. Another regular was a fishmonger known as 'the herring man'. with his dainty horse-drawn cart. At regular times of the year 'rag' women came visiting, carrying on their backs a large sack, looking for old clothes which they would then sell elsewhere. Gypsies, too, appeared, selling bunches of white heather for luck, offering to tell fortunes, and none too pleased if they weren't given something.

For children the streets became an extended playground. Richard was always popping in and out of neighbours' houses for a slice of cake or a 'sweetie'. Also, for a small boy, there was the curiosity of seeing how other people lived. The Graham family across the street were 'quite well educated. Unlike our house they had a lot of books. They had this copy of Dante's *Inferno*, illustrated by Gustav Doré, with gruesome pictures of souls in torment. I always thought it a great treat to get a look at that!'

The Grahams had several sons and one daughter, Nancy, who was something of a tomboy, of whom Mrs Graham, who was a witty and elegant woman, often despaired. Once, hearing a terrible crash, Mrs Graham remarked to Richard, 'That's Nancy fallen again. She's probably stood on her nose!' At the time he thought this the funniest thing he had ever heard. Nancy was the only girl allowed in Richard's gang, in which three of the boys were called Iain. One day they were stopped by a policeman for playing football in the street.

'What's your name, sonny?' he asked of the first.

'Iain – Iain Allison.'

He turned to the next and asked the same question.

'Iain – Iain Cameron.'

By now Richard was already quaking in his boots as the policeman turned to him.

'What's yours, sonny?'

Iain – Iain Wilson!'

'Come off it, none of that cheek, lad!'

'Honestly it is!' replied Richard. In the end they were let off with a warning.

On the other side of Dunlop Street was Greenock Prison, the

high walls of which can still be seen today between the houses opposite. In fact, number 132 Dunlop Street, where the Grahams lived, backed onto the prison, separated from it by a large field which was worked by the prisoners. Richard can remember seeing them drag the plough. In one of several games to do with the prison they had to steal turnips from the field. This they thought very daring. 'We tried to eat them but they were very very raw and tasteless. I suppose it was the idea of stealing from a prison that excited us.' They also used to gather cigarette ends from the gutters and smuggle these to the prisoners when the guards weren't looking.

As with other siblings, Richard and his sister would fight and squabble. 'He used to get more than me on his plate,' recalls Moira; while Richard remembers that he would cry out, 'She's got more currants in her rice pudding,' or 'more chips than I have!' Effie would scream at them in exasperation, 'Stop that fighting. You'll drive me mad!' Her punishment would be to refuse to speak to them, which always upset Richard – the idea of being cut off from his mother's affections. He was, without doubt, his mother's blue-eyed baby, as Moira says, while she was Daddy's girl. When they went out as a family it would be Richard who accompanied their mother, and Moira their father.

Sunday was an important day in Greenock. Just about everyone went to church, twice, while for the children there was also Sunday school. Religion was, and still is, taken very seriously in Scotland although now, as elsewhere, the numbers attending have sharply declined. Today a number of the churches in Greenock have become second-hand furniture warehouses, and the congregations are focused on four main churches. John Wilson was an elder of the kirk but both Moira and Richard attended Sunday school at a different church, Mount Pleasant, which had a lively youth club and drama group which Richard eventually joined. In his early teens he also became, for a time, a Sunday school teacher there. Sometimes the children would accompany their father to his church but had always to be alert to keep him awake 'because he was a great snoozer, our father'. Their mother never went to church. She was not a believer, but this was not a matter they were ever allowed to discuss. The only time Richard can recall seeing his mother in church was for Moira's wedding. But if, on Sundays, Effie stayed at home to cook the dinner, she was strict about the children observing the usual Presbyterian customs. Thus on Sundays the children were not allowed to play out of doors; they might go for sedate walks, but only in their best clothes.

There was never any alcohol in the house; and if Richard's father, like most men at that period, rarely showed affection in a tactile way, Richard never doubted that his father loved him. Both parents did, however, smoke heavily, as did most people, so that daring to smoke was, for many boys as they entered puberty, one of the earliest forms of rebellion. When Richard was twelve, a neighbour, Mrs Steel, reported to Effie that from her upstairs window in Drummond Street she had seen Richard and a group of boys smoking on a bomb site. Effie rounded on Richard, telling him he was never to smoke again without her permission. And he never did. Only when he had left school and was studying for his examinations did his parents give him one or two cigarettes a night.

Often on Sundays, especially when they were younger, John Wilson would take both children with him to his office at Scott's. Richard loved to sit at his father's high desk, playing at keeping accounts; or else he would rummage around in the cupboards looking for old notebooks and ledgers which were no longer needed and which he would carry home. Paper of any kind was always his father's present to him.

One of Richard's most abiding memories is of his father sitting up late at night at home, wearing a green eyeshade, going through the men's overtime slips. Ironically, it was never suggested that he himself should be paid overtime. Being the chief time-keeper at Scott's, which employed a few thousand men, meant that he was responsible for all the other time-keepers. Each foreman had a small book containing overtime slips which, when stamped, showed that the man in question had put in extra hours; he would take this to the ordinary time-keeper, not Mr Wilson, to be

18

stamped. Each man would then enter up how many hours of over-time he had put in, and drop it into an open box.

Ed McClusky, who was an apprentice electrician at Scott's and remembers Richard's father very clearly: 'He knew every man and boy there, both his name and number,' and who now lives with his wife in the Wilsons' old home at 141 Dunlop Street, explained to me how the system was open to abuse. 'The stamps were the kind you could buy in an ordinary shop and there were pads with different coloured inks, which the time office would swop about so that one day it might be red, another green, and so on. One man would go and get his overtime slip stamped and the others would say, 'What colour is it?' If he answered 'red,' they stamped their own slips red and dropped them into the box on their way out, as there was never anyone on duty at that time. So, if you didn't want to work one night you could get one of the lads to stamp your overtime slip for you, and similarly you would do it for him on another occasion. This went on for years.'

Once it was found the system was being abused, the foremen took to checking, with the result that many men were fired for cheating. Richard has never forgotten, as a very small boy, walk-ing along the street with his father, when one of these men swore at Mr Wilson. Horrified that anyone should dislike his father, it was his first intimation of a much harsher world outside.

Just inside the main gates of Scott's was John Wilson's office where the men had to report on arrival for work. He would hand each man a brass disc with his number on it which was then dropped in a box outside. When all the men were in and the gates closed, John Wilson would then come out of his office and hang up the brass discs on a long board. One of Richard's other vivid mem-ories is of standing inside the chief time-keeper's office at the end of a day, looking out at the hundreds of men lined up, waiting for the hooter to blow and the gates to open, and there was his father, in his bowler and raincoat, walking up and down in front of them. 'None of them dared move until the hooter went, when he shot back into the office as phalanxes of men poured out of the gates.'

The presence of a major shipbuilding industry at Greenock

19

meant that it was always likely to be a target for enemy bombing during the war. Almost everyone had a shelter in their garden, or shared one with their neighbours, as the Wilsons did with the Athringtons next door. It was said that as soon as you heard the sirens going the next sound you heard was all the lavatory chains in the tenement buildings being pulled before everyone went to the shelters. Like other small boys (he was only three when the war began) Richard found it exciting having to get out of bed when the warning began, put on his purple siren suit, and make his way down to the Athringtons' Anderson shelter, which was all grassed over, knowing there would be extra cups of tea, biscuits and sing-songs. On one evening, however, when the siren nearest to them, on the prison wall, was late in going off, they didn't have time to get to the shelter and had to crouch under their parents' bed, listening to the whine and explosion of the bombs all around.

Although Greenock had experienced minor raids in 1940 and early 1941, it was the attacks on 6 and 7 May 1941 which are remembered in Greenock as The Blitz. The first raid started shortly after midnight on 6 May when about fifty German planes attacked the town for two hours, causing widespread damage. Worse, however, was to come on the following night. The sirens sounded at 12.15 a.m. on 7 May, with incendiary bombs being dropped around the perimeter of the town, causing a ring of fire from the north side of the Clyde to behind Loch Thom. A second attack was concentrated on the east end and town centre. Unfortunately, the distillery in Inglestone Street, which was quite close to Dunlop Street, was one of the first places to be hit and acted as a beacon for the rest of the bombers. Although still only five at the time, Richard remembers this raid as though it were but yesterday. Such was the force of a bomb dropped at the end of their street that the door of the Athringtons' shelter blew open and, looking up, he saw tracer bullets and a dog fight in the sky, while the youngest of the three Athrington girls was having hysterics. When they got back to their own house they found all the windows blown out and the ceilings down.

The third attack that night came shortly after 2 a.m. when

parachute landmines and heavy high explosives caused widespread damage. It was estimated that some 250–300 German aircraft had taken part in this second raid. About 3.30 in the morning the 'All Clear' was sounded, by which time the whole town appeared to be burning, and many buildings were damaged or destroyed.

Out of a total of 18,000 houses nearly 10,000 suffered some form of damage, and of these, 1,000 were totally destroyed. Both sugar refineries were hit by landmines; the distillery and Rankin and Blackmore's foundry were badly damaged, and Dellingburn power station put out of action. The municipal buildings were also extensively damaged, while both St Andrew's Square church and St Laurence's church were left as shells. Surprisingly, damage to the shipyards was minimal – Lamont's dry dock and Scott's head office were the most serious casualties. Over the two nights 280 people were killed, and over 1,200 injured. Moira remembers a bomb falling at the Thom Street dam, 'when Mrs McCartney was killed ...' Everybody knew somebody who had been affected in one way or another.

It is easy to understand how, after this, Richard was always frightened when his father, who was a fire-watcher, came into the back bedroom to take down his gas mask and helmet from the top of the wardrobe, and he would snuggle down in his bed pretending to be fast asleep. Because his earliest memories are of the war, everything that happened then, such as walking in the blackout, seemed natural to Richard. Occasionally he and his father went to call on relatives or friends, and would creep their way forward in the darkened streets, daring to point their torch downwards for only a few seconds at a time. They had to be especially careful not to crash into the baffle walls which many had built outside their front doors to prevent shattered glass falling in after the bomb blasts.

Similarly, having known nothing else, Richard took for granted the simple food of wartime, with marmalade made from carrots and very little fresh fruit other than apples from local orchards; so that when, after the second raid, says Richard, 'my Uncle Dave from Glasgow, home on leave from the Merchant Navy, suddenly turned up the next day in a lorry loaded with food for us and for our neighbours, it was like manna from heaven.'

During the war Effie worked several days a week at the community centre for the Women's Voluntary Service, helping to prepare meals for the many servicemen from all over the world, some of whom she would invite back to the house for tea. It was when America entered the war that GI soldiers started arriving, wooing the girls with their gifts of nylons, packs of Marlboro and Pall Mall cigarettes, and boxes of chocolates. Not surprisingly, many of the local girls subsequently married GIs and went to live in the States, whilst others married Polish or German prisoners of war. Richard has a memory of one Christmas when an Australian sailor told him to close his eyes and hold out his hand. When he opened his eyes it was to find a tiny black banana, the first he had ever seen.

In the weeks before Christmas there was great activity in the Wilson kitchen, with Effie making currant cakes for all their relatives, using their currant ration, especially saved for months, while John Wilson cut out the greaseproof paper to line the square and round tins. Moira and Richard helped to stir the mixture, but if they tried to taste it their mother at once held up her hand, covered with dough, and said, 'If you don't leave it alone I'll throw this at you!' For Christmas Day she regularly invited cousins and aunts so that there would be about a dozen crowded around the table in the small living room.

At the Christmas just after the Greenock Blitz, when Richard was six, he thought Santa Claus had forgotten him. Each Christmas morning he and Moira got up at six o'clock, while their parents were still asleep, to look at their presents. They began with the stockings at the end of each bed, after which they would start on their bigger presents, placed in two separate piles. On this particular Christmas morning they quickly found Moira's large pile, but there appeared to be nothing for Richard. He was convinced he had been forgotten until, under the living-room table, concealed by the long cloth, they found a wheelbarrow, made by a friend of his father, packed high with gifts. In the continuing aftermath of the raids Richard was often seen on the streets with this wheelbarrow, helping neighbours move their bits and pieces.

When finally he went to school, he had only to walk down the road to the Lady Alice School but, until he was old enough to go on his own, Moira escorted him there and back three times a day (they always came home for midday dinner, as did his father), a task that she often found irksome. About a thousand children attended the school, which was hopelessly overcrowded because the local authority, while building more houses, had failed to build enough schools. With forty children to a class, many had to be housed in community centres for their lessons and extra staff hired to teach them.

Margaret MacLean, who now works as a secretary at Greenock High School, was a contemporary of Richard's at Lady Alice and remembers him as 'quite a clever lad, a joker, but his head was often in the clouds. The teacher would send him off for something and he'd return a few minutes later with a sheepish look on his face, having completely forgotten what he had been asked to do.'

What Richard enjoyed most at this stage was making up stories. Although during the war toys were scarce, he had a toy motorcycle with a rider on it, and he used to invent stories about his bike for the other boys in his class.

Making up stories was the first step towards acting on a stage. Then, at the age of eleven, he made his debut as the King in *The Princess and the Pea*, in which he wore a pair of girl's black gym knickers stuffed with paper to make them look like pantaloons. It was then that he found he could make people laugh.

2

Don't be Stupid, Boy – You Can't Speak!

I have a house where I go
When there's too many people,
I have a house where I go
Where no one can be;
I have a house where I go,
Where nobody ever says 'No';
Where no one says anything – so
There is no one but me.

A. A. Milne, *Now We Are Six*

When Richard was about nine his need for privacy, now a marked feature of his character, first began to assert itself; he would retreat to the loft by putting a chair on a table in order to open the trapdoor. 'That was my secret, my private place. I was still sharing the back room with Moira and so I had nowhere of my own. I loved shutting myself off and away, hearing people moving about below. My father, who was a very quiet man, had only his garden shed where he could be alone. And I had the loft where I used to sit reading my comics and the *Picture Post*.'

One of Richard's earliest secrets was a stray cat he found and which he kept hidden in a cupboard under the stairs for several weeks, feeding it with dried egg and milk, hoping his mother would not find out, which, of course, she did. Toots, as the cat was called, lived on for eighteen years and when Richard eventually moved to London, his mother, in her weekly letter, always included kisses from Toots. He was very upset when Toots died. Although unable to have a cat today he has thought at times of one day running a cattery. When he lived at Tudor Close in Belsize Park, north London, a cat from the flat above, Tiger, used to run out to meet Richard whenever it heard him coming. But he was strict. If Moira came to stay, he would say to Tiger, 'Come and talk to Moira. She's come all the way from Greenock to see you.' And then add to Moira, 'Whatever you do, don't feed him!'

With the ending of the war in 1945 there were street parties in Greenock, and slowly luxuries began to creep back into the shops. Richard remembers Mr Martin, the projectionist at the BB Cinema, calling at their house one day with a tiny tub of Lyons' ice cream, the first he had ever seen, and remarking, 'Ice cream's back again!' Similarly, chocolate biscuits began to appear at the canteen at Scott's and John Wilson would always bring one or two back at the end of the day.

Although he was quite a good runner, Richard wasn't very good at football, and while quite agile – he could put his legs over his shoulders – he was acutely self-conscious about his thin and bony body. 'I used to pray to God to make me fat, and I think it was his failure to do that which finally destroyed my illusions about God. I thought, you're not going to do anything for me, Chum!'

It was while at the Lady Alice that he first saw a boy of his own age who was disabled, and he was deeply moved by this. 'Because I was so gawky, I hated my body so that I got to thinking of myself as freakish and disabled. I knew what it was to be teased and ridiculed. I longed to be like the other boys.'

This identification with those who are in any way crippled or disabled was to become for him a central image which moved him profoundly and was to result, eventually, in a remarkable film, *Changing Step*, about amputees of the First World War, which Richard both devised and directed. For all artists there are certain key images which come to them early in life, for which often there is no rational explanation, and which becomes central to their life and work.

The Lady Alice School, if overcrowded, was fortunate in having a purpose-built stage, complete with wings, which was regularly used by the town's amateurs, although during the day the hall served as the school's gymnasium. For those pupils who had reached eleven-plus it was considered a privilege to stay behind after school and set out rows of chairs for the performance in the evening. After tea they would return to see the show, before clearing the hall, ready for the next morning. 'And that,' says Richard, 'was my real introduction to theatre, seeing all those one-act plays performed by amateurs.' He was also fortunate in that, at that period, Scotland was rich in amateur dramatic clubs, of which there were several in Greenock, as well as drama and speech festivals.

Richard was to graduate from acting in school plays to taking a small part in one of these amateur productions, a play about the burghers of Calais entitled *The Six of Calais*. This won a place in the British finals which were to take place in London. One evening, the director appeared at the Wilsons' flat and Richard was sent to his bedroom. It turned out that the director wanted Richard's part to go to one of the more experienced members of the company, rather than have to take on the responsibility for a schoolboy. It was, says Richard, his first theatrical setback.

From Lady Alice, Richard went on to the Greenock High School where he met Charlie Murray, now one of his oldest friends, whose father was headmaster at Lady Alice. Although Charlie was a year older, he had been doing a science course but decided to switch to art, which meant that he had to repeat a year, and so ended up in the same class as Richard, who was then fourteen to Charlie's fifteen. 'We grew up together in adolescence,' remarks Richard. Until then, his school chums had had games, particularly football, as their main interests, but Charlie wanted to be a painter and, indeed, went on to study at the Glasgow School of Art and became a professional. Today he lives and works on the Isle of Bute while his wife Sheila is a local school teacher. 'So Charlie was very seminal in my growing up, in that he was the first artistic person I had really known or been friendly with.'

Every summer the shipyards closed down for the first two weeks of July. The Wilsons, like many other families, took their summer holiday on the Isle of Arran. Sheets, pillow cases and everything else would be sent on ahead by railway to Ardrossan, and then transferred onto the steamer, while the family boarded a paddle steamer for the five-and-a-half-hour voyage which it took in those days to reach Arran. Moira was often sick, but Richard loved to lean over the side, watching the great paddles revolving, churning the water, as the steam poured out of the funnels and the engines throbbed. It was always a great excitement to him as they neared the island and he could see the white farmhouses spread out along the small fields facing the sea, with open hillsides and stretches of moor behind and, beyond, the distant mountain peaks where once he saw the golden eagle.

On arrival at Brodick the Wilsons took a bus to Glen Sannox where 'Aunt' Peggy, as she was called, kept a small boarding house. Effie Wilson's great friend, Peggy, had married Gibbie McKinnon, a sheep farmer on Arran, a very dour man, but he and Richard's father got on well together and would spend days up on the hills tending the flocks. As soon as she saw the bus approach, 'Aunt' Peggy would come running down to the bus stop to greet them, wiping her hands on her apron. 'She seemed always to be baking,' recalls Richard.

Glen Sannox is at the foot of Goat Fell which, at 2,868 feet, is the highest peak on the island. On a clear day walkers can see Argyll and Ayrshire on the mainland as well as the surrounding islands of Jura, Islay, and Mull; while to the east are the Cumbraes, Bute, the Clyde coast, with Glasgow in the far distance. Sometimes Richard would go on holiday to Arran with the Murrays and then he and Charlie would go off cycling together, pushing their bikes up the road between Lochranza and Brodick, zooming down on the other side. They also shared a passion for building dams, which continued into their teens. On one occasion, away up in the hills, miles from anywhere, they built with rocks a very elaborate dam and then, having built it, sprang it, watching the water escape with a great rush. Wet through, laughing and singing, they returned home that afternoon feeling like Viking warriors.

If Arran is rich in history with memories of Viking and other invasions, Greenock is famous for its association with Robert

Burns' Highland Mary, who is supposed to have lived in Charles Street and whose remains now lie in Greenock Cemetery. Because of this association the first Burns' Club, now known as the Mother Club, was founded in Greenock in 1801. In 1986 Miss Mabel Irving became the President of the Mother Club, the first woman to be elected to this position. She had taught English and drama at Greenock High School, and ran the school's drama society. An inspiring teacher, with a deep love of Shakespeare, she would read all the parts herself with great relish so as to bring the play alive and then get the class to read the play aloud for themselves.

One evening, when Richard was thirteen, he went to Mabel's house in South Street, where she still lives, surrounded by photographs of former students and their children and grandchildren, many of whom still come to be coached by her for drama and verse speaking festivals. Richard had finally plucked up the courage to tell Mabel that he wanted to become an actor, 'and that took some doing because acting was not a profession that was encouraged in a small Scottish town like Greenock. And Mabel replied, "Don't be stupid, boy. You can't speak!" I was absolutely devastated. Mind you, she was probably quite right. I couldn't speak. I had a thick Scottish accent.'

When, a few years ago, Richard, now a star, returned to Greenock to make a short autobiographical film for BBC Scotland, he met again with his old teacher 'who seemed unchanged by the years'. She came up to him (this scene is in the film) and said, 'Iain, I didn't say you couldn't speak. I said you spoke through your teeth and, if you don't mind my saying so, you still do!'

Whatever the truth of the original incident, and Miss Irving now claims that it was not she, but someone else, who said these words, undoubtedly they served to crush Richard's early aspirations and so delayed his entry into the theatre until he was twenty-seven. 'For a long time,' says Richard, 'I was convinced that I couldn't be successful because I was now self-conscious about my speech as well as about my physique. My parents were encouraging but wanted me to do a respectable job. There weren't any role models for professional actors then, certainly not in Greenock.'

There is no doubting that these words were deeply wounding and yet it may well have been the best thing that could have happened to him. By the time he entered the Royal Academy of Dramatic Art he had left home, travelled, seen something of the world, as well as the casualties of war, earned his living and, above all, come to know a little more about himself and about life. The initial setbacks in a career are often seen, from a later perspective, as necessary trials. Schopenhauer, in an essay, observes how, at a certain age, you look back over your life and it seems as orderly as a composed novel and, just as in Dickens' novels little accidental meetings turn out to be the main features in the plot, so also in our lives: what seem to have been misfortunes or setbacks at the time often turn out to be critical turning points.

On Saturday mornings Richard used to help Charlie's father with his Saturday morning cinema club at Lady Alice School. Mr Murray chose the films and set up the projection box; and the films, usually westerns, were shown in the same auditorium where Richard had acted. Mrs Murray sold ice creams, while Richard's task was to control the crowds of children. 'I had this strip of felt which I'd found in the janitor's room. There'd be several hundred unruly children and I used to bash them with it. It was all very high spirited. Sometimes, if they were especially unruly, I would bring in the janitor's Alsatian. I was a bit like a Gestapo officer. Today I'd probably be charged with assault.'

One day they changed reels and the films got mixed up so that what had started as a western suddenly turned into a gangster film. In the evenings there were different films for the adults. The cinema club was used to raise funds for the school and became so popular that its success proved its eventual downfall: the local cinemas banded together to cut off supplies of film.

The other great friend of Richard's youth was Tom Purdie, also at Greenock High School and who, like Charlie, went on to study painting at the Glasgow School of Art. Like Richard he had a passion for acting and shared a weekly elocution class with him, taught by Rena C. Webster who also ran the Gourock Drama Group, which Richard joined. He acted in many of her productions while

Charlie and Tom used to help paint the scenery. Because he had to learn speeches of Shakespeare for Rena's elocution classes, Richard went to the local bookshop, McKelvie's, to buy the *Complete Works of Shakespeare*, only to find that the shop was amply supplied with the works of Robert Burns but no Shakespeare. He had to order a copy. The day that he went in to collect it, he was standing turning the pages when he heard a voice behind him say, 'I'm glad to see my efforts weren't entirely in vain, Wilson!' It was Mr Stewart, his former English master.

'He was a remarkable teacher,' recalls Richard. 'He knew how to make language live, though you did get the feeling that he was slightly fed up with teaching. He would prop up the lid of his desk for long periods and we never knew what he was doing behind it. Some of the boys claimed he was having a quiet snifter. Probably he was. He was a very witty man. When he had to call someone out to belt him, he would say, "Just you tumble head-over-heels out here, boy!" Once, someone put a stink bomb in an ink well and he ignored it for a long time. We all waited to hear what he would say. Finally he said, "I sincerely hope that whoever has caused this abominable smell that it is not from natural causes!" And then he just ignored it for the rest of the lesson. Sometimes he would suddenly lower the lid of his desk and remark, "Pay attention, boy! Have you come here to shelter from the rain?"'

Then there was the science teacher who, if someone gave a silly answer, would let out a loud cry and leap up at the blackboard and hang from the top, which always got a big laugh. Richard also recalls the geography master with a peculiar speech characteristic, who used to keep saying, 'Aye, well, let's turn now, aye, well, to, er, er ...' One day, Richard's class decided to keep a tally of how many times he said, 'Aye, well!' He caught the boy who was keeping the record. 'Aye, well! Come on out here. What is this that you've got, aye?' And he held up the piece of paper which had fifty-five ticks on it for the number of times he had said 'Aye, well!' Naturally they were unable to tell him what it was.

And then there was Miss Biddy Byers, whose mother told fortunes. Tom Purdie describes when Mrs Byers dealt the cards to predict

30

Richard's future. Although she didn't mention the theatre, she did say that eventually he would be in a position of authority either as a parson, a bank manager, a doctor, a teacher, and so on. 'She seems to have had some kind of foreknowledge,' comments Tom, 'because Richard has at least played all those roles on television.'

Although Richard continued to nurture a secret ambition to be an actor, as the time to leave school approached he was faced with having to make a decision about a career. His father wanted him to work in farming (something he himself would have preferred to do) and to take an administrative job with the Ardgowan Estates, which owned the land around Greenock. Mr Wilson knew the factor, but although Richard toyed with this idea he finally decided against it. For a while he also flirted with the idea of joining the Merchant Navy and seeing the world. His mother's brothers were all seagoing and a number of his chums had already decided on the sea as a career. Then he met a friend who, prior to going up to Glasgow University to study medicine, was working as a laboratory technician in a hospital in Glasgow, 'and I thought it would be nice to work in a hospital and do a bit of good for people'. Secretly he also thought it might serve as a stop-gap until he decided whether or not he was going to be a professional actor which, at that time, seemed so unlikely and unreal.

And so, in 1953, at the age of seventeen, having specialised in botany and zoology, and obtained his Scottish Leaving Certificate, Richard left school to train as a laboratory technician at Stobhill Hospital in Glasgow. Moira had left home and Richard moved into his parents' bedroom whilst they went into the back bedroom. He remembers that one of the things he fought for at this time, although they couldn't really afford it, was to have a bureau in his room. His parents gave him one for his birthday, obtained through a mail order catalogue. This desk became a treasured posession (today his office has three desks, each one in use) linked clearly with the memory of his father's desk at Scott's Yard, and symbolising that a new phase in his life had begun. He was on his way, even though, and for some years to come, that way was none too certain.

3

Spreading of Wings

... I'd be prisoned there
But that my soul has birdwings to fly free

Edwin Muir, *The Labyrinth*

Each morning Richard had a twenty-minute walk to the station at Greenock, followed by a fifty-minute train journey; then a walk across central Glasgow to catch a bus, and a final twenty-minute walk to Stobhill Hospital, which he entered through the mortuary gates as this was the shortest route to the pathology department. Opening his locker, he would change into a white coat – his uniform for the next ten years. Some days he arrived an hour earlier so that he could go swimming with the other laboratory technicians in the local swimming baths. Because he had no university qualifications he had to attend night school several evenings a week at the Western Infirmary, attached to Glasgow University, and sit a medical laboratory technology examination which would eventually earn him the initials AIMLT: an Associate of the Institute of Medical Laboratory Technicians, the rough equivalent, he says now, of a poor BSc.

Richard started his career working in the bacteriological laboratory, specialising in the diagnosis of tuberculosis, which meant dealing with samples of urine taken over a twenty-four-hour period, which had to be allowed to settle for a week. When they were opened, the smell, recalls Richard, choosing his description with care, was often astonishing! After pouring off the liquid, the sediment would be removed and spun down into a centrifuge so that it could become a solid residue which would then be cultured to see if it contained the tubercular bacillus. 'That,' says Richard, wrinkling his nose, 'was an even more astonishing smell!' There were also samples of sputum which arrived in little wax containers.

Part of his job involved the inoculation of guinea pigs with the bacillus. Next he killed the guinea pigs and examined their spleen to see if they had TB. 'I did not like that very much. You killed them with a blow on the head from a mallet. We also used rabbits for creating antibodies and these rabbits you got to know over the weeks. They were beautiful animals. And you had to kill them in the same way but first you shaved their necks so that you could cut the vein there more easily. The blood you drew from that was what you used for the antibodies.'

The laboratory technicians took their lunch, tea and coffee breaks in the same room in which they tipped the urine. It was all quite primitive. On one occasion, the consultant bacteriologist, John Stevenson, a flamboyant character with a slight stammer, was escorting a group of businessmen and potential sponsors around the laboratory. The technicians at that moment were having their coffee break in this room and the consultant bacteriologist remarked to the visitors, 'W-w-w-would you like your s-s-s-sons to w-w-w-work here? We have cultured tubercular bacilli running off these w-w-w-walls.'

The train journey from Greenock to Glasgow became a central part of Richard's life over the next several years. Charlie was now studying at the Glasgow School of Art, shortly to be followed by Tom Purdie. The trains were still steam hauled, so, as Charlie recalls, 'If you leaned out of the window you risked getting bits of black in your eyes.' The carriages were filthy and smelt of tobacco smoke; the fabric of the seats was worn and shiny, and there were faded sepia photographs of Highland scenes above the luggage racks. The friends recall that if it was a Friday or a Saturday they hoped the train would leave Glasgow before a drunk got in. If they saw one coming they would put a foot on the door so that it couldn't be opened. But one Saturday a particularly objectionable drunk did get into their carriage. When the train stopped at Bishopton, the drunk asked, 'Where are we? Is this Port Glasgow?' and at once they said yes, even though it wasn't, and he opened the door and got out. Immediately they put their feet up on the door so that he couldn't get back in and the train moved off, leaving him behind on the platform. Since there wasn't another train that night, it meant that by the time he got home he would have sobered up quite a bit!

Homeward we're bound
Homeward we're bound
The click of the wheels
Spells out the sound,
Telling the night
As we hurry in flight
That each tap on the rail
Means we shorten our trail.

Shall we go on?
Shall we go on?
A steaming train
And its homing throng,
Bright lights race by
Blinding the eye
Now a clear space
Through the country we race.

The pace now is slowing
The pace now is slowing
Through country familiar
The train now is going,
Then with grinding of brakes
The whole train vibrates
We've finished our roam
At last we're home.

This poem, which Richard sent to Beatrice when he was stationed in Singapore, catches something of the excitement of that train for these youngsters from Greenock. Glasgow was the first city they encountered, and represented their first contact with a wider world, even though on 'some mornings you could hardly see for the green fog once you got into the city', remembers Charlie. To the actor John Fraser, who grew up in Glasgow, the city was then 'absolutely black'. There were still tram-cars; the Gorbals, one of the most famous slums in Europe, had not then been razed to the ground, while the old Citizens Theatre there stank of size and dry rot. The other abiding memory that Richard, like John Fraser, has is of the overwhelming smell of breweries, with a pub on every corner, and everywhere the evidence of endemic alcoholism, a paralytic drunkenness.

One of Richard's happiest discoveries in Glasgow was the Cosmo, a small art cinema which used to show all foreign films. 'I think it was then that I first realised there was something magical about the cinema as an art form, more than just entertainment.' At the Cosmo, over the next few years, he saw for the first time the films of Bergman, Antonioni, Truffaut, and Jacques Tati whom he regarded as a genius. 'I wasn't aware that I was wanting to do what he did, but I just knew that what he did was so funny. And, in spite of what Mabel had said, deep down I knew that more than anything I wanted to be an actor, which is why I did so much amateur acting at that time, because I was beginning to realise that I could entertain people – and that it was also a way out of not being expected to be anything else.'

What is clear about these early years is Richard's growing realisation that he was different and, as with every adolescent, that there were some things he could not share with his parents or sister. Although amateur acting occupied much of his spare time and creative energies, it is curious that his mother, who adored him, went only once to see him act, and that was in a comedy in which he had to perform as a woman, wearing Moira's 'going away' two-piece suit.

After two years at Stobhill, Richard moved to a better job at

Gateside Hospital in Greenock. With less time spent each day travelling, he had more time for acting. It was also a happier and freer atmosphere, and once again he could get home each day for midday dinner. Gateside used to be the Infectious Diseases Hospital and the laboratory was in an old isolation ward. Over the years, as it developed, portakabins were added on, but in the 1950s it had only one consultant pathologist, Dr Stewar, and one laboratory technician, David Hutton. Richard was one of the first technicians to follow him. Also on the staff was Beatrice McCallum, who began typing up post-mortem reports until she was taken on as full-time secretary, by which time the laboratory had its own consultant bacteriologist. Slowly other departments were added, including microbiology (where Richard worked), pathology, biochemistry, haematology, and blood transfusion departments. Each department had a senior technician in charge, and overseeing the whole laboratory was the chief technician, Stanley Bald.

What Beatrice McCallum remembers most clearly about Richard at this time (she still refers to him as Iain) is the way he made everyone laugh. 'In the afternoons we used to stop work at five o'clock, and about ten to five, when everybody was clearing up, Iain would perform for us. He was always spouting Shakespeare and other speeches. He used also to burst into my office, jabbering away to me in what sounded like French or German, but was in fact just gibberish, but he hit off the accent so convincingly that it really sounded like the real thing. He would make up the words as he went along.' Many years later, the actress Susan Wooldridge recalls being on holiday in Paris with Richard where both she and he would converse in mock French until they collapsed with laughter, unable to keep it up any longer.

Beatrice remembers one occasion in particular when Richard was up on a bench, 'which he did quite often', doing a flamenco dance, and all the other technicians were standing around clapping their hands in rhythm. Suddenly the chief technician, Stanley Bald, came rushing out angrily to demand what all the noise was about. He looked up at Richard and said, 'Wilson, you shouldn't be working in a laboratory, you should be on the *stage!*'

A group of technicians, including Richard, also formed a skiffle group which played at local dances. They practised in the biochemistry department and every now and then one of them emerged to ask Beatrice, 'How did that sound?' Always she replied, 'Terrible!' because it was.

The dozen hospitals in the area at that time have now amalgamated, each a separate unit: surgical, maternity, ear nose and throat, eye and infectious diseases. But in Richard's time, once a year the entire medical staff of these dozen hospitals met at a hotel for a dance, whilst during the year each department organised smaller events for its own staff. Richard, who has always loved dancing, used to make up a couple with Beatrice. In between dances he would often speak of his love of acting and 'I could tell even then,' recalls Beatrice, 'that he was very serious about this and meant one day to further his ambitions.'

And then, says Richard, 'Alcohol came into our lives.' Together he and Charlie and Tom, who were as inseparable as the Three Musketeers, began to discover drinking. 'We couldn't afford to drink regularly,' says Charlie, 'but when we did it was a real blow-out.' Their regular meeting place in Greenock was the Horseshoe Bar, a small pub with imitation green leather seating, and an L-shaped bar. The three would argue about art, politics and religion. The latter they took very seriously. Tom was, and remains, a churchgoer, but Charlie, like Richard, soon rebelled. Richard was nineteen when Moira married Jimmy McLaren, and Charlie remembers how Richard collared the minister at the wedding, inviting him back to tea at Dunlop Street, and then proceeded to grill him. This rebellion against what they saw as the narrow-mindedness of Scottish Presbyterianism was, says Charlie, all part of their growing up. He remembers how, as a child, 'if you chopped firewood on a Sunday you were told you would go straight to Hell.' The regular customers at the Horseshoe Bar soon became accustomed to the three boys' fierce arguments. Often they would stay until closing time at half past nine; sometimes, because the pubs in Gourock remained open until ten o'clock, they would jump on a bus and go into the town to pack in an extra twenty minutes' drinking.

During this period Charlie, Tom, and another of their friends, Angus Stirling who studied commercial art in Glasgow, rented a studio at the top of an old commercial building in Greenock, like a Parisian atelier, looking out over the rooftops of the town. Because the building was number 33 in the street they named it Studio Trente Trois. And because Charlie made home-made wine, Angus had labels printed: Vin Studio Trente Trois. It was the scene of many lively parties at which Richard would recite speeches from Shakespeare.

Among those who gathered at the Studio was Roy Hanlon, who became one of Greenock's first professional actors. From the west side, he had been educated at the one 'posh' school, the Academy. To avoid being called up, Hanlon, who was just finishing at Greenock Academy, asked the Information Centre in Glasgow if there were any colleges that would take someone who had no academic qualifications and was told that there were two: the Glasgow School of Art, and the Glasgow College of Drama.

'Which is the nearest?' he asked.

'Are you serious?' they replied.

The College of Drama was just up the road; so he went and got a form and filled it in. He had then to ask the Rector at the Academy to sign it for him. The Rector, who regarded the theatre as a place of licentiousness and debauchery, signed the form but threw it on the floor, so that Hanlon had to grovel under the man's desk in order to pick it up. In no time at all, to the Rector's horror and to Richard's fascination, the *Greenock Telegraph* splashed the headline: 'Local boy becomes drama student.' In later years Hanlon and Richard were to act together in *Holy City* by Bill Bryden (also a Greenockian) and again in *Normal Service* by John Byrne (from Paisley). Richard remembers talking to Roy Hanlon in Studio Trente Trois about acting, and thinking, here am I, an amateur, still struggling away, and he's just gone and done it!

Richard's first taste of fame as an actor came when he played a leading role for the Gourock Players. He was down in the coal cellar at home, getting a bucket of coal, when the newspaper boy arrived. 'I took the paper off him and read it with my coal-black hands. It said, "Iain Wilson ... a star is born." Although I no longer remember what the play was, I do remember realising again the power of laughter. I knew then, even more than when I was younger, that I had the power.'

By now he was appearing not only in amateur productions, but acting the clown on every occasion. Once, in the back garden, he was swinging a golf club, pretending to be a champion golfer, while his mother watched from the upstairs window. Suddenly he gave it a great swirl and hit Charlie on the head, who fell to the ground unconscious. Effie, convinced that he had killed Charlie, threw up the window and screamed. Charlie, fortunately, was only concussed.

Charlie recalls how Richard used to make his mother laugh a lot. He would do daft things, like pretending to be a surgeon doing a brain operation with Tom as the patient. 'The three of us were always acting, making up plays, and this one grew into quite a drama, my mother being convulsed with laughter as Richard removed the brain, stitched up the cut, and then realised he had forgotten to put back the brains.' Neighbours also have memories of calling at the Wilsons' flat. The door would be opened by Richard wearing a smoking jacket, holding a long cigarette holder, pretending to be Noël Coward, although hardly anyone there actually knew who Coward was. 'In one sense,' says Richard, 'Charlie, Tom and I were very infantile. Even though by then we were well into our teens, we were always fantasising and making up stories, and acting them out.'

Charlie remembers the Wilson home as happy, and thinks it was due in no small way to Mrs Wilson, a great character, full of life and fun. 'She put up with us a lot, suffering us to come in at all sorts of hours, perhaps after the cinema, and hogging the television.' The Murrays didn't have television; few did then. It wasn't until 1953 that Richard saw his first television. The Wilsons owned a set – one of the first in the neighbourhood – after Mr Wilson won £400 on the Pools (the equivalent of £10,000 by the 1990s). Richard was sworn to secrecy about it as Effie did not approve of the Pools. While the three lads sprawled in front of the set in the living room (which still doubled as Moira's bedroom), Effie would be in and out of the kitchen, making sandwiches for the boys, stopping sometimes to watch a programme over their shoulders. Moira by this time was courting, and when she and Jimmy McLaren came back they would find that the three had taken the best seats on the sofa, and they were forced to sit on hard chairs at the back. Moira, of course, could not go to bed until they had all gone. She admits it was a relief when she got married two years later.

Apart from the Horseshoe Bar the three boys used to frequent an Italian coffee shop, the Sun d'Or Café, run by Dina and Pino Signorelli. Dina used to try to teach Richard Italian and it was she who suggested that Charlie, Angus and Tom should have an exhibition of their paintings at the Sun d'Or and that Richard should open it. Richard, who was eighteen at the time, still remembers the theme of his speech, which was that if you live with a painting you learn that it never stays the same and, therefore, if people are thinking of buying a painting they need to remember that 'There's what you see now, but it will change.'

It was through Charlie in particular that Richard became interested in art. 'He taught me, in a sense. I was always saying, "But I don't understand that!" And he would say, "But you don't have to *understand*, it's not an intellectual exercise. If you like it, just look at it, and it will grow on you." And so modern art ceased to confuse me. I learned to enjoy looking at shapes and colours.'

Often he accompanied Charlie and Tom on their painting trips. He preferred oils to watercolours because he could always paint out his mistakes, but in the end gave up the effort. 'I didn't have any talent, but it did help me to appreciate painting all the more.'

There is no doubt that his early friendship with both Charlie and Tom opened many doors for Richard and planted in him an appreciation of visual art. Being able now to afford to build up his own collection, it is typical of him that in doing so he should support the work of young Scottish artists such as Ann Oram, Alison Watt, Alexandra Gardner, and others such as John Byrne. If he fancies a painting he first takes it on loan in order to see if he can live with it, knowing, as he said all that time ago, 'There's what you see now, but it will change.'

Another influential friend at this period was a fellow laboratory technician, James Kennedy. 'He was very much into classical music, which I didn't know much about. We were talking one day and he said to start off with Beethoven's sixth symphony. That sounded a bit difficult to me but I got a recording out of the library. Then I went back to him and told him I didn't like it. He told me to listen to it again. I did and thought it was wonderful!' Even as a small boy Richard had had a toy baton and would put on records in his room and conduct in time to the music. 'He would just lose himself,' says Moira. By the time he was living in London he owned a real conductor's baton, which used to have pride of place on his mantelpiece.

In 1956 Richard entered the Verse Speaking Contest of the Renfrewshire Musical Festival Association, and was called on to render two pieces. The first was the opening chorus of Shakespeare's *Henry V*:

> O for a muse of fire, that would ascend
> The brightest heaven of invention:
> A kingdom for a stage, princes to act,
> And monarchs to behold the swelling scene ...

for which he was awarded 86 points out of 100, with the following comment from the adjudicator: 'Pleasing manner and absorbing audience into the play. The gestures were good but don't overdo them. Like your adjudicator you have conspicuous hands. Your manner of speaking was curiously at variance with your hand gestures. Not "uz" for "us".'

The other piece was Wordsworth's *The Solitary Reaper* for which he received 81 points out of 100, with the comment, 'Well-spoken but lacked lyricism and flow. It was a little dull. It should be quietly contemplative and reflective.'

That autumn, Richard was called up for two years of National Service. Because of his medical background he joined the Royal Army Medical Corps. Both Charlie and Tom were excused military service on health grounds. Richard, however, was instructed to report to the RAMC training depot near Farnham. For the first time he was leaving Scotland. The time had come for him to spread his wings.

4

The Army

The army proved a threshold experience for Richard, 'a shock to the system, as I had never been away from home before, except for holidays to Arran'. In the army he found that he had become a number, 23343162, known by his last three digits. '162 is still absolutely embedded in my mind.' Fortunately he was not the only laboratory technician in the barrack room, which gave him some sense of continuity with the life he had left behind. The army medical training proved so tough that during his twelve weeks at Cookham there were three suicides. 'It wasn't the studies so much as all the drilling and all the shouting which wore you down,' he says. To his surprise, drilling had its positive side: 'When you actually got to stopping all at once and all in unison on the command of *Halt!* there was something very satisfying and aesthetic about that experience.'

After completing his post-basic training Richard was sent north to Catterick in Yorkshire to await posting. While there, the education officer suggested that if he was interested in theatre he should audition for the Carey Garrison Theatre. The first time, he stood outside the huge Garrison Theatre but, being too scared to go in, he returned to camp. The second time, he once again stood outside, feeling decidedly nervous, and if it hadn't been for someone coming up to ask him if he needed help, he might have funked it yet again. Instead he replied, 'Yes, I've come to join!'

While at Catterick he turned down the chance of officer training because it would have meant giving up laboratory work, and he was determined to complete his studies as an Associate of the Institute of Laboratory Technicians and so continue his career.

His first posting was to Bermuda, but because the garrison there was closed down three days before he was due to fly out, he was despatched instead to Salisbury Plain, where smallpox was supposed to have broken out, although he knew nothing about the disease. On arrival, he and his fellow technicians found there was no laboratory, and were 'quarantined' in a building with a white rope round it. For a few hours Richard was one of a team of army personnel dealing with what was a front-page epidemic. In the end it turned out not to be smallpox, and before long he was being flown to Singapore in an RAF Comet.

On arrival at Aden the blast of heat that hit him as the door was opened made Richard think there must be a generator outside. 'But there wasn't; it was Aden. I was very naive then.' They were told that as the plane had broken down they would have to stay overnight in tents. Next day they were finally flown out, but in a plane that had been sitting on the runway, baking in the full glare of the sun. 'I'd never experienced heat like that before,' recalls Richard.

At Neesoon, their first garrison, they were put into huts with grass roofs. Before leaving England they had been instructed always to tuck in their mosquito nets securely long before retiring to bed. Richard obeyed the instructions minutely and that first night climbed into bed with utmost care, determined that no mosquito should possibly get in at the same time. He lay back, exhausted in the heat, but confident that he had not disturbed the net. Then, as he lay on his back, he noticed a HOLE in the slope at the top of the tent and thought, oh, my God, this is terrible! He climbed out of bed, draped a towel over the hole, and crawled back inside with great effort and lay back, with the sweat running off him. Suddenly he saw the towel start to glide, revealing the hole. Once again he got up, replaced the towel, and climbed back into bed. He lay there, very still, exhausted, gazing upwards, only to see the towel once again begin to slide; at which point, says Richard, he gave up.

'I remember the toilets that night as well. There was a huge rhinoceros beetle crawling across the floor and I thought, oh, my God! I don't think I have ever invoked the Deity so much. It was all rather a shock to a young lad from Greenock; but although I didn't like creepy crawlies, and there were quite a lot of them, I soon got used to them.'

Going to Singapore meant being on active service as there was a war on, the Malayan campaign against the Communist guerrillas. Joining the British army were the Gurkhas, the African Rifles, and the Malaysian Regiment, an extraordinary mixture of races, with many more Indians and Malaysians than British. Nor was Singapore as Chinese as it is now. Newly arrived Europeans faced not only vibrancy of colour and intense heat, but also the insidious damp following the monsoons. Everywhere they experienced the exotic smell of the East: of rotting vegetation, fruit, flowers, incense and spices, with food stalls lining the streets, and stir-frying all day and night; all this mingling with the fumes of the traffic. To Richard it was overwhelming and utterly different from the austerity of post-war life in Greenock.

Just as the rivers and creeks were crowded – with boat people living in their sampans – so, too, were the narrow streets, each segregated according to various trades: cloth merchants, silversmiths, shops selling spices, clothes, shoes; while one street was used by families for their dying relatives, an early form of the hospice movement. Occasionally, weaving its colourful way through the noise of the streets, Richard would witness a Chinese funeral. Today, observes Richard, who has been back, it has all changed and become, like so many other places in the world, westernised; but at that time 'it was a wonderful potpourri of every nationality and without colour prejudice'.

A close friend of Richard was Sam Buzza, of the African Rifles, 'one of the blackest men I have ever seen,' whom he helped through a crisis when Buzza's father, in Africa, died. According to the tribal tradition, if the new chief was not in the village when the old chief died, he was supposed to kill himself. Buzza, faced with such a terrible dilemma, was suicidal. 'However,' says Richard, 'I was able to talk him through it.'

A more unexpected friend was Corporal Charlie Connaghan, head of the Hospital Police, the most hated man in the camp, on loan from the King's Own Scottish Borderers, as the Medical Corps did not have their own police. One night when Richard was drinking with a group of friends in the crowded NAAFI canteen, Corporal Connaghan entered and the whole place went quiet as Charlie looked round the room. Finally he came up to Richard's table (everyone's eyes were on them, wondering what they had done). 'Is your name Wilson? Do you come from Greenock?' When Richard said yes, he replied, 'Then you're a pal of mine! I come from Greenock too. The wife's from Greenock also. Come round to dinner one night.'

Richard did go to dinner – the Connaghans lived in married quarters – and got on very well with him, finding him to be a generous and kind man, quite unlike his public persona. He still remembers the New Year's Eve party at Charlie Connaghan's when he had a bagpiper play the 'Lament for the Old Year' on a beautiful moonlit summer evening in Singapore. 'It was very, very moving.' Forty years later on, in Hampstead on New Year's Eve 1995, it was Richard's turn to engage a Highland piper for his annual party. A few minutes before midnight the tall windows of Richard's drawing room were opened and there, floodlit in a well-timed mist, against a background of shrubs and trees, stood the piper in full regalia, playing this same haunting lament.

Not long after arriving in Singapore, Richard discovered that Gordon McCulloch, the son of the family downstairs at 141 Dunlop Street, was stationed not far away. During the Malayan Campaign, many of the European rubber planters had been assassinated by the Communists who wanted to kick the British out of Malaya. As a result there was a desperate need for planters. By the time Richard arrived in Singapore Gordon McCulloch was already running a rubber plantation in Kluang, speaking fluent Malay as well as reasonable Chinese, and living in a large mansion with a lot of servants, a far cry from the small council flat in Dunlop Street.

Since it was the command laboratory for the whole of the Far East, Richard had to deal with battle casualties as well as cases of rare and unfamiliar tropical diseases. He learned that the treatment for tapeworms was to starve them out of the system. 'We used to get these bedpans brought across and you could see this great length of tapeworm, and you had to find the tiny head among the faeces. It has four suckers and eight hooks on it which enable the tapeworm to catch onto the bowel. And so, of course, you had to go through all those piles of shit until you found the head. And until you had found it, you knew you hadn't got rid of the tapeworm. If you only found a length of it, it meant that it was still working away inside the bowel. And although you wore a mask for the work, you still had to peer into all those faeces. Nasty! Nasty!'

Richard was also called upon to take over the serology syphilis test called the Wasserman, a procedure which took all day. A tedious and complex test, calling for the use of sheep's cells, which had to be fresh, the tests were done in batches of a hundred a week. Just after Richard took over, the Australian Regiment was leaving Malaysia and the authorities decided that every man in the regiment should be given the Wasserman before returning home. It was only the second time he had carried out the test and suddenly Richard found himself swamped by hundreds of samples. To this day he remains uncertain as to how efficient he was at the beginning. 'It was very tricky and it was always going wrong at some stage or another.'

Richard told this story in 1994 at an Australian Day lunch, when he was in Australia making a travel film for the BBC, saying, 'There may be some of you here tonight whom I tested.' Then he added, 'Sometimes, of course, it can lie dormant for twenty years.' It didn't go down too well, comments Richard. They weren't too pleased.

By this time he was a corporal with a billet of his own, off the blood transfusion laboratory. He remembers one night in particular, lying in bed with no clothes on, it was so hot. 'I woke up, put on the light and there, coming down the wall and right across my body, was this column of ants. They then climbed up the opposite wall. They were carrying bits of cockroaches they had killed. I looked up and there they were, carrying these cockroach wings and walking straight across me. I didn't scream. I just jumped up and brushed myself down. It was extraordinary. There must have been thousands of them. I don't scream a lot but I do jump easily if I touch something. And there were some huge insects out there. In the rubber plantations there were quite a few snakes, some of them dangerous, such as the bandit krate for which there was no known antidote if it bit you.'

Sometimes Richard would do 'turns'. On one occasion in the canteen, when a group of them had been drinking, he decided to recite Hamlet's 'To be or not to be', which had been among his repertoire in the Studio Trente Trois days. He was standing in the middle of the canteen, with a cup of coffee in his hand, reciting, when one chap burst out laughing. Slowly Richard walked over to him and poured his cup of coffee over the fellow's head, saying, 'Do not laugh at Shakespeare, you moron!' He was quite a big guy, recalls Richard, 'and could easily have clobbered me. I suppose I wanted to bring a bit of culture into the place.'

The laboratory technicians used to do a certain amount of private work for outside laboratories and the money received enabled them to have a party once a month. For his twenty-first birthday they held a special celebration for Richard (he even wore a suit and tie). Not surprisingly everyone drank a good deal. The colonel in charge, who was nicknamed 'Toffee' because he was bald and had a brown head, left the party in his MG and apparently went round the roundabout outside the gates four times before he could find the road.

A few months after this, in September 1958, Richard returned to England aboard the *Nevasa*. Arriving at Southampton he took a train straight to Cookham to be demobbed, only to discover that he had lost his kitbag. 'If you've lost your kitbag,' said the sergeant, 'you can't leave the army!' Somewhere between the train and the depot it had been mislaid. Richard was in agony, unable to bear the thought of being kept on, 'after the huge joyous expectation of going home'. Also, all his presents for the family were in that kitbag: watches for his mother and Moira, and a cigarette lighter for his father. He had already sent on in advance a lot of other things, especially china, which in Singapore was very cheap. In the end his kitbag was found and he was on his way home. He didn't even want to visit London, but got on a train for Scotland to return to work at the Gateside Hospital. But not for long. 'I think I knew on my return that I could not stay in Greenock. I had tasted freedom.'

And so, within a year, he left for London.

Whatever Richard's parents may have felt, they did not oppose his decision. Repression of emotion is very much part of the Scottish temperament and there is no doubt that one of the freedoms which acting has given to Richard is that of being able to release and express emotion. Although all his spare time was devoted to acting, his parents – concerned that he should have a steady job and get on – did not take this seriously. Thus, he could not share with them the fact that he nurtured 'this secret desire to be an actor'.

It is possible also, as Richard admits, that even he did not take it all that seriously at first, in that he still thought he was incapable of doing it as a job. The words 'Don't be stupid, boy! You can't speak!' were to continue to reverberate over many years, like a prophecy of doom.

He knew for certain, however, that the confines of a small Scottish town could no longer contain him and so, like another Richard, he set out for London town but, alas, without his cat. Toots had to stay behind.

5

Arrival in London

On his arrival in London in the late autumn of 1959 the first job Richard was offered – at University College Hospital – he turned down because he thought: I don't like London. It all felt such alien territory. He used to walk the streets at night, looking down into basement flats, seeing families around fires, and think: why am I not back in Greenock? He was terribly homesick. Even the thickness of his accent alienated him from people. 'I remember I had to say everything twice because no one understood me. My Scottish accent proved almost unintelligible.'

Much of what he felt is expressed in a film script which he wrote during his first two years in London, which depicts the arrival in London from a small Scottish village of a young man anxious to find work. Though determined to better himself, he has no conception of what a big city is like, 'but from the moment he puts foot on the platform at Euston Station he finds himself confronted with its strange bewildering ways. At first he is dumbfounded by the size of everything: buildings, streets, crowds, the general sense of urgency, the anxiety to get everywhere and anywhere as quickly as possible, and the barbaric conditions in which people travel, baffles him completely, while his first response to the high prices he finds everywhere is one of shocked surprise.'

Richard's mother, writing her weekly letter to him, observed drily, 'It's not till you live there that you realise how much dearer it is to live – of course you knew that before you went, and remember, old man, no one asked you to go! It was your own wish!'

While looking for a job Richard lived in north London in the Belsize Residential Club in Belsize Square. His testimonial from his commanding officer in the RAMC – 'A laboratory technician of outstanding ability and competence who has obtained the highest possible army qualifications in his trade' – and his Diploma of Associateship of the Institute of Laboratory Technicians, which he had completed during his military service, soon secured him a job at Paddington General Hospital in the Haematology and Blood Transfusion Unit, at a salary of £10 a week. While continuing to do research work he was also responsible for taking blood samples which, as he always wore a white coat, often resulted in patients calling him 'Doctor'.

On one occasion, at the end of a long day carrying out injections, he was busy filling in the forms for the previous patient when he heard the next come in. Over his shoulder he said, in his thick Scots accent, 'Roll up your sleeves.' He then heard a frightened woman's voice saying, 'Oh, doctor, I didn't think it would come to this!' Turning round he found a West Indian woman unbuttoning her blouse, thinking he was going to inject her heart while Richard, not realising she could not understand his accent, thought she was making sexual advances. It was a situation worthy of the medical series he was to make years later, *Only When I Laugh*.

In a letter dated 23 October 1959, his mother reveals that his father is sending him 10s, 'and he is the man who keeps saying to me, "I wouldn't send him money, he has got to learn to stand on his own feet." And then he does exactly what he tells me not to do!' Soon, gifts of food began to arrive from Scotland – 'a cake, I thought you would enjoy it at supper time with your cup of tea' – and enquiries about his laundry, news of Moira's first pregnancy, and always she concluded with news of his beloved cat: 'Old Toots seems to be looking for you. I can't get her to stay in the house, and she sits right down at the gate. I keep telling her she will have a long look.'

Once Richard had settled into his new life he enrolled in acting classes at the City Literary Institute. On 5 November his mother wrote, 'Glad you are enjoying your classes. By the tone of your letter they seem to be very interesting and no doubt you'll make the most of them if it's going to help you to be an actor. Who knows I'll maybe see your name in lights yet (ah, ah, ah!)'

His father also showed interest. 'Glad to hear you are getting on with the night classes. I suppose you will meet some very interesting people and at the same time make good progress in your studies. We are all keeping quite well and of course missing you. I think this affects me more at bedtime when I go to put Pussy in or out, and wonder if Iain will be late as *usual*. I suppose Mum may feel your absence more when she doesn't take in your morning tea. Of course your letters keep us quite near to you. Thought I could have sent you five bob but I'm afraid you are out of luck, but for goodness sake let me know if you should be in *financial* straits. Toots still outside in the coal box at nights, although she still looks in good shape. Love from all at home, Dad.'

When, in December of that year, he was tempted by a more lucrative job as a travelling salesman for medical supplies, with a car expense account (even though he could not drive), his father wrote a letter which reveals much of the cultural ethos in which Richard was brought up.

'Dear Iain, I'm writing this in the office in the usual rush. I meant to write last night when Mum was out at Forfar Road with Moira, but I fell asleep at the cosy fireside with Toots for company ... The suggestion of your becoming a medical representative with car expense account appears quite exciting and I'm sure a bit tempting, but remember, dear boy, money isn't everything. Maybe I'm old-fashioned but I still feel you're giving a service to the country in the job you are doing now which all the money in the world won't pay for. However, I'm never likely to forget that you are level-headed and not likely to let yourself down. Glad to know you have got fixed up with a room. It will be a bit more homey for you.'

The room was a north London bedsitter at 25 Lyncroft Gardens off the Finchley Road. Up two flights, on the side of the house, it was a dark room, with a single bed in one corner, and a washbasin in the other, a gas fire with a chair on either side, a Baby Belling gas ring for boiling a kettle, and a gas meter which had constantly to be fed with coins, or so it seemed. The bathroom and toilet along the corridor were shared with other tenants in the house, as was the pay telephone. Richard Howard, the actor, who often visited Richard there in the late 1960s, says, 'I am astonished that he lived in it so long.'

Each day Richard travelled to work on the number 28 bus to Westbourne Terrace and then walked to the hospital, passing the police station on his way. He recalls asking one of the laboratory technicians, an Australian, why the hospital always got so many people on a Monday morning who claimed to have fallen down the steps of the police station.

'Come on, Iain, you know why!'

'No, I don't.'

'It's because they get beaten up by the cops at the weekend!'

Richard, who had been brought up to look upon the police as bastions of the law, was shocked.

Life became a little easier when old friends turned up from Greenock. He was joined at Lyncroft Gardens by Charlie Murray, who came south to try his luck as a painter. Tom Purdie was studying to be a teacher so he visited London only occasionally and, when he did, stayed in a small hotel nearby. More of their peers from Scotland were to follow: Angus Stirling and Ron Sanford, both of whom were artists, and Duncan Miller who now runs an art gallery in Hampstead specialising in the work of young Scottish painters. Ron Sanford, who had been at school with Richard and later studied art with Charlie at the Glasgow School of Art, had come to London to teach art at St Martin's School of Art, as well as at the Royal College of Art. 'He was quite well off,' remarks Richard, 'whereas I was quite poor. Ron was always very generous and would pay for me. Today when people tell me I am too generous I always reply: listen, once people used to buy me meals.'

Charlie and Ron were champion drinkers and used to drink everything, recalls Richard. A beer? Right! How about a vodka now? Right! A Scotch? Right! Let's have a Scotch! He remembers waking up on Sunday mornings at Lyncroft Gardens, lifting his head off the pillow to see how he felt and thinking, oh God, it's going to be another three hours! It was, he says, terrible, terrible! Today he has a strict regime of three dry days a week.

Richard's arrival in London coincided with the opening of the Hampstead Theatre Club in the church hall at the back of the Everyman Cinema, before it moved in 1962 to its present site at Swiss Cottage. It was here that Richard was to direct his first London productions. In 1956, at the Royal Court Theatre in Sloane Square, John Osborne's *Look Back in Anger* had exploded onto the English stage and with it came a new wave of directors and writers, both in the theatre and the cinema. Realism and naturalism became the battle cries of younger film-makers in the late 1950s. It was a perfect time for the young Richard Wilson, who was himself to become one of the most austere of the new Realist directors, to arrive in London. He joined the British Film Institute and, as his small pocket diaries of these years reveal, would, either on his own or with Charlie, spend three or four nights a week at the National Film Theatre. He and Charlie also experimented a lot with a camera, as many early photographs show: Richard once more posing as a world-weary Noël Coward; Charlie in a bowler hat with a long cigarette holder made from a length of glass tubing; Richard as a corpse.

Richard also attended several BFI summer courses and helped to make short films, whilst a select group used to accompany Paddy Whannel, then head of BFI Education, to watch films all day, particularly the influential work of the Japanese directors such as Akira Kurosawa and Yasujiro Ozu. The latter's *Tokyo Story*, the portrait of a dysfunctional family, was especially a revelation to Richard. 'I was astonished that the Japanese could show me nuances of family existence which the British cinema hadn't even smelt. It was mind boggling to watch. It was a stunning film and I think we must have been among the first people in the UK to see it.' He was to be deeply influenced by the minimalist playing of the actors, and from then onwards the long mirror in Richard's bedsitter took on a very practical purpose related to his acting classes. He would spend hours in front of it, practising *non*-acting, trying not to do anything, attempting to eliminate all personal ticks and mannerisms, just *being*, allowing the thought and the feeling to come through without any demonstration on his part.

On 16 January 1960 Richard's mother, in her weekly letter, reports to him on Moira and Jimmy's first child, Kenneth, and sends news of a lodger, a young apprentice, whose rent, she says, will provide her with extra pocket money. She also tells Richard that she is sending him £5 towards an air fare. 'I want you to fly home when you come. If you can put your train fare towards it I'll put the rest for your flight. It would be much quicker and warmer this weather.' Then follows the very moving expression of how much she is missing him: 'I now have your visit to look forward to. The sooner the better, for *I am wearying for a look at you.*'

Early in 1960 his mother collapsed at home with a brain tumour. The young lodger found her on the floor, ran across the road to telephone Mr Wilson at Scott's Yard, and she was taken to the local hospital. Richard took time off from work and travelled up to Scotland.

'I went with her and my father in the ambulance to a specialist hospital outside Glasgow. It was quite a long journey and we diverted to pick up another patient, and I thought: this is not right. If this had been royalty there would have been a helicopter. I always felt that was wrong.'

He stayed up in Greenock and went visiting regularly with his father or with Moira. At one time it looked as though Effie was getting better and that the hospital would be able to operate on her to relieve the tumour, so he returned to London in order to carry on with his job.

On 5 April his father wrote to him: 'Dear Iain, still no change. I had a chat with Sister today, the one you call the pessimistic one. I asked her what the doctors thought. She said they couldn't do anything until they were able to work on the case. She did say that Mum's blood pressure and temperature were down, and that this condition was being maintained.

'I took Mum's hand in mine again and thought she tried to draw hers away but I think it was just my imagination. She lies there

55

quite relaxed and breathing easily. The half hour with her today was like nothing on earth.

'I phoned tonight about 10.30 but it was another Sister. Still no change. Will finish this in the morning. Hope you are sleeping well. Moira and I are doing well in this respect. Must close and get pussy in. Off to make a cup of tea. Fond love from all. Dad. Toots XXX. P.S. Thursday a.m.: still the same.'

A few weeks later, quite suddenly, Richard's mother died, aged fifty-seven. Richard returned home at once. 'It was quite late when I arrived, pouring with rain, and there were no buses; in those days I never thought about taxis. As I walked from the station to Moira's house, in the pouring rain, I kept thinking how dramatic it was that the night my mother died I was getting soaked to the skin. I was upset and grieving, thinking of all that I was going to miss – her love and her humour and her vitality – and I was think-ing of what her death had done to me. But she had gone and she was out of pain and that was that. And I had to remember what she had once said to me, "If I die, you must never grieve. You must cremate me, not bury me." She was very specific about that. She said, "You know, I've had a good life, and I don't want you to grieve over my death." So that was very helpful to me.'

But it didn't help his father at all and he never really recovered from her death. He was devastated; immediately after Effie's death he never cried. And then one night, alone with Richard, talking late, he suddenly broke down. Richard had never seen his father cry before, or show so much feeling. John Wilson also worried about what form the memorial in the crematorium should take, but Richard said, 'I don't care what you do. Do what you want. I'm not going to have anything to do with that. I don't need it. I have my memories and I want to keep them happy ones.' And so he left after the funeral. 'I was going to a concert in London that night. I got on the train, took off my black tie, and that was it. I was going back to carry on, as I knew my mother would have wished.'

When eventually Richard was able to cry over his mother's death it was a great relief. He recalls crying on the tops of buses quite unexpectedly. 'And I remember one night in particular at Lyncroft Gardens. Charlie and I hadn't spoken much about my mother's death. Then, on this evening, we were going out for a drink and Charlie switched on the radio and it was playing Handel's Largo. "Please turn that off!" I said. It had been played at my mother's funeral. Suddenly I just flipped and I talked to him all night about her death and the funeral. Then we went to the pub and it carried on there. That was a great relief. It was only when I got back to London that the loss really hit me.'

After his mother died, his father took up the pen and continued the weekly letters his mother had used to write. 'My father was a neat writer. His letters were meticulous with detail. He could conjure a sentence out of the simplest thing such as a cow in a field. And being a clerk his handwriting was very tidy. He was also a very neat man, something I have inherited from him, as well as his eye for detail.'

The first production in which Richard appeared at the City Literary Institute was Jean-Paul Sartre's *The Flies* on 20 and 21 May 1960, directed by Lawrence Hayes, in which he played the High Priest and doubled with the part of a soldier. Other productions followed and he was spotted by Roger Booth who, as an amateur, was already acting in, writing and directing revues. 'I first saw Iain, as he was then known,' recalls Booth, 'singing Coward's "Mad Dogs and Englishmen Go Out in the Midday Sun!" I was immediately impressed by his great ease with the material and the fact that he was very popular with the audience.' As a result Roger Booth invited Richard to be in his next revue, *Bring Your Own Tuba*, which had music by Geoffroy Millais whom Roger had also recruited from the City Lit. The production opened at the Twentieth Century Theatre in Westbourne Grove in May 1961. Apart from performing, Richard wrote three solo sketches as well as two others with Roger Booth. He also wrote the lyrics for two songs: 'How Could We Dream?' and 'Anatomy of Love', the latter sung by Anthony Stevens, now a psychiatrist, Jungian analyst and author. Clearly the words of this lyric were inspired by Richard's medical background:

Now I would give a kidney to you
Since I don't really need the two
It may even prove to be fun
To go through life with one
And if my stomach would do any good
I would go without my food.

I could live without water
Unless you want my bladder
And if you were in need of a leg of mine
You could have it with all my love
The left the right one or even the two
So long as they're for you!

CHORUS:

Please, please remember
Though there are lots that I'd dismember
There is just one thing that I'd like to hold
If I may make so bold
Please let me keep my heart
Since it's such an essential part.

If your blood was like water and caused you to totter
Have a pint on me
There's just one thing I'd better tell you
Before you go ahead
That I'm blood group A and you are blood group B

And if we mixed the two
There would be no more of you
If your brain became a little soft
I would give you my cerebellum
I don't mind losing a brain cell or two
Providing they're for you!

CHORUS

If your globus pallidus was not up to scratch
You have certainly found your match
Have mine, I wouldn't mind it
Providing you can find it
My biceps and triceps and axis on atlas
I could never keep to myself
And even if I had a dose of flu
Don't worry, I would pass it over to you
And there's one other thing that I would give
Though as yet I haven't got it
But it would fill me with bliss to give you
A touch of Rigor Mortis.

In those days professional producers such as Michael Codron regularly attended amateur shows looking for fresh talent, and in this way amateurs made the break into the professional theatre, including Roger Booth himself, when he made his first professional appearance in a revue at the Hampstead Theatre which he cowrote with Piers Stephens. Following this he played Victor in my production of Noël Coward's *Private Lives*, only his second appearance on the professional stage.

The following year Richard appeared in another revue by Roger Booth, *Squeeze the Trigger Gently*, which was mounted on a shoestring at the old Unity Theatre, near King's Cross, in February 1962. This was followed in January 1963 with *Refresco* at the small Chanticleer Theatre, in which Richard performed one solo sketch and four duologues, as well as appearing in company numbers. The set was designed by Ron Sanford, and the business manager was Roger Booth's wife Barbara, later to become secretary to Mrs Norma Major at 10 Downing Street. Typical of this period are some of the cuts demanded by the Lord Chamberlain in the texts of the revue. One example is from a sketch entitled *Danger, Priest Working*, performed by Richard and Roger. On the first page is the following dialogue – the passages underlined being those that the Lord Chamberlain required to be cut and no substitute to be provided.

Priest: Our Lord once said, 'Come unto Me and I will refresh you.'
Foreman: <u>Not in my time He doesn't!</u>

Again, on page 2 we find:

Priest: There's hardly enough time for midmorning communion. The welders, especially, have to gulp their wine. Ten
minutes is their limit, no more!
Foreman: <u>Honestly, this factory 'as gone mad on this communion business ... I've 'eard them in the spindle galleries:
'Which do you prefer, Burgundy or Chateau-neuf-du-Pape?'</u>

Faced with such petty-minded tinkering it is little wonder that
the 1960s saw the battle to abolish the Lord Chamberlain as
theatre censor reach a climax. His theatrical powers were finally
extinguished in 1968.

The revues were rehearsed in hired pub rooms, one of which
was on the first floor of a large pub off the Old Brompton Road, a
typical Edwardian establishment with mahogany panelling and
engraved mirrors, but all a little run down. Anthony Stevens, who
in 1959 had just completed his premedical studies at Oxford, and
had arrived in London to do his clinical training at Charing Cross
Hospital (at that time just off the Strand, close to Trafalgar Square),
recalls their common bond was their belief in Roger Booth's talent,
which lent itself so marvellously to that now virtually extinct
genre, the revue. One critic indeed referred to Roger Booth as 'a
veritable Ustinov with a large scale comic talent'. 'None of us then,'
says Stevens, 'had the slightest idea that Richard (or Iain as he was
then) was destined for such fame. He was a good, competent, reli-
able, reasonably talented amateur, with a Scottish accent that he
was trying, with varying degrees of success, to lose. We were all
very fond of him. And I thought, even then, that the roles which
he filled most effectively were those in which he expressed indignation and frustration. At this he could be very funny.'

Roger and Barbara lived in a two-roomed flat and it was there,
after shows, that the company would gather for a party. Roger also

bought an old Austin car for £5 and on Sundays he, Barbara and Richard would go off for picnics to Taplow, the Chilterns or to Epsom Forest. Eventually the car collapsed outside the British Museum and, because Roger could not afford to have it towed to a garage, he took it away in bits.

In one of his diaries there is the following glimpse of a typical outing: 'Iain and I went for a walk through the beech woods near Ellesborough. Iain and I suddenly went mad, snorting and galloping through the trees, shouting and swinging from branches, behaving like two dray horses turned loose in a field. Barbara plodded patiently behind us like a nurse in charge of two mental defectives.'

Richard now left Paddington General, but without knowing what he was going to do. He only knew that he had to quit, just as earlier he had known that he must leave Greenock. In the words of Joseph Campbell, he was about 'to follow his bliss'. He would become either an actor or a social worker. At a party he met an actress who told him that he had lived long enough in London to qualify for a grant from the London County Council to train as an actor. Roger Booth, sensing his restlessness, urged him to apply to the Royal Academy of Dramatic Art. As he observed in his diary in 1963: 'I met Iain today for lunch at a pub in the Harrow Road. He is still temporarily at the hospital in order to pay his rent, but has applied to RADA. I do hope he gets in as I think it is his final chance to make an assault on the acting profession.'

Like many amateurs Richard had pooh-poohed professional actors, believing that drama schools only spoiled people with talent. He still thinks this is true although, hopefully, the talent can be rediscovered once the technical training has been mastered. None the less he pressed ahead and began to prepare his audition speeches, one of which had to be from Shakespeare and one from a modern play. For the latter he chose a solo sketch from a Roger Booth revue. 'People said to me, "Oh, no, you must choose a proper playwright!" At the time I was much more easily swayed by other people's opinions than I am now, but on this occasion I stuck to my guns. And I did it myself without anyone helping me.'

Roger's sketch was about a rather pathetic man for whom everything he touches turns out a failure. There were lines like: 'I took up pigeon racing but the birds never returned,' or 'I was married to a nice girl but she sent the ring back in a Beecham's pill-box ... I think what she wanted was something a bit more flamboyant, with coloured lining to his mackintosh ... I took up cycling but the other club members used to hide in the bushes.'

Richard's instinct proved right. The adjudicators, having sat through endless Chekhov and Rattigan, were relieved to hear something different but, as the Principal, John Fernald, later told Richard, in the end the judges were split down the middle and it was only by Fernald casting his vote for him that 'I just slipped in by the skin of my teeth!' When the results of his acceptance arrived, Richard was so excited that 'I did the very theatrical thing of crumpling up the letter and throwing it in the air!' Having won his place at RADA he then had to go before a panel of judges at the LCC and audition for them. They gave him a Major County Award of £13 a week.

As the time drew nearer for him to start at RADA he became increasingly frightened. Having so often criticised drama schools, pronouncing that they produced the wrong type of actor, he was now having to eat his own words. There was also, he admits, a fear that he would be found out, that he would be laughed at. 'My inferiority complex was so huge.' None the less he knew that the moment which he had long awaited, and of which he had dreamed – to be allowed to act all the time – had at last arrived. There could be no turning back.

6

The Royal Academy of Dramatic Art

'You're a regular wreck, with a crick in your neck, and no wonder you snore, for your head's on the floor, and you've needles and pins from your soles to your shins ... and a feverish tongue and a thirst that's intense and a general sense that you haven't been sleeping in clover ... .'

On a warm day in early October 1963, from an open window of an upper-floor studio at the Royal Academy of Dramatic Art in Gower Street, there could be heard, above the noise of traffic, the sound of young voices chanting a tongue-twister, '... but the darkness has passed, and it's daylight at last, and the night has been long – ditto, ditto, my song – and thank goodness they're both of them over!'

Thank goodness indeed! gasped Richard as he staggered out of Clifford Turner's voice classes, relieved that such a vocal ordeal was over for a few hours. 'I had this very broad Scottish accent which used to drive my teachers to despair. When I did something like King Lear, "Blow winds and crack your cheeks! Rumble thy bellyful!" Clifford Turner used to burst out laughing. He'd look at me and say, "Oh, Wilson, Wilson! I don't know *what* I am going to do with you!"'

Being already self-conscious about his voice, Richard admits to being more acutely aware of this because Clifford Turner, who had been an actor, had a superb vocal instrument of great range and flexibility, albeit of an older school of verse speaking. None the less, Richard took to having private lessons with him at his tiny flat around the corner from Gower Street. He never thought of himself as having a distinctive voice and yet today, as Susan Belbin, the producer and director of *One Foot in the Grave*, says, 'Richard's voice is vital to the characterisation of Victor Meldrew. His enunciation is wonderful, the way he bites off the words and munches them.'

By the time of his final term in the summer of 1965 Barry Smith, who had taken on much of the voice work at the Academy, was able to write on Richard's report: 'Latterly you have really begun to make progress and seem to have cottoned on to what voice and speech in the theatre is really about. Your OH and OO sounds are too narrow still. You are limited in vocal range and colouring. You should work on carrying lower resonance into your upper range, but its light dry quality matches your comedy.' It wasn't that Richard wanted to lose his Scottish accent because he was ashamed of it, but that he didn't want just to be a Scottish actor. He wanted to be able to play a variety of roles and knew that there were better parts around if he wasn't bound by his accent.

The English accent that he acquired at RADA and which he has put to such hilarious use in many television roles has also, as Alan Rickman observes, inhibited him at times. It was after seeing Richard perform in the revival of Joe Orton's *What the Butler Saw* at the National Theatre that, over dinner, Rickman told him he needed to do more work on his voice, 'because all I can hear when you're playing someone English are those dying Scottish falls'. It seemed to Rickman that with Orton's long sentences Richard needed a vocal energy which would carry him forwards. 'I thought that he should look cold-bloodedly at where he could flick the lines up in order to help himself; otherwise he is constantly coming downwards vocally and then having to scrape himself up off the floor. If he did this then he'd have an energy which would carry him through the play. I've said all this to him but you can only say that kind of thing once, you can't keep going on about it. Richard's big success is with Victor who, interestingly, is Scottish and so his humour has rhythms. As soon as he puts on an English accent it freezes him and that's what was happening at the National. If he is going on to take on a major role in theatre then it is going to have to be with a Scottish accent.'

Once through the first term Richard began to enjoy RADA, although he continued to feel that all the emphasis on technique stifled his spontaneity, what he calls 'free-wheelingness'. 'The technical work was such a trial to me that I stopped acting. It seemed to me that improvisation was what acting was about and that was something which RADA didn't offer. Never mind verse-speaking I thought, just be *believable*, be a person. Which is why I have always admired Brando as an actor.' He tried to persuade John Fernald to send RADA students out into prisons, hospitals, and the community. 'I had this fear that actors tended to copy actors and not people, that they didn't even observe or listen, let alone communicate with, ordinary people.' Feeling inhibited by the technical restraints placed upon him, he became prominent in student revues because these allowed more opportunity for spontaneity on stage.

He encouraged this spontaneity in his fellow students via games that he invented. Clive Francis, who was just eighteen and in the same class, remembers how they all looked up to Richard, and how he would take some of them to an art cinema in Oxford Street to see the kind of films which he felt would open their eyes to what acting was really about. On the way, 'He would get us to improvise games; we would have to pretend to be spies and things like that.' For the spy games they all had to draw marked slips of paper from a hat. 'G' indicated membership of the Gestapo; 'S' that the person was a British spy. The game consisted in seeing how long everyone could go without being found out.

Patrick Dunne, another student, and Richard used regularly to assume 'characters' when they went to lunch. 'We would put on an accent and talk gibberish and the task was to see if we could succeed in appearing very ordinary.' If they attracted people's attention this meant they had failed. On one occasion, in the cafeteria of London University, they pretended they were food experts. Every time Dunne took a sip of milk he masticated it many times until finally Richard leaned over and asked, 'Excuse me, I hope you don't mind me asking, but why are you chewing your milk?' To which Dunne replied, 'Recent research has shown that you should masticate your milk.' Whereupon Richard started masticating his milk, chewing each sip many times. They had to remain absolutely serious and not collapse into giggles. Such a scene might be a sketch with Peter Cook. Indeed, after Richard and Peter Cook had worked together so well in 'One Foot in the Algarve', Eleanor Bron describes how she was working with Cook on a new entertainment for the theatre and when she asked him who he had in mind to direct, he replied, 'Why, Richard, of course!'

During Richard's first term at RADA he was asked by a friend at London University if he would lead some improvisation classes. 'But I'm only a first year student at RADA!' he protested. However, his frustration that RADA had no such classes encouraged him to take on a challenge which seeded many ideas he was to develop several years later at a weekly gathering of professional actors. Perhaps, too, he reflects, 'There may have been a subconscious desire to direct, although at that time I had no idea of ever being a director. The thought had never entered my head. My one consuming ambition was to be an actor and the more I could learn about that, even if it meant my leading such a class, was all that mattered to me.'

For some time, however, at RADA he continued to feel awkward, self-conscious about his body, and his voice. 'I was far too gauche,' he admits. 'I didn't know who I was. I was very gawky and confused – like all Presbyterians.' It wasn't until Peter Barkworth's acting technique classes that he experienced for the first time a teacher who gave him real confidence and who really encouraged him. Ask any actor or actress who went to the Academy in the late 1950s and early 1960s to name the teacher who influenced them the most and they are likely to reply, 'Why, Peter Barkworth, of course!'

Once, when asked why he was an actor, Peter Barkworth replied, 'I think it is that, on television especially, the actor is able to reveal the privateness of ordinary people. Most public faces nowadays are cover-ups, masks, but the actor's task is to make as true a revelation as he can of the most complex emotions. It is his task to show what it is to be lonely, ecstatic, anxious. It is an entertainment but, at the same time, it is stretching the audience into a revelation of what life is about.' Such a statement also sums up Richard's philosophy, both as an actor and even more so as a director. But, during his two years at RADA, the actor in him was still in the melting pot.

Clive Francis admits, 'I have to say I never could see his career going anywhere. He was not a very good straight actor and he had this adenoidal problem which was his main setback.' It was Fernald who continued to believe in his talent, chastising him when necessary, as in a letter written to him on 1 April 1964:

Dear Iain Wilson,

I am writing to you because though I have liked very much all that I've seen of your work I have more than a suspicion that you don't really work hard enough. You have a valuable natural talent and a valuable personality which will always please an audience. It is doubtless perfectly possible for you to be lazy without quite realising it and to rely on what you've got, and to just leave it at that. This, however, would be fair neither to you nor to your talent – and it is not what you are here for.

In his final term Fernald threw Richard an unexpected challenge, casting him in the role of Macheath in *The Beggar's Opera*, not the most obvious casting. Roger Booth remarks, 'I sensed that he and Fernald had a rather special relationship in that, because Iain was more mature, they had a particular rapport.' Richard himself describes the incident as follows.

'In your first term at RADA you were given a singing audition and if you were any good you then went on to have singing lessons as part of your training. I was so appalling that it was decided not to give me any lessons! And then, with my last term, Fernald decided he was going to do a musical in the Vanbrugh, but everything was kept under wraps until the last minute. When the notices went up, announcing the productions and the casting for the final term, we all crowded round the board. And there it said, *The Beggar's Opera* by John Gay, ... Macheath: Iain Wilson! So I went straight to the Registrar and said, "There's been a mistake. On the board

I've been cast as Macheath in *The Beggar's Opera*." And they looked at the list and said, "No, no, that's right." "But I can't sing!" I replied. "What about the singing?" And I was told, "You're starting singing lessons tomorrow!" Apparently Richard Carey, who was directing, thought I had the best acting potential for the role.'

On his final report Richard Carey wrote, 'In the most difficult role of Macheath he developed during rehearsals and gave an excellent performance, with good comedy sense, timing and charm. Every time he played the part he "matured", without in any way distorting the original intention. He should be very useful in the professional theatre.'

And in his final report Fernald, who had done so much to foster his talent, wrote, 'An erratic actor, highly intelligent and sometimes unexpectedly very good indeed. Consistency is a professional virtue and consistency can only be achieved with the confidence of a fully acquired technical mastery. I am not quite sure whether you have as yet achieved this, but I am quite sure that you *can* achieve it. And when you have – your qualities of personality and wit and genuine talent will come into their own. Good luck. John Fernald.'

Prophetic words indeed. Perhaps, on reading Fernald's comments, Richard thought of Bruce and the spider and the words, 'If at first you don't succeed, try and try again!' Few actors have worked so hard or with such singleness of purpose to achieve mastery of their craft.

John Fernald had been appointed Principal of the Royal Academy of Dramatic Art as a successful director with four productions running in the West End, including Peter Ustinov's *The Love of Four Colonels*. The first professional director to be Principal of RADA, he proved a great innovator. Classes were reduced in size from a staggering and hopelessly unmanageable thirty, or even more, to about a dozen. He trusted his staff and loved his students, and introduced a much more personal relationship between the two. He was always willing to listen to people and, if convinced, to change his own opinion. He wanted the Academy to feel more like a professional theatre than a school. It was also his policy to encourage 'late vocations' to the theatre, welcoming the valuable contribution that more mature students, such as Richard, could make.

In his final term a major crisis erupted that was to exercise Richard's skills of political leadership. Out of the blue, the RADA's Council requested the resignation of Fernald as Principal. The Student Council, led by Richard, wrote to all Council members on 2 June 1965 to protest:

> The Student Body wish to proclaim their wholehearted support of the policy and find the Principal's methods both in the administration and teaching entirely satisfactory. We realise, as a student body, that we are only a transient factor of the Academy, but we must point out that any break in the continuity of the Principalship at this stage for the present students would have a serious effect on the development of their studies. We also regret, as fee paying students of the Academy, the amount of publicity this matter is receiving in the National Press, and the contradictory nature of this matter.

The letter was signed by Joyce Bell and Iain Wilson.

Richard followed this letter with a demonstration in which around one hundred students paraded for about an hour outside the Academy in Gower Street as a protest against 'being kept uninformed of the issues'. One press report states, 'Their leader, Mr Iain Wilson, aged twenty-nine, who leaves on Friday, the end of term, said, "We want to know from the RADA Council the full reasons for Mr Fernald's resignation. So far we have been told nothing. We are paying 95 guineas a term and that entitles us to know what is going on. If the issue is one of policy, then we want to know what that policy is."'

In a further letter to the Council the students wrote, 'We will continue to support Mr Fernald until such time as the Council will divulge to us satisfactory reasons why we should not do so.'

Sir Felix Aylmer, Chairman of the Council, sent a telegram to Fernald referring to the picketing and stating that he expected him 'to maintain discipline'. In turn, Fernald sent a telegram back expressing his deep concern about the situation, saying that everything would be done to maintain such discipline 'in most exceptional circumstances', and that the students' action was without his knowledge or approval. In fact, Fernald went out into Gower Street on four occasions to ask the students to cease their silent protest but each time Richard, as their leader, refused, saying to the press, 'We don't want to embarrass Mr Fernald. He is still the Principal until December. But we politely told him that we wanted to carry on the protest a bit longer.'

There is little doubt that Sir Felix and certain members of the Council behaved in an insensitive and autocratic manner that would not be possible today, although a number of the Council, led by Peter O'Toole, did try to press for the reinstatement of Fernald, but in vain. The students were incensed. Clive Francis, who had just been presented with the Ronson Award by former RADA student Richard Briers, telephoned Briers to protest. He remembers standing in the phone booth on the main staircase of the Academy with all his class, including Richard, listening as he said to Briers, 'You have to reinstate John Fernald or ... ,' leaving Briers stammering at the other end.

The following day, an Extraordinary Meeting of the Council was called. The students lined the street and the main staircase of the Academy in silent protest, forcing the entire Council, including Sir Felix Aylmer, to walk past them.

With this flexing of his political muscles, and the exercise of his powers of leadership, as well as a growing confidence in his ability as an actor, Iain Wilson was now ready to become Richard Wilson, a change of name forced on him when Equity reported another Iain Wilson already in the profession. At first this came as a shock to Richard but, once he had got over it, he thought it an improvement. 'I couldn't change the family name, but because Iain Wilson was not a particularly good sound, and was also very Scottish, I didn't mind changing, and I also thought Richard Wilson sounded better.' For a while it was confusing when people called out 'Richard!' and he didn't respond, but today, if someone were to call out 'Iain!', Richard would assume it was someone else. 'Now I don't think of myself as Iain at all.'

The change of name was also, as he realised, symbolic of his new life and image. It represented his new identity. With it, his career as an actor, a dream he had long nurtured, had at last begun. His only sadness was that his mother was not alive to share in it.

7

First Steps in the Theatre

Although Richard failed to win any awards at RADA, he did get himself an agent before he left and went straight into a job, playing an important role as a stonemason in *The Phantom Piper of Tannochbrae*, episode one of the seventh series of *Dr Finlay's Casebook*, starring Andrew Cruickshank and Bill Simpson, which was rehearsed and filmed in August 1965.

He was paid £85. 1s. (this fee included the sum of one guinea for overtime), with an additional sixty guineas for any repeats. Richard remembers his debut as a professional actor for one incident in particular. On the third day of rehearsal he was approached by a much older actor who had only a small part in the episode.

'Is this your first Finlay?' said the older actor.

'I don't know what you mean.'

'Is this the first time you've done a *Dr Finlay's Casebook?*'

'Yes. This is my *first* job!'

'Oh, really? Where have you been?'

'I've been at RADA.'

'When did you leave?'

'Last Friday.'

The actor then looked at Richard haughtily and said, 'What about rep?'

'Well, I'd like to do some repertory around London,' replied Richard, 'because I've got a bedsitter in West Hampstead.'

'Well, take my advice, laddie, and do some work in the provinces. Make your mistakes there!'

Years later, when Richard had become not only a celebrated actor but a director of some influence and power, he was casting a new play and someone mentioned this actor who had tried to cut him down to size and made him feel very small at the beginning of his career. 'I think you know him; he'd like a word with you.'

'No, thank you,' replied Richard sharply. 'I don't want a word with him. I don't see why I should.' Richard subsequently commented, 'He'd been extremely unkind and cruel to me, and even though I was twenty-nine at the time, I was just starting out in the profession. Clearly he has forgotten that I was that young actor. In this game it pays to be kind. Ours is a very fragile profession. It is all too easy to undermine another person's confidence.'

Richard's appearance on television gave his father much cause for pride. 'I think,' says Richard, 'if I'd still been in Greenock, my father, with his canny Presbyterianism, would have had something to say about my becoming an actor. But he was thrilled when I appeared on *Dr Finlay's Casebook.* That made me respectable!'

Richard next joined the repertory company of the new Swan Theatre in Worcester, where he was to have his first experience of theatrical digs, in a freezing cold attic with only one electrical bar for heating. Standing in the theatre bar, talking with the theatre's artistic director, Teresa Collard, and looking out through the windows at some swans swimming across a large expanse of water, Richard commented, 'What a wonderful situation it is here on the edge of this lake.'

'Oh, no!' replied Teresa Collard, 'that's not a lake, that's the race-course. It's flooded!'

Only then did Richard observe the winning post sticking up above the water.

That Christmas John Fernald, still deeply shocked by the way in which he had been treated by the Council, resigned as Principal of RADA. Richard decided he wanted to do something to acknowledge the debt of gratitude which he and past students felt they owed him and so, although he was busy rehearsing in Worcester, he managed to organise a cabaret, performed by former students, which was presented in the Vanbrugh Theatre. 'How you managed to achieve this when you are already working at Worcester,' wrote

Fernald to Richard, 'I just don't know, but the gesture of love is appreciated just as much as the magnificent exhibition of professionalism.'

After three plays at Worcester there followed periods of being out of work when he took any job just to pay the rent. 'Every time you got a job, you earned just enough to pay your debts and then you were broke again. There have been times when I was so broke that I would walk down the road to the next bus stop in order to pay a lesser fare.' But although things were often tight, he never went hungry. He also did cleaning jobs – until he discovered that one of the people he was cleaning for was with the same theatrical agency as he was 'and that didn't seem right to me. In any case, I hated housework.'

He took a job as a security guard at London's Olympia exhibition centre, where he was put in charge of a stand of lamps. When one of the lamps was stolen Richard found himself, like some character out of a Whitehall farce, walking round the exhibition, bent double, looking under tables in search of the missing lamp, and trying not to be noticed, as in one of the games he used to play with Pat Dunne at RADA.

In 1966 Richard was invited by Tom Browne, a producer for Danish radio, to mount a revue to be presented in Copenhagen that summer. Entitled *English Spoken*, the show was devised and directed by Richard, with a company which included, apart from himself, Gyda Hansen (a Danish actress), Tom Browne, Barry Bryson, and Maggie Ollerenshaw who is now one of his oldest friends. Since the revue was evolved from improvisations the producer, Louis Miehe Renard, was often puzzled and kept asking Richard, 'But where is the script?'

English Spoken was such a success that it moved to a second theatre and played for three months altogether. In two of the sketches Richard developed that predilection for inventing mock languages that he had first tried out on Beatrice McCallum at the Gateside Hospital. One, clearly influenced by *Tokyo Story*, used a mock Japanese while another, *And Quietly Flows the Borishnolovoff: An Upper Slobvian Play in One Act with Subtitles* (see Appendix II) used subtitles in mock Russian. But the great success of the show was a mimed parody of a circus troupe, performed with manic energy. As one critic wrote in *Anmeldesser*, 2 July 1966, 'The coup of the evening is an acrobatic number, *The Boldinis*, which the actors throw themselves into with much whooping, sweating and dancing, and alarming energy, and out of all that fuss comes a little hop! Deathly pale, nearly fainting with exhaustion, the Boldinis accept the applause. It is the evening's most harrowingly funny number.'

Richard also performed a parody of Marcel Marceau, the famous mime. As Maggie Ollerenshaw says, 'He just imitated what he saw and it was so funny.' The amount of physicality in the show is particularly interesting given that for many years Richard had been convinced he could not be successful because he was so physically inadequate. At RADA, however, he had come under the influence of two brilliant movement teachers, Madame Fedro and Molly Kenny, who each encouraged him to work on his movement. This, together with his love of dancing and squash, gradually resulted in his filling out until, finally, he learned how to own and inhabit his own body and no longer be ashamed of it.

As a result of that summer in Denmark, and his contact with Tom Browne, he was employed to write a weekly comic sketch for Danish radio, often acting in some of them. For several years to come this provided him with a sinecure, as well as a regular trip to Denmark to record the latest batch of sketches. Following his return from Denmark in September 1966 he went up to Scotland to appear in James Bridie's *The Queen's Comedy* in Perth. The play centres around the Trojan Wars and the intrigue of the gods in the outcome. His performance as Vulcan was singled out by the *Scotsman*, while the *Glasgow Herald* wrote, 'All the parts give scope for humorous emphasis, if not actual caricature, and most opportunities were taken – a little gem being Richard Wilson's sketch of Vulcan, a Scots-spoken engineer who moves in a breath from an explanation of how to split the atom to domestic plumbing repair.'

The following year saw Richard at the Close Theatre Club, attached to the Citizens Theatre in Glasgow, where he appeared in a season of documentaries under the generic title, *Theatre of Fact Season*, based on a similar season which I had inaugurated at the Hampstead Theatre the previous year. This was followed by *Three Goose Quills and a Knife*, a new play by Lesley Storm, at the main Citizens Theatre, directed by Michael Meacham, in which he played a hellfire minister, and doubled with the part of a soldier who had only one leg and one arm, which meant, therefore, using a peg leg that he had to strap himself into by tying back his right leg, which was very painful, and then strapping up his left arm. 'It took a long time to get ready and I did feel particularly disabled.' He felt even more disabled on the first night when, at the curtain call, the peg leg snapped and rolled away down the stage, leaving Richard hopping about the stage, to the amusement of the rest of the cast and, presumably, the audience.

His next move, and one that was to prove crucial in ways he could not have foreseen, was to the old Traverse Theatre in Edinburgh. The Traverse, housed in a former brothel in a seventeenth-century tenement, had opened in 1963, and under its first artistic director and presiding genius, the American Jim Haynes, had swiftly won international fame in its first three years. Mounting debts and Haynes' frequent absences led to his being forced to resign in 1966, when Gordon McDougall was appointed his successor, with Max Stafford-Clark as general manager.

Whilst McDougall co-ordinated policy and directed new and classical plays, Stafford-Clark was more interested in the new American avant-garde theatre. Encouraged by McDougall, he developed a link between the Traverse and La Mama Troupe of New York, so that in the spring of 1967 he directed at the Traverse a triple bill by Paul Foster, who had worked with La Mama. The most notorious of these plays, *Balls*, consisted solely of two tennis balls bouncing backwards and forwards, with all the dialogue prerecorded. Later that year Paul Foster and La Mama came to the Edinburgh Festival to mount four productions in association with the Traverse, including a new work by Foster, *Tom Paine;* but it was one of the other plays, *Futz*, about a relationship between a man and a pig, which, inevitably, was blown

Richard with his sister, Moira.

Richard at the Lady Alice School, top row, third from left.

Play-acting in the back garden at 141 Dunliop Street, Greenock.

Effie and John Wilson, Richard's parents.

Toots, his first cat.

With Effie and Moira.

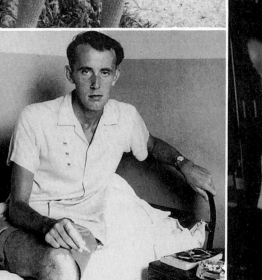

National Service in Singapore

(above) Swabbing down!

(left) As Corporal in the Royal Army Medical Corps.

(below left) In his room.

(below) With Tiddles, an adopted cat.

(top) Laboratory technicians at Gateside Hospital, Greenock, with Richard second from left.

(above) With Margaret Dyer.

(left) With Effie.

(below left) The Laboratory skiffle group, with Richard top, far right.

(right) The three inseparables: Charlie Murray, Tom Purdie and Richard.

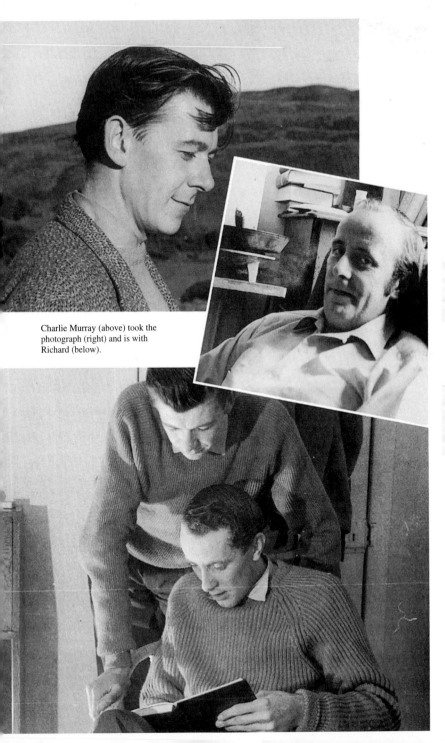

Charlie Murray (above) took the
photograph (right) and is with
Richard (below).

(above) Charlie Murray catches Richard posing as
world-weary Noël Coward and as a corpse (right)

(below) Richard's photographic revenge:
Charlie Murray.

(above) Rehearsing for *Bring Your Own Tuba*. To the left of Richard, top centre, Veronica Castang and Anthony Stevens; to his right, Roger Booth and Anne Hyde. With the tuba, Geoffroy Millais.

(below) Rehearsing for *Dark of the Moon*, a production at London's City Literary Institute; Richard is far right.

(above) Richard, with beard, kneeling, with laboratory team, Paddington hospital.

(left) A press shot for *English Spoken.* a revue devised and directed by Richard in Denmark; Maggier Ollerenshaw on right.

up into headlines such as 'Filth at the Fringe'. Thus it was, writes Joyce McMillan in her engrossing *Traverse Theatre Story*, 'under the supposedly mild mannered McDougall, the Traverse actually reached the height of its notoriety in Edinburgh with wildly exaggerated stories circulating about the drinking, dope taking, drug dealing, and lurid sex practices that were supposed to take place there. At the time the Traverse was a powerful focus for respectable Edinburgh's fantasies and fears about the new "permissive" age.'

To many, such as the young actress Dinah Stabb, the Traverse was Bohemia, 'the centre of everything exciting and avant-garde'. Never before in a British theatre had artists, writers, actors and directors worked together under one roof. There were paintings by Roy Lichtenstein, Patrick Heron, Jasper Jacob, Elizabeth Blackadder, Mark Boyle and many more. The theatre was open every night, with late-evening shows and discussions as well as the main production; and because the bars everywhere else shut at ten and weren't open on Sundays (not even during the Edinburgh International Festival) the Traverse became the place where everybody in the arts gathered.

Inevitably Richard was attracted to the Traverse and to McDougall's belief that theatre should be a means for 'communicating that there are things that need doing about the way people live'. He also responded to McDougall's exploration of documentary theatre in such programmes as *The Vietnam Hearings* (December 1966), *The Denning Report on the Profumo Affair* (January 1967), and the various talk-ins on local issues. Hearing that McDougall was planning a special Christmas production of Samuel Beckett's *Waiting for Godot* which he intended staging as a protest against the hypocritical attitude of the Edinburgh middle classes towards the tramps on their own doorstep in the Grassmarket (where, ironically, the new Traverse now is), Richard persuaded him that he should play Vladimir to John Sheddon's Estragon.

Not only was this an unconventional choice of play for Christmas, the production made it even more controversial. Before rehearsals started, the actors and their director, dressed in cloth caps and long raincoats, spent a day among the down-and-outs who, having been thrown out of their hostels at nine o'clock in the morning, stood around the Grassmarket for most of the day. 'We chatted to them about their lives,' recalls McDougall, 'though most of them were fairly woozy with having just woken up, or were suffering from hangovers. The police never actually paid much attention to them. There were three hostels in that area and it was accepted that the Grassmarket was where the drunks and tramps would congregate, so the respectable burghers of Edinburgh gave it a wide berth. It was something that was never dealt with or talked about, and it just felt to me that Edinburgh was a hugely hypocritical city.'

In Vladimir and Estragon Beckett has fused two immemorial archetypes, those of the tramp and the clown. As Peter Vansittart observes in his book *In The Fifties*, they were two Laurels without a Hardy, with further echoes of Chaplin and Keaton, with their training in music hall and vaudeville; two tramps trudging towards nowhere, awaiting a sign from 'the great cold, the great dark'. Like Mrs Rooney in Beckett's *All That Fall*, they dream of other roads, in other lands, of another home. Like her they seem to be struggling with a dead language. The bleakness of Beckett's vision and the heroic stoicism of his characters, as well as his dark comedy, are peculiarly suited to Richard's temperament and outlook. Having rejected all religious belief in his teens he, like Edgar in *King Lear*, simply believes that

> Men must endure
> Their going hence, even as their coming hither.

On his frequent trips home to Greenock from Edinburgh Richard always called in at Gateside Hospital to see Beatrice. She describes how, after one visit, some of the new technicians came into her office to ask, who was that? 'He was always dressed very smartly,' says Beatrice. 'Even then he wore beautiful shirts, suits and ties, and had such an air about him. That was very much something he had acquired since going to London.' Today Richard dresses with a flamboyance of style and colour, mainly from Armani and

Paul Smith. He is a great buyer of clothes but also enjoys clearing out his wardrobe in order to make way for new purchases.

Robin Hooper, the actor and writer, describes how, when they were fellow judges for the Mobil Playwriting Competition, they had to go to Manchester for the awards and 'I don't know whether I was looking a little scruffy or what, but he did say, quite discreetly, that he had several articles of clothing which he felt would fit me and that if I was interested in going over to his flat I might like to pick up a few things. So I drove over and had a drink. "I've put the clothes out in the guest room," he said. Well, the bed was simply covered with clothes, bags of shirts, trousers, suits, and lines of shoes! It wasn't just one or two things he was throwing out, it was practically a whole wardrobe. I was set up for the next five years.'

After *Waiting for Godot*, in the following year McDougall formed a company to do three plays: Thomas Middleton's *Women, Beware Women*; Chekhov's *Uncle Vanya*; and a new play by David Wright, *Would You Look At Them Smashing All Those Lovely Windows?* In *Vanya* Brian Smith played Dr Astrov to Richard's Vanya, while Richard Howard played the Professor. 'I always think,' says Howard, 'that they were the best Vanya and Astrov I've seen, and Richard's Vanya was a very tortured and funny creation.' McDougall confirms this. 'Richard is a wonderful Chekhovian actor. He has that quality – absolutely essential in Chekhov – of preserving the tenderness, the sadness and the tragic feeling, with an immensely comic aspect, and Richard is one of the few actors who has a real gift for combining the two. The moment when Vanya goes off to get the gun and tries to shoot the Professor and says, "Missed him again, have I? Oh, hell and damnation!" and then, throwing down the gun, collapses into a chair, crushing the bouquet of flowers in it (which in the previous scene he had brought for Elena but, finding her in the arms of Astrov, drops in the chair) was sheer magic as Richard played it.' Nancy Meckler, the director, who saw Richard repeat his performance as Vanya in a revival at the Oxford Playhouse some years later, describes it as 'unforgettable; it was as though the man and the part were made for each other'.

Richard also performed in the late-evening shows at the Traverse, acting with Max Stafford-Clark, in which they would improvise on any subject given by the audience. These 'games,' as Richard describes them, were very much the precursor of similar acting games now made familiar by television on the show *Whose Line Is It Anyway?* In a typical example, says Richard, two actors would be told: 'You are a surgeon, and you a school teacher, and you both meet in the middle of a swamp. Go!' In the audience two batons, one red, one white, were handed around. If the white baton was held up the actors would have to 'freeze' at once and one actor would be replaced by another before the scene was resumed exactly where it had stopped. If the red baton was held up, the actors would be given new characters and a new situation, and asked to adapt at once. Apart from providing fun for an audience, such exercises clearly help expand an actor's imaginative and technical skills. One evening, however, they were stymied by a rival theatre director: Richard Eyre, then running the Lyceum Theatre in Edinburgh, threw such impossible subjects that Richard finally protested, saying 'That's not fair! We're not going to do that; it's just not reasonable. We are going to do something else!'

If the Traverse was a vital, formative experience for Richard, something even more exciting was to follow. By April 1968 McDougall had, in only two years, mounted fifty-four shows, including thirty-five world premières, in an organisation that was constantly in serious debt, with himself and Max Stafford-Clark (who would succeed him as Artistic Director) and all the staff, working seven days a week.

McDougall now left Edinburgh for Manchester, to start a new theatre company for Granada Television. Although the Stables Theatre, as it was called, survived for only just over two years, it would prove an important seed-bed for a number of new writers, including Trevor Griffiths, Peter Ransley, Bill Morrison, and John Bowen, as well as a turning point in Richard's career.

When Richard left Edinburgh it was with three key friends for life: Dinah Stabb (whom he was later to direct in two of his productions and with whom he now shares a race-horse), Max

Stafford-Clark (for whom he was subsequently to work both as an actor and a director at the Royal Court Theatre in London), and Gordon McDougall, who was about to open up a whole new world to him. Above all, like Stafford-Clark, Richard had been inspired by the experience of La Mama and the idea of a company creating its own work, an idea that would lead Stafford-Clark to form, with William Gaskill, Joint Stock, a company which evolved plays through a workshop process.

While waiting to join the Stables company Richard received a letter, dated 30 September 1968, from the manager of the Finchley Road branch of the National Westminster Bank:

Dear Sir,

I thank you for your letter of the 27th inst. and confirm that your overdraft, at the moment, is about £12 ... in connection with your request for further overdraft facilities, I should be glad to know, before considering the proposition, ... whether you are able to deposit any acceptable security.

Little did the bank, let alone Richard, foresee how dramatically, within a very few years, his financial affairs were to change, or that he would leave the National Westminster Bank and transfer to the Royal Bank of Scotland.

ACT II

8

The Emergence of a New Talent

'The idea of the Stables,' remarks Richard, 'was revolutionary. It was to be a repertory company of actors, designers, directors and writers, working in television as well as theatre, evolving new plays which could then be translated into the medium of television; using, whenever possible, the same actors.' Even more important at that time, it was possibly one of the only theatres with a special budget to commission new plays.

The ideal of a permanent company of creative individuals has been a recurring dream in theatre over the past hundred years, from the Moscow Art Theatre of Stanislavsky, to Jacques Copeau's Vieux Colombier, and Michel St Denis' Compagnie des Quinze, to the Group Theatre of America, and Peter Brook's International Company in Paris. McDougall's project was different. Here, for the first time, was a television company sponsoring a group of artists to create productions for both theatre and television. Above all, as McDougall wrote in his manifesto, 'to conduct a true experiment one must have the right to fail'. However, he was realistic enough to know that such a theatre had to be run economically: 'One cannot have the right to fail in a very costly enterprise. So one needs a small adaptable area with a live audience reaction.' The Stables was, as Benedict Nightingale wrote in the *New Statesman*, 'the first professional theatre in Britain where deserving failure may take place without recrimination; a kindergarten where stumbling dramatists who seem to have something are helped to walk.'

In order to house this experiment Granada took over derelict stables (hence the theatre's name) at the back of its Manchester studios. The stables, which had been part of one of Britain's first railway stations, were around three sides of a courtyard: on the left, accommodation for dressing rooms, props and administrative offices; on the right, the theatre bar, and in the centre, the hundred-seat theatre. As one of the original company of twenty actors, Richard received a letter from Granada in May 1968 informing him: 'You will play as cast in not more than eight television plays. You will receive an annual salary of £2000, payable weekly in arrears' – a sum considerably higher than that earned by actors in the average repertory theatre at that time.

Granada had in twelve years shown itself different from the other commercial television companies. Its origins had been in cinema between the wars. In television its creation of the twice-weekly series, *Coronation Street*, demonstrates its commercial acumen, but it also had a sense of social purpose in creating current affairs series such as *World in Action*. This sense of *gravitas* came from the top and its chairman Sidney Bernstein. Jack Rosenthal, who worked with Granada from its inception and rose through the ranks to being a writer and producer, describes Granada as being like a Jewish family business. 'You didn't leave; they would have regarded that as a betrayal.'

In those days Manchester was an exciting place to be. The city centre had not then gone into decline, nor had the unsightly Arndale Shopping Centre been built. The buildings were still black as they are in Lowry's paintings, and one could pass Lowry in the street or, as I once saw him, eating a solitary lunch at the Great Midland Hotel, with a large linen napkin tucked into his shirt collar. George Best was *the* footballer, and Manchester United was *the* football team, but George Best was the icon, even more so than Bobby Charlton. There were boutiques everywhere (including George Best's own); and every disco or nightclub that Best attended was packed with hundreds of girls eager to see him. Into all this excitement came the Stables. When the actors arrived for its launch in January 1969, among them was Maureen Lipman who remembers picking her way through scaffolding and planks, feeling like an advance army. 'It was very moving when we opened the first season and we felt we were doing something terribly new.

They were days of great enthusiasm when everything seemed possible. We felt we were trail blazing.'

The theatre itself was just a space with beams in the ceiling and yet, as Richard Howard, who was also in the company, says, 'You felt that anything could happen there.' For Gordon McDougall's production of *The Cherry Orchard* the audience was seated on benches among an orchard of silver birches. At one end was the Nursery scene for Acts 1 and 4, and then, after Act 2, which was played among the audience, the spectators turned round to face the other end which had been set for the ballroom scene of Act 3.

For each production the space changed, recalling the early experiments in Russia of Okhlopkov whose first action, on being appointed director of the Realistic Theatre in Moscow in 1930, was to strip out the stage and auditorium seating. Since then, of course, there have been many experiments with the use of theatre space. Perhaps the most seminal work came in the 1970s with Jerzy Grotowski's Polish Laboratory Theatre. Grotowski, above all, was concerned with the role of the spectator, so that each production evolved a form of staging that would test the different aspects of the relationship between the spectator and the actor. Thus in *Kordian* the action was set in a psychiatric ward and the entire space was filled with beds, so that the spectators found themselves having to sit among the sick. In *Dr Faustus* the spectators sat alongside the actors as guests at Dr Faustus' table in the monks' refectory. In 1969, outside the Stables, however, no one was experimenting with theatre space in such an imaginative way.

The whole place was alive with experiment, the actors working all hours, rehearsing main productions, late-night shows, television plays, mini-plays (lasting less than fifteen minutes) and micro-plays (lasting less than four minutes), as well as taking part in workshops. Someone had only to say: Strindberg's *Miss Julie* and Gordon McDougall would say, oh, yes! and it would get done. Maureen Lipman and John Shrapnel performed a long one-act play by Israel Horowitz, *It's Called the Sugar Plum*, which they did in two weeks, rehearsing each day for an hour – in their tea break. They then performed it as a late-night show. McDougall remembers, 'It was eleven o'clock on a Friday night when they first did it, and when they came off they just fell into each other's arms, rolling about in hysteria that they'd actually got through it.' It was such a success that it became a main production and was subsequently televised the following year. Things got done by dint of people wanting to do them. Richard used to organise the late-night shows and Maureen remembers him rehearsing a revue and managing to persuade everyone to come in on Sunday, their one day for lying in. Everyone was so committed to the theatre and the audience, 'it just felt hugely liberating to have that space to work in'.

Because of the better than average salaries, the actors didn't have to live in the usual theatrical digs. John Fraser took an elegant flat close to the theatre, albeit in the red light district, and cycled to work; Maureen Lipman lived in Frog's Lane, Didsbury. Richard Howard, who had a motor-cycle, preferred to be outside Manchester, as did Bill and Jane Simons who rented a cottage at Mobberley, and drove to work. Richard lived in a large Victorian house, built of Pennine stone blackened with dirt, with an overgrown garden, which he shared with John Shrapnel, Ewen Solon and the latter's Alsatian dog.

The Stables bar was the focus of social life for both the actors and the audience. 'It became Granada's bar,' recalls Jack Rosenthal, 'and was always full of *Coronation Street* people and visiting celebrities.' That the theatre had a bar was thought surprising, given that Sidney Bernstein was teetotal. Richard Howard recalls how 'Mr' Sidney, as he was known, would often come round the Stables 'looking in drawers and cupboards, searching for booze. He was very strict, very heavy, about booze on the premises, and so he would have these periodic checks.' Richard Wilson also remembers the occasion, before he had met him, working late one night in the Stables office, when the door opened and in walked a man in a raincoat.

'Can I help you?' enquired Richard.

'I beg your pardon?' replied the man, looking round 'What do you mean?'

Richard repeated his question, whereupon the man replied, 'I'm Mr Sidney.'

A year before Richard joined the Stables, he went one night to the City Literary Institute, to see two new one-act plays, written by members of the City Lit's writing course. The plays were performed by amateur actors from the various acting classes, those same classes which Richard himself had attended in 1959 on his arrival in London. The first play was so poor that in the bar during the interval there was some discussion as to whether they should go back for the second half. Fortunately they did, for the second play was *Disabled* by Peter Ransley. It would prove a seminal moment in Richard's career.

'I was very excited by the play and after meeting Ransley in the bar afterwards I told him that I would like to try and get it done professionally. I had no idea at the time of directing it myself.'

He was as good as his word. He showed the play to Gordon McDougall, who liked it, and so the Stables took an option. Ransley thought this meant the Stables were definitely going to do it, 'which led to that terribly hopeless period of anguish – because you're terribly naive, aren't you? – of having told everyone. And then they came back, saying, "No, no, we want to do a rehearsed reading," and I didn't even know what that meant.'

As a result of the reading Richard was 'delighted and amazed' to be asked to direct the play as part of a season of one-act plays. He and Ransley worked closely on the text, both for its stage production and later for television. It proved to be one of the best results Granada had hoped to achieve from the Stables experiment.

Disabled is the story of a semiparalysed old music-hall veteran, played by Ewen Solon in the original production, who struggles around his bedsitter in a wheelchair, fighting a running battle against the welfare workers who insist on doing good to him. In rehearsal there developed the most ferocious arguments between Solon, who wanted to play the character for sympathy, and Richard who wanted the performance to be realistic, knowing that Ransley had based the character on a real person whom he knew, who was not only disabled but cantankerous and difficult, wanting sex from the home help, from the social worker, and anyone else; all of which was woven into the play. There came a point, says Ransley, when Richard felt he couldn't continue, Solon felt likewise, and it looked as though the production would collapse.

By dint of compromise the play eventually opened – to excellent reviews, with the *Guardian* hailing Ransley as 'an exceptional new playwright'. Solon, in particular, received rapturous reviews: 'Superb, he slurs his words, twists himself fiercely around his chair, sits pigeon-toed and grimacing, to create a character who is almost too large for the tiny stage. The climax, when he begins to dance slowly round the set, filthy and sweating, with smears of make-up on his face, at once proud and pathetic, thrilled and exhausted last night's audience … the finest production I have seen in this theatre yet.'

The last sentence especially delighted Richard who now knew that his instinct about the play had been confirmed, and that his very first stage production had proved so successful. As a result, at the end of the first year, he was made an associate director of the Stables, with an office to himself. '*And* a desk!' he adds, 'And a secretary, even though I had to share her with Gordon, but I could *dictate* letters. I loved all that!'

Following the success of *Disabled*, the Stables, acting on Richard's initiative, commissioned another play from Ransley, *Ellen*, which Richard directed in 1970 with Maureen Pryor in the title role. Ellen was an old tramp whom Ransley had met on a London doorstep in 1966. Her real name was Nelly Ellen O'Connor-Manczak; her mother was German and her father a Manchester man who bred and trained horses, a job which took him all over the world. Ellen spoke fluent French, German, Russian, Polish and English, though her pronunciation of the latter was thick. She told him many weird stories: how she had been born in Moscow, gone into a German film that was never finished, eloped with a rich Pole, then lived an erratic, bizarre life in Germany and Paris during the late 1920s and 1930s. This was all mixed up with some story about her 'documents being stolen by the Church of

Scotland', and being unable to cross certain roads because of mysterious electric currents. She was medically labelled a schizophrenic and because of the absurdity of the electric currents Ransley imagined that everything else she had told him was absurd. 'I got the biggest shock of my life,' he says, 'when one day she produced pictures and documents to show that most of what I, and certainly her doctors, had taken to be fantasy was fact. And that was the germinal point of the play.' If it had not been for Richard and the Stables, Ransley doubts that he would have put pen to paper, since naturally every author writes for performance and hesitates if that seems unlikely.

The play revolves around John Sutcliffe, a successful young playwright from up north, married to Clara, the daughter of a psychiatrist, and both living in Kensington. Their inability to have children creates tension in their marriage. The play opens with a sleepy, irritable husband trying to produce a sperm sample with the help of a gramophone record at nine o'clock in the morning, in order to rush it through London's traffic for a hospital test of his potency at ten o'clock. John is trying to write a play about Ellen, a tramp who, rather like Alan Bennett's true life example, camps on his doorstep and tells him stories about her exotic past in Paris and her many lovers. To Clara, Ellen seems simply a paranoid schizophrenic in need of treatment, whereas to John she symbolises the freedom he has lost in pursuing success.

The first performance of *Ellen* coincided with the television transmission of *Disabled*, under the title *Dear Mr Welfare*, directed again by Richard, so that both he and Ransley had that rarity – a double first night. 'I owe my career to Richard,' says Ransley, but that career nearly came to an end that evening when, after the usual first-night party, 'at which I got absolutely plastered,' he ran his car into a tree on his way back to his digs. 'The next thing I knew I was in the Manchester Royal Infirmary, having lost so much blood that they couldn't even do a blood test. I awoke to find Richard standing at the end of my bed, followed by Maureen Lipman and Jack Rosenthal bearing the biggest bowl of fruit I had ever seen. It was three months before I was able to walk, so I finished up at the Stables being disabled myself! I thought for a time I was disabled for ever. I had broken bones in my foot, an arm, a leg, but they healed and after a time I went back to work.'

During the run at the Stables the play was seen by Albert Finney whose company, Memorial Productions, took an option on it, hoping Elizabeth Bergner would play the leading role. Richard went to visit her. 'She told me that if I would get rid of the sperm in the first act she might do this wonderful play!' He replied that it was an integral part of the play and could not be cut. Instead, he cast Mary Merrall in what was to be his first production at the Hampstead Theatre Club. John Peter in the *Sunday Times* praised 'Richard Wilson's meticulous direction', while Nicholas de Jongh in the *Guardian* spoke of the amazing performance that Richard conjured from his leading lady. 'Mary Merrall provides in the second act the most marvellous acting from a veteran I have seen. With staring and enormous pale blue eyes, a voice and a body insulated from artifice, she projects a glowing sense of past rapture almost as if redeeming the glories from long ago.' Ransley himself watched with fascination in rehearsals as Richard coaxed from his septuagenarian actress a rare performance, 'though from a different generation of acting she blossomed under his enormous patience'. For both Ransley and Richard their meeting was a special marriage of talents at a crucial stage in their careers. As Richard wrote at the time in *Stables News*, 'I suppose the day has got to come when I direct plays by other authors than Peter, and other actors outside the Stables, and both departures are bound to be more than a little painful.'

In the first year at the Stables, Granada bent over backwards to make the experiment work. Realising early on that the actors needed a Green Room, somewhere they could relax between the shows or during long waits, a notice appeared on the board: 'Your Green Room is ready. It is Room 608 on Floor 6 of the main Granada building.' Maureen Lipman recalls the excitement as they all went scurrying over, to find that Granada had literally given them a *green* room – green walls, green floor, green curtains, even green furniture. 'And you had this picture of the bemused Granada executives saying, "Oh, well, for God's sake get a tin of green paint and paint the bloody walls if that is what they want!"' In the end it didn't really get used because it meant checking in at the reception in the main building and then going up in the lift, and the whole point of a Green Room is that it should be close to the stage.

The opening production of the new season, *Professions*, was billed as 'an evening of incredibly short plays' (the average length of each was five minutes) with contributions from Henry Livings, Brian Friel, Stephen Gooch, Stanley Eveling, Jonathan Powell, Fernando Arrabel, David Brett and Richard Howard. This was followed by the first full-length play by Trevor Griffiths, especially commissioned by the Stables, *Occupations*, in which Richard played the leading role. The play explored the takeover of Italian factories by Communists in 1920, their successful running by workers' control, and the eventual collapse of the experiment when a national referendum of workers accepts a compromise offer from the employers.

It is impossible to over-emphasise the importance to Richard of his two years at the Stables, playing not only a variety of roles but discovering his talent as a director. Maureen Lipman says of Richard at this time, 'He was always a bit of an elder statesman to us younger things. But you knew that you could trust him. And you wanted his approval as well. If he laughed, you felt that you had succeeded. If you got a word of praise from him you felt it was honest and true because he wasn't "theatrical" in any way. He was his own man and had an inner authority.'

Above all, his experience of working first at the Traverse and then at the Stables confirmed his preferences. In *Stables News* edition 4, September 1970, he wrote:

I am totally dedicated to the small theatre idea and I feel that a three-sided audience is perhaps one of the most exciting shapes – the spectator and the audience then make up a total ambience which, when it is working, is hard to surpass. Assuming we have a good play, well done, the audience in this situation is also required to give a great deal, any antipathy is immediately felt by the players, but if the audience is a generous one then the atmosphere is, to say the least of it, electric. At the end of such a performance, the actor feels like thanking the audience as much as they him.

I don't feel this communion can be achieved in a large proscenium arch theatre. I find, on entering the huge cavern of your 'normal' theatre, a coldness which is hard to overcome because of the gap between the audience and the stage. Also I find that the large theatre necessitates a style of acting that one can only call 'big' and 'stagey'. I think it is the possibility of keeping one's acting so close to naturalism in a three-sided arena that makes it so exciting. There is no chance for tricksy or glib actors to get away with half-baked performances; you are in there, and could have someone gazing up your nostril for all you know, so that concentration must be a hundred per cent all the time and it is this intensity that helps to bring about such a joyous totality.

To this day Richard still prefers acting and directing in small theatres such as the Hampstead Theatre, the Bush, and the Royal Exchange in Manchester, or the Minerva Theatre at Chichester, where in 1996 he directed Alan Bates in Simon Gray's *Simply Disconnected.* In 1995, while performing in Joe Orton's *What the Butler Saw* at the Royal National Theatre, he remarked, quite late in the run, 'Only now do I feel that I can control the Lyttelton theatre, by and large, but there are times when I'm standing there and feel I'm shouting. And I don't feel I am anywhere near a *character.*' It was only when he was re-rehearsing the play with Isla Blair, who took over from Nicola Paget, and they did a run of the second act in the rehearsal room that he admitted feeling that, for the first time, he was giving a good performance. 'I just don't like big theatres. I never have, nor as a director.'

Sadly, in the second year of the Stables, the experiment came under increasing stress, ending up £63,000 in debt. Yet today, when all too often original creative work in television, or on radio, is sacrificed to the imperatives of accountants, with an all too apparent decline in quality, it is inconceivable that any television company would initiate, let alone sponsor, such a project as the Stables.

The Stables had been a brave experiment which worked best in theatre terms, and in discovering such new writers as Brian Clarke, Trevor Griffiths, Peter Ransley and others. Unfortunately for

Granada, too few of the plays transferred to the medium of television. As John Fraser remarks, 'The link between stage and television didn't really work. The shows that were done on television, with one or two exceptions, seemed always to show their theatre roots.' One by one the actors left, some even after the first year. 'There was no big party at the end,' says Richard Howard, 'we knew it was grinding down. It's like our business anyway – you know you have to move on.'

The final production was, in fact, Gordon McDougall's imaginative staging of *The Cherry Orchard* and the programme carried the following sombre note: 'From 19 December 1970 Granada TV will no longer undertake to support the financial loss of the Stables Theatre Club. This is therefore the last production which will be presented by the Stables Theatre Company on its present basis.'

Richard, both as the company representative and then as an associate director, had played his part in trying to keep the theatre open, employing all his skills of diplomacy but, finally, on 19 November 1970, he received the following letter from Lord Bernstein (he had been created a life peer the previous year):

Dear Mr Wilson,

Thank you for your letter of November 5th. We all regret that the original project for the Stables Theatre has not worked out. After most careful consideration by everybody involved we came to the conclusion that the problem could not be resolved and we, Granada, should not continue.

9

Onwards . . .

'Richard would often be quite uptight by the end of a day's rehearsal,' recalls the designer Saul Radomsky, 'or irritated if the actors wanted to end rehearsal earlier on a Friday so that they could get a better train back to London.'

The year was 1974 and Gordon McDougall had been appointed Artistic Director of the new Oxford Playhouse, with Richard as Associate Director. Radomsky, the resident designer, describes how he would walk into the rehearsal room 'and there would be a distraught-looking Richard at the far end, and so I would often pull his leg and try to make him laugh. He was inclined to very serious!' Radomsky recalls that at this period Richard was much thinner, 'very debonair and handsome, and with long hair'.

Richard was also commuting regularly to Manchester, playing Jeremy Parsons Q.C. in the highly successful Granada series, *Crown Court*, a role he took for four years. He became hugely popular, says McDougall, who was originally responsible for getting him the job, 'and rightly, because he was so good. He took great pains and really learned his lines instead of reading them as many of the actors did.' William Simons, who was also in the series, reiterates this, 'It was fascinating to watch the amount of study and the detail which Richard put into the part, and into each episode, far more than any other actor did. The character of Jeremy Parsons, terribly refined and precious, was entirely Richard's invention. I can't think of any other actor, except Peter Barkworth (who, of course, taught him), who puts in so much work.'

At the Oxford Playhouse Richard directed John Fraser in Dennis Potter's *Only Make Believe* and Fraser also comments on Richard's meticulous attention to detail as a director. Other productions followed, with Richard playing Uncle Vanya once again, this time to Anton Rodgers' Dr Astrov. The administrator of the Playhouse was David Aukin who was married to the director Nancy Meckler, and it was through him that she learned she had a fan in Richard 'which, in those days, was somewhat unexpected, since it wasn't particularly fashionable to employ women directors. It wasn't an "in" thing. Women didn't have a very high status at that time, so it was very gratifying to know that there was someone who was aware of what I was doing.' Richard persuaded McDougall to invite her to direct at the Playhouse. Having founded the experimental theatre company, The Freehold, in the late sixties, she was surprised to find herself directing *Kiss Me, Kate*. So began a friendship between the Aukins and Richard that remains today.

In 1975 Richard's father was rushed to hospital in Glasgow, suffering from an aneurysm. He was seventy-nine and since his retirement had been living with Moira and Jimmy. Richard used to travel from London or wherever he was working to visit him. He would joke with him and say, 'You'd better make up your mind whether you are going to live or die, as I can't keep coming up and down like this!' The last time Richard saw him in hospital he had the feeling that he was finished, that he had had enough. Death wasn't mentioned but his father said something like, 'Well, I think I'll have a good sleep now.' He died suddenly after six weeks. Richard was amazed by the turnout at his funeral, as if all Greenock was in mourning, and by the number of people who came up to shake hands and say what a marvellous wee man his father had been.

Early in 1976 David Aukin returned to London to become administrator of the Hampstead Theatre, under Michael Rudman, and it was in that year, says Nancy Meckler, that the three of them, she, David and Richard, quit smoking. They made their pledge in a restaurant by signing a paper serviette and agreed to meet on the first day of each month to discuss progress. It was 8 April and Nancy remembers the date for a very special reason. She had been wanting to have another child and, at last, after a few months, discovered she was pregnant. Her son Jethro was born on

8 April 1977. 'It really made us laugh, the idea that the anniversary of us not smoking was that we had this baby!'

For Richard, giving up smoking was a fierce struggle. He would wake in the night with terrible pains in his stomach, knowing that if only he had a cigarette the pains would go away. But he refused to give in. He was so determined, as he is about everything he undertakes, that he was prepared to go through anything to break the habit. Nowadays he is a passionate anti-smoker, taking part in campaigns, and won't allow anyone to smoke in his presence.

It was during the August of 1976 that Nancy Meckler found Richard especially supportive. Already pregnant, she had got herself into a situation where she had agreed to look after three children whose ages were four, five and seven. 'I was having a lot of sickness and we were also going through a heatwave. Richard used to come round and cook hamburgers and fish-fingers for the children, and play games with them. He would run out into the garden and throw buckets of water over them, which they loved! I couldn't have got through those few weeks without him, because the children were quite stressed. So, when Jethro was born, it was natural that we should ask Richard to be his godfather. And since he was born on 8 April Richard gave him eight premium bonds, each with the number 8 on them!'

Many have commented on Richard's love of children and it is his one great sadness not to have had children of his own. His friend Dr John Collee observes, 'He has this way with them, this knack of completely focusing when he is speaking to you – which babies especially respond to.' Family remains very important to Richard, and his especial delight when his nephews were growing up was to spend time with them. He would play with the two boys, go for long walks in the hills above Greenock, and take his turns at preparing meals, helped by the elder, Kenneth, who then went on to study hotel management and now runs a hotel in Nigeria, while Moira's other son, Ian, went to work for the *Greenock Telegraph*. It is not surprising that Richard is in much demand as a godfather!

1976 was also the year in which Richard moved to his first flat in Tudor Close, Belsize Park. It was his fortieth birthday and the telephone engineer who arrived to install a telephone on the same day couldn't believe that it was the first telephone he had owned. After years of living in one room Richard found it took a while to get adjusted to the extra space. 'I would walk up and down, looking at the way the light came in, thinking "This is wonderful!" I thought it was enormous, and hoovering it seemed endless.' In reality it was quite a small flat with a sitting room, bedroom, bathroom, tiny kitchen, and a spare room which he always meant to turn into a dining room but never did. 'Tudor Close was when he went public,' says Dinah Stabb, 'because he could now invite people to where he lived, and he never had before – because if you have a bedsitter you don't. And suddenly it was open house!'

Anna Massey recalls a meal at Tudor Close when she was filming with Richard in *Virginia Fly Is Drowning* (one of the few straight roles on television, and with a love interest, that Richard has played). The other guests included Alan Rickman, Rima Horton, Antony Sher and Jim Hooper. 'He kept saying at rehearsal, "I don't know whether you are going to like what I've prepared for tonight." And what do you think he gave us? *Tripe and onions* served with a white sauce and a *baked* potato! It was very odd, and when I was told that it was the lining of a cow's stomach, well, I just couldn't swallow it! I don't think Jim Hooper did terribly well either. After that he tended to buy sirloins of steak at Fortnum's, and smoked salmon.'

Anna always felt the flat unlived in. Certainly the walls were bare of all pictures, photographs, mementoes; no identifying signs of the person who lived there, whilst in the living room there were no chairs. 'I was so minimalist,' laughs Richard, 'that I had only cushions on the floor, like in *Tokyo Story*, but then I noticed that older people had some difficulty and so I had to get a sofa and armchairs.' The real centre of the flat was the study, where Richard worked and to which few were admitted. It was at Tudor Close that Richard began his annual New Year parties which are now famous among his friends but because of his strictures about smoking he had Antony Sher prepare two signs, one saying 'No Smoking' and the other indicating a room set aside for smokers. 'He gets very tetchy,' says Sher, 'if people don't observe these signs. He himself is a great respecter of territories, his own and other people's.'

Richard and Antony first met while appearing in a television film, *The Sheik of Pickersgill*, which was part of a series, *The Pickersgill People* written by Mike Stott, author of *Funny Peculiar*, and *Lenz*, which Richard directed at Hampstead. *The Sheik of Pickersgill* is an extremely funny script, hilariously performed by Richard, whose performance is amazingly reminiscent of Alastair Sim, in which he portrays the principal of a small language school for foreigners in a northern town, while Sher plays a rich Arab sheik who comes to learn English. Their two performances are a delight, each taking wing from the other. It is extraordinary that no one has thought to pair the two of them since, except for a small cameo role for Sher in an episode of *One Foot in the Grave*. As Sher says, 'We hit it off straight away and we laughed so much that we kept corpsing on the set. The director and the crew were not so pleased because they were racing against time, but it was such a delight to find that this very professional and rather severe disciplinarian could corpse!' They became firm friends.

'Throughout my life,' says Sher, 'I always used to have a best friend, and I am very much aware that Richard has become that – *and* a best friend with whom I have had fierce arguments about acting! I used to think that our tastes were quite similar but now I'm fairly resigned to the fact that actually my work is basically not to his taste. I find it quite enjoyable, really, his constant going on about minimalism in acting. It's quite useful having someone that close who is as fiercely critical as he is. I don't think he has enjoyed anything I've done for years! And whenever he comes to a show, it's grit your teeth, oh God, Richard's in, he'll hate it! And yet that is a terribly useful thing to have in one's life. One's close friends daren't do anything but be incredibly supportive, seeing how much you're sweating blood and tears, and then along comes this terribly severe sort of school teacher, rather like a Scottish dominie! Actually, he enjoyed *Travesties* at the Royal Shakespeare Company; that's the first performance of mine that he's enjoyed for years.

And, of course, when he does enjoy something, then it's like manna from heaven; you glow!'

What also brought the two together was their discovery that although they come from different backgrounds (Sher is from South Africa) both have the feeling of being trespassers in the British theatre, each having come from the kind of background where theatre was not considered a suitable career. They both share the sense of having travelled a great distance. Each has journeyed a long way from his background, 'and we've noticed, for example, how we have both developed a posh English way of talking which is not our natural accent.'

Richard's perfectionism, that attention to detail which has contributed so much to his deserved success, stems from a fastidiousness which is reflected even in his domestic life. Edie, his housekeeper for more than twenty years, who does all his shopping, washing and ironing, and buys fresh flowers each week, describes how he has to have all his clothes in different compartments. 'All his white shirts have to be on hangers, so that they won't crease, while his sports shirts go in one drawer, his pants in another. Everything has to be very orderly for him. If there are special things he wants doing he will say, "Can you just wipe those fingermarks off that door." He was very upset after his first Christmas party in the new flat, when drink got spilled on the carpet.'

Even Richard's more spacious office in his new home is a model of tidiness. Each of his three desks has papers laid out in orderly fashion, relating to the different areas in his work. It is as though everything in his life has to be tightly controlled. He is also not only obsessively tidy but strict about punctuality. He can be quite severe with friends who are late, and is easily thrown if things do not happen exactly as he has planned them. He will say, 'I can give you one hour,' and woe betide the visitor who is even a few minutes late or a few minutes early. Equally, if he says he will do something he keeps his promise even if he is not well. Jenny Topper, artistic director of the Hampstead Theatre, describes how she once bumped into him when he had a temperature of 102 and was feeling quite ill. She learned that he had just spent the afternoon on top of a double-decker bus taking part in a rally to save University College Hospital. She at once put him into her car and drove him home. He exerts an iron discipline over himself and expects the same of others. 'He feels guilty,' says Dinah Stabb, 'if he doesn't keep a promise, and then wishes he hadn't said yes. So his diary gets filled up and all the time he worries. He is such a hard task-master that it would be almost impossible now for him to share his life and home with anyone else, to have to adapt to the different rhythms and patterns of someone else. He likes people to behave in a proper manner, and everything to be done in an orderly fashion. He has an almost obsessive need to keep chaos at bay.'

Richard not only moved house when he was forty but began to learn to drive. Until then he had always resisted learning because he felt that travelling on public transport was essential for an actor. 'I love observing people. When Jennie Stoller and I go off on holiday to Amalfi or somewhere, we love sitting at our table and gossiping about the other guests. Once you're in a car you're cut off and insulated from people. It's an actor's job to look at people. Now they look at me all the time.'

However, because an actor is called upon to rehearse in so many different parts of London, he realised that it would be more efficient and less time-consuming to be able to drive to rehearsal. He bought a second-hand car from a cousin and for its first outing the actor Pip Donaghy drove him to Dartington to visit one of Richard's productions that was on tour. Just as they got to the motorway the car broke down. Although Donaghy kept putting his foot down, the car wouldn't do more than 35 mph. Richard had bought a dud.

Once he had learned to drive, Richard drove a BMW, but today he favours a Mercedes 500, which he changes every two years.

Early in 1979 Richard was invited by Michael Rudman, then artistic director of the Hampstead Theatre, to direct Mike Stott's *Lenz* with Jonathan Pryce in the title role. Also in the same year Antony Sher suggested to Bill Gaskill and Max Stafford-Clark, co-directors of Joint Stock, that they should talk to Richard about doing a production for them, especially as he liked to use improvisation and workshop techniques when rehearsing a play. At the interview Richard was asked what project he was working on and he replied that he wasn't, that he was just a jobbing actor and director looking for new plays. However, he added, he did have one idea but it was intended to be a film, not a play, about amputee soldiers returning from the Front at the time of the First World War. Both Stafford-Clark and Gaskill were excited by this and told him that if he could get David Halliwell to write the script (he had written *Little Malcolm and His Struggle Against the Eunuchs*, in which John Hurt made his first starring appearance in the West End) they would give him the go-ahead. And so *The House*, as it was called, went into production.

During the workshop period the actors visited old soldiers at the Star and Garter house in Richmond, talked to VAD (Voluntary Aid Detachment) nurses who had served in the First World War, and did many improvisations, including writing letters home, as their characters, describing their experiences at the Front. Dinah Stabb improvised a dream sequence in which, as the music of a Schubert quartet was played on an old gramophone, she wove bandages round the soldiers in slow motion until they were all intertwined with the bandages. 'It was,' admits Richard, 'quite extraordinarily beautiful and moving' but, in his search for total realism, which is his forte as a director, he could find no way of using such impressionistic material. At the end of the workshop period Halliwell went off to write the play and then the actors reassembled to rehearse it. The play opened at the Institute of Contemporary Arts in London on 29 October 1979, before going on tour. Michael Coveney, writing in the *Financial Times*, referred to 'Richard Wilson's clean and devastatingly accurate production . . . [which] shows an entire world of human relationships sharply etched in a carefully researched and illuminated setting'.

Already Richard was beginning to impress critics and others with the meticulous care and detail of his work as a director. One of these was Dusty Hughes who, from 1976 to 1979, had been artistic director of yet another of the growing number of fringe theatres in London, the Bush, working in a triumvirate with Simon

Stokes as technical director and Jenny Topper as business manager. Having directed regularly at the Bush during these years, Dusty Hughes decided in 1979 that he wanted to try his luck as a writer before it was too late, and so had taken a sabbatical in order to write his first play, *Commitments*. He sounded out one or two actors who had worked for Richard, who said what everyone says about him, that, 'He is the most marvellous director for actors; and so, since I had written a very naturalistic play which needed an actor's director, I suggested to my colleagues at the Bush that Richard should direct it.'

Commitments represents very much the kind of writing to which Richard, as a director, is attracted. His primary interest is in new plays that reflect the social and political issues of the age in which we live. Spanning the months of the downfall of Edward Heath's government, with the miners' strike, the three-day week, sudden power cuts, blackouts and IRA bombs, the play's action is set in the flat of a disenchanted intellectual, played by Alan Rickman, who finally leaves the Workers' Party, confessing he had only been in it for the girls.

John Elsom wrote in his review for the *Listener*: 'Those who believe the play is a kind of debunking of the Workers' Revolutionary Party have missed the play's underlying strategy. The five activists in the play may be muddled in their motives, they may find that their political and personal commitments get hopelessly tangled, they may misread the political situation around them through an excess of jargon and misapplied theory: but what essentially goes wrong is that they underestimate the strength of that historical imperative which should sweep them to power on a tide of workers' support.'

For Alan Rickman the experience of acting for Richard was to prove a turning point in his career and work. 'I had just been doing a season at Stratford with the RSC where all I was learning to do was shout. It was only by leaving and meeting Richard that I began to discover myself. He is one of the most profound influences in my life. He absolutely changed its course. If the word "mentor" means anything, then he is that.'

Rickman arrived late for his first meeting with Richard at Dusty Hughes' flat. Being late, as he learned then, is to Richard a real sin, whose opening words to Rickman were, 'I don't think we've got off to a good start, have we?' He is rigorous as a director, comments Rickman, 'but it is a clean rigour, and not about punishing. It's just that he has a real austerity which I find really refreshing and which gives shape to the day. And so I read for him, and it was such a relief to be in a room with someone who said, "Don't act! Don't try and make an impression, don't over-energise, just read it and don't interfere with it!" That was such a relief. I sighed, thinking: thank God, I'd had the courage to get out of Stratford, and then along comes this man and this play at exactly the right time. At a very crucial period of my life there was Richard. He's the great guru, but he's also a human being, and it's all very practical. He has a sense of humour, a sense of the ridiculous and the extravagant, so that working for him is both bracing and fun.'

London's theatre critics gave the play their 'Most Promising Playwright Award' of 1980. When, two years later, it was produced on television, again directed by Richard, Peter Fiddick in the *Guardian* wrote, 'It is galling for a TV critic to find a play like Dusty Hughes' *Commitments* coming up on TV. It is contemporary, intelligent, testing political stances in a way rarely seen on the box – creating an ironic, compassionate counterpoint between the political and personal lives of its characters. It is funny and it is moving. It is altogether a rare piece in the way it sets out to engage a contemporary audience with contemporary life. And it comes from the theatre . . . if the box and the modern theatre can work together in such a way, there is hope for us yet in the world beyond Shepherd's Bush.'

It was also in 1979 that Richard began to appear in a new comedy series which was first to bring him to the attention, as an actor, of a wider public. *Only When I Laugh*, written by Eric Chappell (author of *Rising Damp* and other such successful series) for Yorkshire Television, was produced and directed by Vernon Lawrence, with a cast that included James Bolam, Peter Bowles and Christopher Strauli as three contrasting patients in the same ward of an NHS Hospital. Richard played Dr Thorpe, the house surgeon, a man very conscious of his own importance but who covers up a basic insecurity with a swagger and a forced cheerfulness in his bedside manner. As the doctor, Richard reveals himself as the master of the rising inflection and the pursed lip, a Lady Bracknell of the wards. In viewers' minds *Only When I Laugh* singled him out as a comedy actor. The idiosyncratic way in which Richard pronounced 'Figgis', the name of James Bolam's character, resulted in people asking him to repeat it for them. Little did he know that other catchphrases were to follow.

Only When I Laugh ran for four consecutive years until 1982, and was repeated in 1995. There were twenty-eight episodes in all as well as a Christmas special. The first series was due to go out in September 1979, but owing to a strike, ITV was off the air for eleven weeks. Ironically, during this period, the BBC put out a new series, *To The Manor Born*, with Penelope Keith, which also made a star of Peter Bowles, so that when *Only When I Laugh* was finally shown, Bowles already had a large following. Launched on 3 November 1979 the series went straight into the top twenty – in itself unusual – and, during the first series, rose to be number one.

Few viewers watching this, and similar situation comedy series, realise how intensive is the work involved. The company used to assemble at midday on Sunday at the Sulgrave Boys' Club in London to read through that week's episode with the author. Next, Vernon Lawrence blocked the moves and business for a second run-through. At five-thirty the actors would break to start learning their lines. The following morning they reassembled to rehearse the first half, and then went home to learn the second half which would be rehearsed on the Tuesday. On Wednesday there was a technical run-through for the lighting director, the costume designer, the camera man and the sound supervisor, who would have travelled to London from Yorkshire TV's Leeds headquarters, so that this run was very much like a first performance. Starting at ten o'clock on Thursday morning the actors had three run-throughs, including a 'speed' run when moves and dialogue are taken very fast. This makes the actors more aware of the overall rhythm and pattern, as well as helping to eradicate any slack. After this the company travelled to Leeds and were in the studio by six o'clock, ready for a rehearsal on the set, without costumes or lights, but with everything else, including the camera man and the boom operators, so that the camera man could see what the shots were, and whether any prerecording might be needed, in which case it was always done immediately.

The following morning, Friday, saw a run-through in the studio, with two more after lunch, then a full dress rehearsal at the end of which Vernon gave his final notes to the actors and crew, after which the actors went to their dressing rooms to relax for half an hour. The audience were admitted at ten to seven, the professional warm-up man would entertain them, and then would introduce the author and actors. From the start Richard made a point of chatting with the audience beforehand, something at which he is quite brilliant, and has made a practice of ever since, as those who are fortunate to attend a recording of *One Foot in the Grave* know. Many actors are frightened of an audience and want to keep a distance, but Richard finds that by establishing contact it makes for a more relaxed performance. As far back as the Stables Theatre he encouraged the actors to mingle with the audience in the bar after a performance.

After the warm-up, the recording of *Only When I Laugh* began promptly at seven-thirty, ending at about a quarter to nine. 'People talk about weekly repertory,' remarks Vernon Lawrence, 'but with sitcom you only have one crack at it. If something major goes wrong, you have to go back at once and reshoot it, and that can alter the audience laughter and response, which is being recorded. Sometimes the audience will laugh even more in anticipation when this happens, or else they laugh in the wrong place. It's the worst form of purgatory anybody ever invented. Drama is straightforward by comparison.'

In rehearsal actors get used to where the laughs should be, so that at the recording they can be completely thrown if the audience laughs in a wholly unexpected place; which is, observes Vernon Lawrence, when the great comedy actors, like Richard, come into their own, because they will keep their performance the same size as they rehearsed, and not be tempted to enlarge it because of an unexpected audience reaction. 'Of course,' says Vernon, 'if the actors don't get laughs that can be bad also, because the automatic reaction is to increase the size of the performance in order to try and get a laugh and, on television especially, that is disastrous. Sitcom before a live audience is indeed the most difficult of all genres to do.'

The secret of *Only When I Laugh*, apart from the writing, lay in casting actors rather than comedians. Each actor knew comedy and would adopt the role the author had written and play that part, allowing the laughs to come out of the characters and the situations and not out of the jokes. This, too, is one of the reasons for the great success of *One Foot in the Grave*. Richard loved playing the doctor but, because it was quite a small part, used to get bored and would ask Eric Chappell to write in another scene for him, even if it wasn't used, so that he would have something more to do than sit around; but he enjoyed watching the expertise of Bowles and Bolam. He also used to nag Bolam, who had a bad chest, to give up smoking, which he finally did. Vernon, who in those days smoked up to eighty cigarettes a day, says with a grin, 'Richard was a pain in the arse to us all about smoking. He carried this flag to stop us all smoking. And I have!'

In 1982, while continuing to appear in episodes of *Only When I Laugh*, Richard acted at the Royal Court Theatre in G.F. Newman's politically provocative play *Operation Bad Apple*, directed by Max Stafford-Clark. When it was over, he went on holiday to Crete with Anna Massey, the first of three such holidays together. They were joined unexpectedly by Alan Rickman, not yet a star, and Rima Horton, who stayed in a bed-and-breakfast place, joining Richard and Anna each evening for dinner.

Anna describes her and Richard's daily routine: 'Breakfast alone, then umbrella on the beach, not talking, hardly at all. I would be reading masses of novels. Richard's not a terrific reader, if he read one book that holiday it was a miracle! We sunbathed. He sunbathed a lot. He was a lot browner than me. Quite competitive,

Richard! A very competitive man. He swam. A *lot*. He's a very powerful swimmer and would go off for long snorkels. Then we would have lunch, then siesta in our separate rooms. At five o'clock we would go for a swim in the pool and then we would always have ouzo on our balconies. He was always a much better host than me, he used to get crisps and olives and things to eat with the ouzo. I'm not nearly so good an entertainer, whereas he is the most generous host and much better organised.

'We would have dinner, followed by a little stroll. And then we came to a lot of difficulty because Richard is someone who likes to go to bed very late and, of course, it's awful to be abandoned by your holiday companion around nine o'clock, which was when I would want to go to bed! So that was a bit of a difficulty, but because Alan was there, he and Richard could stay up late talking.'

That Richard lives alone means that everybody, especially his friends, are the beneficiaries of his success. Richard loves holidays and will often treat friends to a shared holiday. 'He's great fun to holiday with,' says Antony Sher, 'although we do fight a bit! We're both quite controlling people and so if there are any decisions to be taken there can be quite a bit of tension.' Once, in the South of France, they decided to walk into Cannes, assuming it to be an easy walk. It turned out to be endless, as bay succeeded bay, with the road twisting and winding, so that Sher's feet began to bleed from where his new shoes rubbed against the skin. 'Richard, of course, wore shoes that were properly broken in, and was wholly unsympathetic. He just strode ahead while my little legs were struggling to keep up and not quite managing it!'

In 1983 Richard directed a remarkable play by Robert Holman, *Other Worlds*, at the Royal Court. Based upon a true story of a monkey, the sole survivor of a Napoleonic shipwreck, washed up on the English coast, whom the local people in their ignorance thought was a Frenchman and promptly hanged, Holman's play was set in Robin Hood's bay in North Yorkshire, a landscape he knows well. Although it was Holman's fifteenth play this was his first in a large theatre and with a big budget. Indeed, it proved to be the most expensive production mounted at that time by the Royal Court, with the costume for the monkey alone costing some £3,000. Superbly designed by John Byrne, the cast included Rosemary Leach, Juliet Stevenson, Jim Broadbent and Paul Copley, while Richard's assistant was Alan Rickman. 'It was typical of Richard's generosity,' says Rickman 'that he actually let me direct. It wasn't just a question of getting his tea and running errands. There were actually dual rehearsals going on.'

After the first week of rehearsal Richard took the company in a hired van for the weekend to Robin Hood's Bay, so that they could visit the places mentioned in the text. The actors were also given individual subjects to research: from land enclosures to living conditions of the period, attitudes towards 'Boney' and the French, and so on.

The play itself was savaged by the daily newspaper critics. 'It was a shock to us all,' says Holman. 'It was my first play in a big theatre. It looked stunning, and was beautifully acted and directed. They weren't just bad reviews, some of them were vitriolic – "How dare this be put on the stage!", that kind of thing. We waited for the Sundays, hoping they might be better, but they were even worse.'

There was one performance when there were only fifteen people in the audience and the actors were close to rock bottom. Then followed a rearguard action, with letters in the press from various people saying it was a disgrace the way in which the play had been treated and urging everyone to go and see it. But although audiences began to pick up it was too late to save it. 'It was a very delicate play absolutely destroyed by the critics, something they should still be very ashamed of,' reflects Alan Rickman.

Sheila Hancock, who at that time did not know Richard, and had never worked for him, says of the production, 'It just blew my mind.' Afterwards she went backstage and recalls the actors saying how wonderful Richard had been, 'and that's rare, because usually if a show is a flop the actors turn on the director. They have to have someone to blame and it halves the pain if they can say the director made a hash of it. But nobody did. And Richard was still giving notes and nurturing the actors. That's very rare.'

Clearly Max Stafford-Clark thought the same because he wrote to Richard to thank him 'for sustaining the high morale of your cast and the whole staff during the run of the show. When houses are small it is easy for standards to slip and I thought it remarkable how the play was sustained throughout its whole run.'

Throughout his career Richard has always displayed these qualities of leadership and responsibility, whereas too many directors never put in an appearance after the first night.

In the same year Richard directed a film for BBC1's 'Play for Today' series, entitled *Under the Hammer* by Stephen Fagan, set in a famous London auction house. This had no connection with the television series *Under the Hammer*, written by John Mortimer, and also set in an auction house, in which Richard was to star some nine years later. Richard's direction of this one-off television play demonstrates the way in which he takes pains to build up the minutiae of life. From the corseted, almost strangulated upper-class tones of the directors to the gossip of the porters' room, he creates for the viewer the sense of being an eavesdropper on conversations. There is one masterly scene, beautifully underplayed by Peter Bayliss, in which the directors visit by night a semi-retired restorer. The quality of stillness and concentration as the Bayliss character works at repairing a damaged masterpiece is punctuated only by the nocturnal cry of a cat and the clink of mugs as coffee is made. To achieve such ensemble playing Richard once again started with games, developing an atmosphere of trust and reciprocity among the actors, for he knows that acting is primarily about reacting and interacting.

While rehearsing *Under the Hammer* Richard received a call from his agent saying that David Lean was making his first major film after a gap of fourteen years, *A Passage to India*, based on the E.M. Forster novel, and wanted to see him.

'I can't,' replied Richard. 'I'm too busy.'

The agent rang back a little later to say, 'He will see you in an evening after your rehearsals. Just pop down to the Berkeley where he is staying.'

And so began a new adventure for Richard, combining his love of travel with work, when he was to be in India for over six months, playing Turton, the Governor of the district, in what proved to be David Lean's last film, acting alongside Peggy Ashcroft, Nigel Havers, James Fox and Judy Davis.

10

... And Ever Upwards

At their first meeting David Lean asked Richard about the television film he was directing. 'What do you fear as a director when you're acting?' At first Richard didn't understand what he was talking about so that Lean had to repeat the question. When, finally, Richard realised that he was talking about acting *and* directing at the same time, he replied, 'Oh, no, no, no! I would never act in a production I was directing.' They went on chatting for a time until Lean suddenly remarked, 'I think you will enjoy Turton,' and then said goodbye. It was only much later, when Richard was in India filming, that he said to Lean one day, 'You know when I came to see you and you said you thought I would enjoy Turton? It was a bit confusing because it sounded as though I had got the part,' to which Lean replied, 'Well, you had! You got the part the moment you walked into the room.'

'But that's terrible! You shouldn't do things like that!' answered Richard.

'I hate interviews,' said Lean. 'I'd seen your photograph and when you came into the room you sort of frightened me and so you got the part.'

Lean asked Richard what he did when he was casting.

'Oh, I have to get to know people first,' replied Richard, and they then had a long discussion about casting techniques.

He found working for Lean a wonderful experience. 'He was a great painter of pictures, and had this extraordinary eye for detail.'

Richard recalls one incident when they were filming a scene of arrival at the station, and all the leading actors, as well as a company of soldiers from the Indian Army, a brass band, and hundreds of extras, arrived at the railway station to film the scene, and it poured with rain so that they couldn't do anything. During the day Richard came across Lean standing by himself on the platform, looking at the steam engine that was to be used in the film, and said to him, 'I'm sorry, David, about the weather. It's terrible.' Lean replied, 'Yes, yes, dear boy. Look at the front of that engine. I think it would be much better black than red, don't you?' So a painter was sent for and he had the front of the engine repainted. When it was finished he turned to Richard saying, 'Yes, yes, that's much better! Don't you agree?'

Having been an ex-editor, all the technical side of filming was very important to Lean. 'He was terribly fussy about light and about the way the film was printed,' remarks Richard, 'but he was often criticised for not being good with actors.' For one scene, where Richard and James Fox come back in the train from the caves – the visit which forms the climax of the book and the film – the two actors worked on the scene together, even going back to the novel. When they took the scene to Lean he said, 'Oh, you chaps have been working hard on this, it's wonderful. And you've been back to the book, wonderful, wonderful!' Then he set about changing it all. He was, says Richard, less interested in the scene between the actors than in a particular visual effect he was after: as the train pulled out he wanted the camera to close up, not on the actors but on the guard passing the open door of their carriage, waving his flag.

In many ways Lean was a pragmatist as well as a perfectionist. 'I think,' says Richard, 'that the crew, by and large, didn't like him very much because he kept changing his mind. They felt at times he didn't really know what he wanted because he would change things on a whim, when the crew might have spent a lot of time setting something up.' None the less Richard, as a director, learned a great deal from observing Lean at work, much of which he was to apply when he came to direct his first film, shot on location, *Changing Step*.

'David was a very generous man,' observes Richard, 'and would lavish us all, regularly taking the actors out to dinner, buying the best wines and champagnes.' Once, when they were around the pool at the hotel, Lean came up to Richard and said, 'I hear you are a Socialist, Richard. We must have a chat about that some time!' As though, adds Richard, having had a little chat he would suddenly become a Conservative. On another occasion they were discussing money when Lean remarked to him, 'When you're a millionaire, Richard, you will understand.' And Richard laughed at the very idea.

Listening to Richard it is clear that he and Lean had a special rapport which may well have sprung from the fact that the two men were alike in many ways. Another director, Michael Powell, once said of Lean, 'He's very cloistered in his life,' whilst Katharine Hepburn observed, 'David understands loneliness. He understands passion. He understands desperation.' The same may also be said of Richard. Powell also remarked of Lean, 'Passion and ice,' and Richard, too, especially when he is directing, can appear very grim and austere. As one of his friends has observed, 'Often he can seem rather cold and forbidding, stern even, and rather scary, but that's just his way,' whilst another friend, John Collee, remarks, 'What has always struck me about Richard is that he is such a soft-hearted man, yet he is blessed with this incredibly grim face, so that there is a dichotomy between his external stern appearance and his warm-hearted nature.'

The secret of Richard's comedy as an actor lies in the vulnerability behind that severe countenance which is often like that of an old-fashioned Scottish dominie. But there is more to it than a physiological explanation. Although his favourite word about acting is 'open' he remains, as Antony Sher has remarked, a very closed person. Often in thinking of Richard I find myself recalling these lines from Robert Frost:

> I have been one acquainted with the night.
> I have walked out in rain – and back in rain.
> I have outwalked the furthest city light.

or, again, in these lines from Frost's poem, *Desert Places*:

> They cannot scare me with their empty spaces
> Between stars – on stars where no human race is.
> I have it in me so much nearer home
> To scare myself with my own desert places.

Just as he was due home for Christmas 1983 Richard went down with a severe chest infection. 'In Bangalore they dilute the petrol with water so that all the buggies and other vehicles give off terrible fumes which are mixed with the red dust from the roads, and if ever you caught a cold it was very difficult indeed to get rid of it.' He remembers the panic of trying to get his suitcase closed and being unable to because he was so weak. On the way back they all had to stay overnight in Calcutta and while the rest went out on the town, Richard just lay in the damp room of a cheap hotel, feeling absolutely miserable. On the plane back home he was in delirium and Moira came down from Scotland to nurse him. When he had recovered he returned to do a final four weeks on the film.

On the film's completion, Lean invited Richard to a private viewing, keen to know what he thought. Richard congratulated him, adding, 'I love the silences.' Richard was fascinated to see how Lean had put it together. He could not, however, attend the royal première of the film at the Odeon, Leicester Square, in March 1985, in the presence of the Queen Mother, as he was then on tour at Leicester in a new play by Hugh Leonard, *Some of My Best Friends Are Husbands*, in which he was starring with Peter Bowles. None the less he was determined to get to the reception afterwards at the Savoy Hotel and remembers driving down the motorway at about 120 miles per hour in his dinner jacket. 'Well, it was a big event,' he says, 'David Lean's first film for fourteen years.'

In 1984 came another play at the Royal Court by G.F. Newman, *An Honourable Trade*, a political farce of Tory life, directed by Mike Bradwell, in which Richard played the central role of Sir Walter Purser, the Attorney General, who is embarrassed at having to charge 481 Metropolitan Police detectives with corruption following the independent enquiry which had been the subject of

Newman's previous play, *Operation Bad Apple*. Sir Walter is further embarrassed at being caught raping a prostitute whom he has been seeing for several years, and saddened by the discovery that his wife is having an affair with the Party Chairman, one of his best friends.

Michael Ratcliffe wrote in the *Observer*, 'Mr Wilson is embarrassment incarnate, playing the Attorney General like a man in the barely delicious agony of trying to remember whether he is still wearing silk drawers while addressing the House of Commons or, worse, whether he has taken them off and, if so, where.' As a moral broadside against corrupt politicians the play was prophetic of a general political sleaze that was to overtake the Conservative Party in the 1990s.

The following year, 1985, Richard directed a revival of Charles Dyer's *The Staircase* for Theatre of Comedy, starring John Thaw and Dyer himself. A young actor, Frank Stirling, who acted as Richard's assistant, remembers especially a meal in a fish and chip restaurant across the road from the Palace Theatre at Westcliff-on-Sea. They had reached the end of a very long day and were to open the following night. After about five minutes of the final dress rehearsal, Dyer suddenly came to the front of the stage to announce that he could not possibly carry on because of his, heretofore completely unremarked, laryngitis. He then left the stage mumbling something about saving himself for the performance. John Thaw was left on stage looking surprised, while Richard was absolutely speechless.

'How we ended up in the fish and chip shop,' comments Stirling, 'I can't remember, but I think it was probably a case of emergency comfort eating.'

There were four of them there: Richard, John Thaw, the company manager, and Stirling. The shop was owned by a sweet and rather shy Chinese couple who were slightly awed to have both John Thaw and Richard in at the same time, and were giving them VIP treatment. One must remember, says Stirling, what enormous founts of diplomacy Richard had had to draw upon for the previous four weeks. He was now, through no fault of his own, barely on speaking terms with Dyer and, in fact, Frank Stirling had been having to pass on Richard's notes while pretending they were his own, in order for them to have any effect.

Richard looked to the back of the restaurant and a gleam came into his eye for there, in the corner, resplendent and clearly taking pride of place was an upright piano, brand new – and *bright orange.* He asked the proprietors about it who nodded and beamed, saying it was their pride and joy. 'Then it started,' recalls Stirling. 'Four weeks of self-restraint collapsed and the stream of withering invective directed entirely at the piano and its ridiculous colour was astonishing. We were all concerned about the feelings of its owners, but the more Richard went on about it the funnier he was, and the more hysterical we became, and were quite unable to stop him.'

The further Richard went the more obvious it became what he was talking about and it gradually became apparent that the proprietors thought he actually liked it! As they smiled and nodded so Richard was goaded into still more torrents of abuse at the poor inoffensive instrument. As they finished their meal the others finally shut him up; by which time the Chinese couple had at last got the message but were more concerned about the state of Richard's health.

'We left them, I think,' says Stirling, 'with a lasting impression of a somewhat unbalanced group of actors in the grip of a strange hysteria and with an unreasonable hatred of pianos.'

This is one of the very few recorded instances of Richard letting down his guard and revealing his feelings.

In December of that year and over into 1986 Richard was filming *Whoops, Apocalypse,* having by now acquired a new agent, Jeremy Conway. Although he had no idea at the time, this film was to prove crucial in the development of his career. Directed by Tom Bussman, it was written by Andrew Marshall and David Renwick, based upon a television series of the same title. The film opened at the Cannes Festival in May of that year and was released in London in March 1987, starring Peter Cook in his best Harold Macmillan imitation, and sporting a hook for one hand, as the Prime Minister of a Conservative Government, with Richard as his Foreign Secretary.

The film is a wild satire on world leaders, Anglo and American bureaucrats, military top brass, international terrorists, and the Royals, with the Falklands as its target. The Prime Minister sends a task force of 48,000 troops to free a small remnant of the British Empire (population 750) which has been occupied by a neighbouring South American dictator (played by Herbert Lom), while a female President of the United States (played by Loretta Swit) attempts to mediate. The task force is led by a gay Rear Admiral Bendsh (played by Ian Richardson) who has among his crew a Royal Wren, Princess Wendy, who accidentally castrates a sailor while shaving him. It is that kind of broad comedy. When the Princess is kidnapped, the Prime Minister threatens to unleash the atom bomb and plunge the world into Armageddon. Meanwhile, back home, the PM is convinced that the high rate of unemployment is caused by pixies and that the only cure is to have workers jump off a cliff in their thousands, thereby making way for the unemployed. Those members of his Cabinet who disagree, among them the Foreign Secretary, are crucified. It was the look on Richard's face while this scene was being filmed which was to give David Renwick the idea for Victor Meldrew, as we shall see.

In March 1986 Richard directed J.B. Priestley's *An Inspector Calls*, designed by Saul Radomsky, at the Royal Exchange in Manchester, with Graeme Garden as the Inspector, Russell Enoch as Arthur Birling, and the then unknown Hugh Grant as his son Eric. Although for once not a new play, it is clear that Richard was attracted to it by its social background, in which the most acutely felt divisions in society, and therefore of living standards, are those of income and wealth. He found calculations based on the tax records for 1911–33 revealing that eighty-seven per cent of the country's total personal wealth was concentrated in the hands of a mere five per cent of the population while, at the other end of the scale, nearly a third of the country's male manual workers who, with their wives and families, added up to something like 8 million people, had to get by on less than 25s. a week. A contemporary account describes people on that level of income (and Richard would have seen something of this as a boy in Greenock, and still today in Glasgow) as 'under-housed, un-fed, insufficiently clothed, their growth stunted, their mental powers cramped, their health under-mined'.

The following year Richard was again at the Royal Exchange, directing a remarkable new play by a young Scottish writer, Iain Heggie. *A Wholly Healthy Glasgow*, which had won the Mobil Playwriting Award, and later transferred to the Royal Court Theatre in London, concerns an eighteen-year-old idealist, Murdo, who comes to work in the massage parlour of a sleazy Glasgow health club, having set himself the task of transforming Glasgow into a city of 'perfectly proportioned, sinuous, non-drinking joggers with reposeful and alert minds'. By 1990, he declares, he hopes to have a wholly healthy Glasgow.

The play caused an uproar during its first performance in Manchester when a local businessman, Bryan Nolan, led a walk-out of some twenty members of the audience after only ten minutes, protesting at the play's tirade of filthy language. Shouting out, 'This is a disgrace to the English language, you should be ashamed of yourselves!' he and his party headed for the foyer, looking for someone to complain to, while staff tried to hush them up.

What such protesters fail to realise, of course, is that it is exactly the task of theatre, as Hamlet observes in his advice to the Players, 'to hold, as t'were the mirror up to nature,' knowing that there are strata of society where such language is the norm. This play, perhaps more than any other that Richard has yet directed, reflected his desire to see theatre give a voice to those sections of our society which many people would prefer not to hear.

Also in 1987 Richard acted with Robbie Coltrane and Emma Thompson in John Byrne's *Tutti Frutti* about a failed Scots rock band, the Majestics, which John Naughton in the *Observer* described as 'the sickest, slickest, funniest television series since Dennis Potter's *The Singing Detective*'. Richard played their manager, Eddie Clockerty, a likeable loud-mouth whose idea of a pleasantry is 'Get away and boil yer head!' and whose perpetual irritability is directed at his secretary, Miss Tonar (played by Kate Murphy). Just to hear Richard say 'Miss Tonar' in syllables which he could invest with an amazing range of expressive meaning was a delight to thousands of viewers, and proved to be the second occasion when he created a catchphrase. Once again, as with 'Figgis' in *Only When I Laugh*, people would stop him in the street to hear him say it. It was, says Richard, a very special kind of job, 'the kind that doesn't come along often,' and because it was filmed on different locations in Scotland, he enjoyed the bonus of exploring parts of his own country that he had not visited before.

Later that year six scripts arrived on his desk for a new series in which he was absolutely delighted at being offered, for the first time, a leading part – 'I was even more excited when I had finished reading them.' The series was *Hot Metal*, for London Weekend Television, written by the *Whoops, Apocalypse* authors, Andrew Marshall and David Renwick. Not only would this bring Richard greater media attention, it would also strengthen the relationship between him and David Renwick who, as yet unknown to Richard, was to create especially for him the series *One Foot in the Grave*, which finally brought him stardom.

Sharper and more realistic than *Whoops, Apocalypse, Hot Metal* was a scathing satire on Fleet Street hypocrisy and the inordinate lengths to which tabloid journals will stoop in order to boost their circulation. As Janet Street-Porter wrote in *Today* (12 March 1988), 'I know of several national newspaper editors who consider *Hot Metal* to be essential viewing,' and, she concluded, 'under the easy laughs, *Hot Metal* raises some very important questions about the kind of newspapers we choose to buy.'

Robert Hardy played two characters, the first a Murdoch/Maxwell newspaper proprietor, 'Twiggy' Rathbone, who appoints a new managing editor, Richard Lipton (played by Richard), a former TV presenter whose hopeless ambition is to civilise the tacky tabloid, the *Daily Crucible*, edited by the obnoxious Russell Spam (also played by Robert Hardy). In the first episode, Spam is discovered launching a new column with the following announcement: 'God, the creator of heaven and earth, speaks frankly through His mouthpiece, Sergeant Ken Lutterworth, every Thursday. Yes! God joins the *Crucible*'s award-winning team!'

Peter Tory, writing in the *Daily Express* about the puritanical figure of Lipton, praised Richard who 'plays the role with the indignation of a High Church Vicar who finds himself employed in a
bordello. He is in a constant state of outrage.' Little was Tory to
know that this last sentence would prove prophetic of Richard's
ultimate role as Victor Meldrew, a character who is in a constant
state of outrage when faced with today's society. In a curious way
the part of Richard Lipton is an older version of Murdo, the eighteen-year-old idealist in Iain Heggie's *A Wholly Healthy Glasgow*,
and there is a similar innocence in Richard's performance, which
shines with good intentions.

But fame, in the sense of being a household name, and a face
recognisable anywhere, had not yet come to Richard, as he discovered in September of that year when he accompanied Susan
Wooldridge to the première of the film *Hope and Glory*, directed by
John Boorman, in which Susan had a sizeable part. As the film was
set in 1940 everyone was invited to wear clothes evocative of the
period. Richard wore a navy blazer and a RAMC tie, while Susan
wore an ankle-length red dress hired especially for the occasion.
They arrived and walked down the red carpet and 'the phalanx of
photographers turned from us, they were not in the slightest interested!' laughs Susan. 'Which is interesting when you think how,
only two years later, Richard's career was to change dramatically.'

After the film they went to a ballroom in Tottenham Court Road
for the after-première party, done up like a 1940s canteen. Susan
and Richard were among the last to leave and were climbing the
stairs to depart when John Boorman's wife turned to Richard in his
handsome blazer, thinking he was the manager, and thanked him
for the use of his hall for the evening. 'Richard, without hesitation,
and this is the measure of the gent he is, bowed to her and replied
what a pleasure it had been to have her there! He never gave the
game away.'

It was during 1987 that one of Richard's closest friends, the
actress Caroline Hutchison, developed cancer. A great friend of
Dinah Stabb, Dusty Hughes and Susie Figgis, she was, says
Richard, 'part of our inner circle'. But although she was

surrounded by lots of friends, she and Richard recognised each other as loners, 'not in the sense that they spent time alone,' remarks Dinah Stabb, 'because each had lots of friends, but each of them was a solitary'. Also, being single, they were able to spend a lot of time together.

Caroline always had something wrong with her, says Richard. 'There were allergy problems, an inflamed colon and so on. When she became ill with cancer we all used to meet to discuss how we were going to deal with her illness and probable death. I remember well those meetings, everyone had different ideas about how to cope! She had a lump removed from her breast and returned home feeling much better. We were all thrilled and took her out to lunch to celebrate. Then it got worse again and she was feeling quite ill when I drove her up to Derbyshire where she stayed with a healer who put her on a very strict regime. She had this huge chart on the wall indicating what pills she had to mash down, when to take her enemas, and so forth – and she'd already gone through the whole Bristol Cancer Centre treatment before that. I was always rather suspicious of the man she went to because he smoked, and I thought – he can't be a healer if he smokes! Caroline and I would go for long walks and talk about dying and the need to accept death and yet, at the same time, not give up. She did get a lot better and came back to London. Then she was ill once again.'

Finally, Caroline returned to her healer's house, this time in the south of England. Richard and Dinah drove down to see her. By then she was very weak, and could hardly speak. They each realised they would never see her again. He and Dinah saw her separately. Dinah said 'goodbye'; Richard just said, 'I'll see you,' but they both realised they wouldn't. 'I knew,' says Richard, 'when I left that room that she had said "goodbye" to me.'

Three days later, about midnight, Caroline's father telephoned Dinah to say she had died, 'and I just cried, and went on crying all through the next day,' recalls Dinah. 'Much later on, when talking with Richard about loss and how crying was like washing away the pain, that it was important she cried, he commented,

"Don't you think that's a bit indulgent, Dinah?" She replied, "No, it isn't. It's how not to get ill, how not to be damaged by grief." '

'I was trying to help her,' comments Richard. 'I'm a fairly cool person emotionally. I worked in medicine so I've had to deal with a lot of high octane emotions, dying and pain. And being from a Scots Presbyterian background you're taught to be stoical. Certainly, when eventually I was able to cry over my mother's death, it was a great relief. But when I see people on television beating on coffins, and everyone trying to hold them back, my reaction is "I don't believe it." That is, I always feel, a sort of public display of grief.'

At Caroline's funeral Dinah Stabb remembers looking down at the lid of the coffin where it said 'Caroline Hutchison, aged thirty-nine years' and she thought: life begins at forty; for Caroline it hasn't, but for me it must. And so she decided to do everything she wanted to do. 'I thought, I'm not going to wait until I'm rich and famous. So with a girl-friend I bought this horse. Richard laughed at the time and thought it was wonderful. Then the other girl found she couldn't afford to continue with it, and I was telling Richard about this, saying it was a bit of a blow, when he said, "I'll take over her half!" So Richard continues to pay for half her keep. He's also ridden her a few times. When I go to events to compete they announce "Miss Stabb on Mr Richard Wilson's *Tally*!"'

Although he could not be present at Caroline's funeral, Richard was able to take part in her memorial service at St James's Piccadilly, on 20 March 1988, when he and Martin Jacobs spoke the lament from *Cymbeline*:

> Fear no more the heat of the sun
> Nor the furious winter's rages.
> Thou thy worldly task hast done,
> Home art gone and ta'en thy wages.
> Golden lads and girls all must
> As chimney sweepers come to dust.

Richard was fifty-three. Within twelve months the long years of discipline and hard work were at last to reap their reward and in a way he never could have imagined. His growing skills as a comedy actor on television were to land him a role that would make him a household name.

'There he was,' comments Antony Sher, 'being a very good supporting actor, doing very nicely but clearly never going to be a star, and suddenly he is a super-star, one of the biggest in the country.'

11

One Foot in the Grave

For twenty-five years Richard had rarely been out of work, his reputation growing with every part and, with every television series, his popularity with the public. But it is *One Foot in the Grave* which, late in his career, has made him a star, a national icon, and has led to various awards, as well as an OBE for his services as an actor and director. The series has changed the style of his life. He carries his success, and the burden of responsibilities which such success brings, with humour and a philosophical detachment and, above all, a modesty. He enjoys his success and yet is realistic enough to know that it could vanish overnight. While it lasts he uses it to promote those causes in which he believes. But that success nearly didn't happen.

'I was trying to go away on holiday when Jeremy Conway rang to say that the BBC were sending me three scripts by David Renwick for a new series to be produced and directed by Susan Belbin. I read the scripts and I really didn't fancy them at all. I didn't think they were all that good, and I thought Victor was rubbish because I felt he was too angry for too long. I couldn't imagine the audience would believe in him.' Richard acknowledges, however, that there may also have been some resistance in him to the idea of playing an old man. In his early fifties he was being asked to play a sixty-year-old. So he wrote to David Renwick a polite note saying he was not interested.

'It was such sadness when Richard turned it down,' says Susan Belbin, who had first met Richard when she was a student stage manager in 1966 at the Glasgow Citizens; so she wrote to Jeremy Conway saying that David Renwick had written the series specially for Richard and didn't want anyone else to play Victor Meldrew. Would he read three more scripts? Having read the new scripts Richard began to see what Renwick was after and eventually agreed to make the series, with Annette Crosbie as his wife, Margaret.

David Renwick remembers the moment during the shooting of *Whoops, Apocalypse,* when, in retrospect, the Victor Meldrew character first appeared before him. Richard, as Foreign Secretary, was being crucified, strapped to a giant cross on Queen's Park Rangers football stadium and then hauled upright. 'It was bloody excruciating and I was frozen!' recalls Richard. Because the director wanted to capture the setting sun behind the cross, they ended up doing twenty takes. 'And,' says Renwick, 'as the cross went up and down, up and down, you could see the irritability etched on Richard's face every time that cross went up. Oh, no, he was not a very happy man!' He could hardly have known, then, how the look of suppressed rage on Richard's face would later become his trademark. Had Richard not been crucified, not once but many times, there might never have been Victor Meldrew.

Although it appeared to begin with yet another settee and two armchairs in a suburban home, as people began to tune in to the series they realised that it was different, that it had a satiric blackness to it, and Richard was all for this. He didn't want the series ever to get cosy. Viewers and critics alike, however, took their time to be persuaded. At its launch in 1990 its viewing figures were a modest but respectable 9 million. Then, as it went into repeats, as well as a new series, it became apparent that the grumpy Victor Meldrew, in the tradition of Punch (with shades of Mr Growser from the 1940s children's classic, *Toytown*), had touched people's hearts.

On many levels the relationship between Richard and David Renwick emerges as the magic behind the series' appeal. Renwick admits that without Richard there would be no show at all. 'Over a period of time,' he says, 'the writing has become cross-fertilised by Richard's performance. It doesn't matter how funny the script is, because so much is down to the performer and how funny he is. Richard happens to be a very funny performer indeed and such people are like gold dust. I think the public were on to him rather ahead of the media. They had a real feeling for his brand of pissed-offness because they were experiencing it themselves, and he articulated it for them.'

Renwick also relishes Richard's incisive diction, the way, as Susan Belbin puts it, he bites off words, the gusto with which he says a phrase like 'He's a *foot fetishist!*' The manner in which Richard handles such a phrase is reminiscent of Joyce Grenfell's superb diction, which reaped such comic effect from lines like 'May I be allowed to divest you of your *plastic mac?*' and 'Did anyone tell you you've got *provocative eyes?*'

In the world of situation comedy *One Foot in the Grave* has broken fresh ground with its uncompromising bitterness and sudden leaps into tragedy. 'That is what is so good about David's writing,' comments Richard, 'that he constantly confounds expectations. I think Victor's popularity has a lot to do with the expression of anger – Victor lets it all out, which a lot of people can't do. So it is very cathartic for the viewer.'

In David Renwick's writing, comedy and tragedy often overlap. In *One Foot in the Algarve*, one of the Christmas specials, Renwick has someone falling to their death over a cliff, and he uses this twice, once in a moment of high drama and the other for farcical effect. He appears, as so often in the series, to be playing with our expectations and his comedy always has an air of tragedy, and vice versa. In the episode, 'Dramatic Fever', Victor attends a rehearsal of Margaret's amateur dramatics society when a stage hand falls from the lighting rig through a window of the set, shattering his legs; an actress falls from a balcony; and part of the set falls on the actors. Each of these incidents is real, yet Victor, thinking they are part of the play, falls about in hysterics. And we, as an audience, laugh too, but only at Victor laughing at the events, not at the events themselves. Those members of the public who write angry letters (and there have been many complaints about this series, as we shall see) often fail to see what Renwick is trying to do.

Victor Meldrew is a man with a short fuse who finds it hard to deal rationally or moderately with the irritating events that constantly assail him. Tilting at imaginary as well as real windmills, with his 'Bloody this!' and 'Bloody that!' he projects onto other people his own dissatisfaction with life in the Britain of the 1990s, as he rants against juvenile delinquency, litter louts, British Telecom, long queues at the surgery:

'An hour and a quarter I had to wait in that bloody place, for a simple repeat prescription. The National Health Service overstretched and three million unemployed, you'd think people would have something better to moan about!'

'There are other patients, Mr Meldrew!'

The first episode of *One Foot in the Grave* opens one Monday morning when Victor turns up for work at Mycroft Watson Associates, where for the past twenty-six years he has been a security officer, and finds himself faced with early retirement. Even more humiliating, he finds his successor is a security alarm. 'Officially I'm now a lower form of life than a Duracell battery. I've been replaced by a box, standard procedure for a man of my age – the next stage is they stick you in one!'

Suddenly, from being an 'employed' person he has been demoted to 'senior citizen – retired'. His daily routine is no longer mapped out for him; he feels useless and inadequate. As far as he is concerned the next stop is death. From now on small incidents begin to assume epic proportions. It is almost as though he needs to create a sense of drama and activity in his otherwise monotonous suburban existence in order to fill the void that has suddenly opened before him. In this, Victor all too clearly mirrors not only the experience of many senior citizens today in an increasingly ageing population, but also that of thousands of men who, almost daily, are being declared redundant.

It is a dilemma that Charles Lamb vividly conveys in *The Super-Annuated Man*, which tells of a fifty-year-old clerk in a London counting house where he has worked for thirty-six years. One day his employers summon him for what he assumes will be the sack only to find, to his amazement, that he is to be retired on two-thirds of his wages, out of gratitude for his past achievements. He is stunned and overwhelmed. He thinks he is happy and then begins to realise he is not; he has more time on his hands than he knows how to manage. Very soon he turns into the kind of man all too familiar in our society today, seated on park benches or in public libraries, unwanted and unnecessary. 'I am no longer a Clerk to the Firm of — ,' he says. 'I am Retired Leisure. I am to be met with in trim gardens. I am already come to be known by my vacant face and careless gesture, perambulating at no fixed pace, nor with any settled purpose. I walk about – not to and from.'

Victor, of course, has more of the fighting spirit, as he struggles against this loss of identity. In many ways he resembles the central character in Brecht's play *The Unworthy Old Lady* who refuses to fit into the role society has created for her, and causes consternation by what is regarded as her waywardness, her insistence on experiment, change and lack of supervision. It is not so much that 'ever at my back I hear Time's winged chariot hurrying near', which haunts those in mid-life today but, rather, the inescapability of a long old age which is now secretly the new dilemma. There's an episode of *One Foot in the Grave* in which Margaret says to Victor, 'You're like that car, you're still stuck in the wrong gear. You've got to change down. *Slow* down, adapt into a new routine. You've got a whole new way of life ahead of you – I mean, you've hardly started, Victor. You've got it *all* to come.' To which he replies, 'Yes, that's what scares me!'

It is not that Victor is old but, by being forced into retirement, he has been labelled 'elderly–retired', yet his energy and drive, and the need to be doing something useful, reflect what countless men today feel, especially when, increasingly, women become the wage-earners and the men are left at home. It is significant that Margaret goes out to work each day in the local florist's shop, a point which is underlined in the very first episode when Margaret announces cheerily, 'Right, I'm off to work then!' to which Victor answers, 'Yes, that's right! Rub it in! Those of us who've still got *jobs* to go to!'

'I admit it!' answers Margaret. 'I've got a job! Forgive me, but society is to blame!' She glares him into contrition and then adds, 'Try making yourself *useful*. You can always hoover up the house.' That *One Foot in the Grave* should be so popular reflects an underlying anxiety in today's society, in which the question of 'ageing' has become one of increasing social, psychological and political urgency.

Since Victor no longer has a goal, the trivial things of life now become the focal point of all his energies: getting the car repaired, mending a fuse, looking after the garden, buying a stamp, having a haircut: these become three-act dramas that strain Victor's limited patience to breaking point. In the first episode Victor, left on his own, hearing the letter-box clatter, goes to collect the mail. 'A bloody Wickes catalogue! Why is it, whenever life is at its lowest ebb, when you really need some good news to cheer you up, the only thing that comes through your letter-box is a bloody Wickes catalogue!'

Victor is blessed with the fact that his wife is far more adjusted than he is. While understanding her husband's frustration, and sympathising with many of his difficulties, she is able to maintain a more balanced and philosophical view of the world. However, this does not prevent her sometimes being driven to distraction, especially when Victor, like so many suddenly retired husbands, gets under her feet. 'Oh, for God's sake, Victor, will you sit down and stop fidgeting about! I'd get more peace with a family of orangutans swinging about the room!' shouts Margaret when she is trying to read a book and Victor is inspecting the newly shaved doors in the sitting room. Nevertheless, there is a deep bond of affection between them, as when in 'The Eternal Quadrangle' she embraces him, murmuring, 'You silly old fool!'

As Margaret, Annette Crosbie provides the perfect foil to Richard's Victor, a still centre for all the preposterous incidents in which he gets involved.

'The partnership of Richard and Annette,' observes Susan Belbin, 'makes a totally believable marriage and relationship while the fact that they are both Scottish makes it even more complete.'

The two, indeed, share much in common and not just in being Scots and growing up in fairly strict Presbyterian milieus. Annette is as intensely private as Richard. Just as he says, 'I'm not prepared to share my innermost secrets with anyone except very close friends,' so, too, Annette says, 'I don't like answering questions from total strangers, answers which will be seen in a newspaper read by thousands of total strangers. I'm a completely private person. I hate being asked questions. I won't even fill in questionnaires.'

Although Richard has a steady track record of comedy on television, Annette's reputation had been as a straight actress until *One Foot in the Grave*, having won two BAFTA awards, one for her performance as Catherine of Aragon in the BBC's *Six Wives of Henry VIII*, and another for her role as Queen Victoria in ITV's *Edward VII*. For Annette, therefore, it was her first taste of comedy on television. 'When you're thought of as a straight actress,' she says, 'there's a certain respect. But all that's changed now. Nowadays people come up to me in the street and ask me how I can bear to live with an awful man like Victor – as though I really were married to him! Margaret's a saint really. I don't know why she's not on tranquillisers. If she hadn't a job to go to I think she'd go bananas with Victor under her feet all day.'

'Annette's character,' adds Richard, 'is very important in making Victor a bit more sympathetic. Victor is a man under siege, frustrated by the idea of being on the scrapheap. This actually makes the irritations of life much harder for him to bear. But the fact that his wife can live with such a difficult man and still love him, makes it work.'

Surprisingly, despite his being a morose man, people do tend to be on Victor's side. His heart is in the right place, and there's usually a reason for his explosions. But it is the dark humour of Renwick's writing which is, as Richard is the first to admit, the secret of its success; it is that which gives the series an edge. It means the audience can't settle into a mood of cosy expectation.

Like many of their viewers, like many retired people, Victor and Margaret frequently spend their evenings in front of their television set, Victor often laughing inanely while eating peanuts by the mouthful. But there is a difference now for, as he sourly remarks, 'It whiles away the daylight hours!' Thinking perhaps that he can do better than much of the mindless television he watches, Victor (in 'Dramatic Fever') sets out to write a TV sitcom. When he finally shows Margaret the script she pronounces it drivel. Rather plaintively, and it is such moments that Richard always plays with a quiet truthfulness that endears us the more to Victor, he replies, 'Five weeks' work down the drain! I've really enjoyed doing that. I thought at last I'd found something I was good at.'

The real crisis that overtakes so many men who are declared redundant, or who reach retirement, is that they suffer a loss of identity. They can no longer say, 'I am a bricklayer, an insurance agent, an accountant, a butcher,' but only 'I'm retired,' which in itself carries resonances of the word 'tired'. Growing older is a social process as well as a biological one, and while the obligations required of the retired person are few, this is not quite as attractive as it might appear, since it is the very lack of obligations, the feeling of being useless and no longer *needed* by society which so many, like Victor Meldrew, find upsetting. Unless an individual has initiative and resilience he, or she, is likely to be trapped in this loss of identity.

To those who are forced into retirement, at whatever age, it is not just their identity which is threatened but their income, and that means loss of status, as, for most working people, their income level will be much lower than that of an employed person. There are many today who are forced to withdraw from society for reasons of poverty, disability, or isolation; especially is the latter true in rural areas where there is often now no public transport, and where many do not, or cannot afford to, own a car.

The mystery about the Meldrews is how they manage to live in comparative comfort. Surely not on Margaret's wages from the florist's, whilst the pension for a security guard after twenty-six years is unlikely to be large, yet they seem not to experience financial stress of any kind and are able to enjoy holidays abroad. None the less, Renwick stresses, 'We have always tried to play the comedy against a context of reality rather than the cosy pseudoreality of many other TV sitcoms.'

It is the strength of the series that it is able to address itself to the more painful aspects of ageing, and even death, in an essentially comic context. As Richard says, 'David's humour is very black and he quite often takes things to the edge, but he knows how to make people laugh.' And yet there will always be those who take themselves too seriously and so are quickly offended.

Thus, on 25 April 1992, the Chairman of the Scottish Pensioners' Forum in Glasgow attacked the series for making fun of pensioners and giving the elderly a bad image, overlooking the fact that, at sixty, Victor is neither elderly nor even qualified to be an old-age pensioner.

Earlier, on 15 February 1990, the *Kent Evening Post* published a letter from the Chairman of the Association of Retired Persons, saying that he was 'appalled by the programme which was insulting to all mature people. This kind of crass characterisation is counterproductive to any bridging of the generation gap ... When, in order to get a laugh, TV producers and script-writers have to resort to destroying the dignity and self-image of a whole group of people who are a very worthy and important part of the community, is it any wonder that we lose our sense of humour?'

In the same year, on 11 November, the BBC also received complaints concerning an episode in which a live tortoise had been buried, albeit unknowingly, by Victor, along with garden refuse, in an incinerator and then set on fire, while a second tortoise, at the end of the episode, was buried alive under the assumption that it was dead. These incidents, including also one of a dead cat in the freezer, aroused angry protests from animal lovers.

On this occasion asked to explain himself to the Chairman of the BBC, Marmaduke Hussey (himself a senior citizen), Renwick wrote explaining the cathartic nature of the show. 'You will always offend,' he wrote, 'even though you don't set out to. Horror and comedy are closely related genres and we watch them for their escapist values. Disasters are always funny when they're happening to other people.' One wonders how some of these critics would have responded to Harry Graham's *More Ruthless Rhymes* which contains the following:

> *L'Enfant Glacé*
>
> When Baby's cries grew hard to bear
> I popped him in the Frigidaire.
> I never would have done so if
> I'd known that he'd be frozen stiff.
> My wife said: 'George, I'm so unhappé!
> Our darling's now completely *frappé*!

But the episode which aroused even more indignation was 'Hearts of Darkness' (the title alone ought to have provided a clue) which depicts a scene in an old people's home in which an elderly resident who is reluctant to go to bed is struck across the mouth by the matron and knocked to the ground, where he is then kicked by one of the nurses. In another scene inmates are shown being locked into a cupboard as punishment.

Mrs Garner of East Yorkshire and four other viewers wrote in to complain, as did others from different parts of the country, remarking that some of them were involved in the care of the elderly and they considered the scenes inappropriate and liable to cause distress to people who had relatives in care.

Each letter was carefully considered by the BBC Complaints Department, which replied that it did not consider the scenes out of place in a programme whose concerns with the frustrations and anxieties of later life is one of its most characteristic features. However, while recognising 'that the series has a tradition of including subjects which are themselves serious and require sensitive handling in a comic context, the Committee did consider that on this occasion the treatment of the issues, particularly the depiction of the assault, would have exceeded the expectations of many of the audiences and could have caused distress'. This particular episode, however, one of the most memorable in the series, perfectly illustrates the sharp edge of Renwick's comedy and its social comment, for he is not only trying to make people laugh; he is also trying to make them think.

The treatment of the elderly in both public and private nursing homes cannot be ignored, as was made apparent in a report to the *Independent* on 8 September 1995 when Dr Paul Knight, clinical director of geriatric medicine at Glasgow Royal Infirmary NHS Trust, gave warning to delegates at a conference that up to 500,000 old people today are at risk from abuse. Similarly, in the previous year, the Central Council for Nursing, Midwifery and Health Visiting published a report on standards of care in nursing homes, revealing a frightening catalogue of complaints of physical and verbal abuse, financial mismanagement and unsafe administering of medicine.

'Although *One Foot in the Grave* is primarily an entertainment,' wrote David Renwick in a statement to be used in the event of future complaints, 'and it is not our intention to shock people for the sake of it, we have tried to play the comedy against a context of reality ... And it is because of this sometimes dangerous approach that it is screened after the 9 p.m. watershed. The scenes in which the old people were being mistreated would only have been offensive if we were asking people to laugh at them, and obviously this was not the case. As a society we tend to treat the elderly quite shamefully and I like to think that by showing Victor tackling the injustice on their behalf, we were offering a small message of hope.'

As a character Victor often mouths the author's own sentiments, as when he says of Christmas, 'It's just a four-month trade fair, nothing to do with Christmas.' This is also another example of how Renwick needles the viewer into asking questions, challenging the excessive commercialisation of Christmas. He even has Victor being cynical about Christmas as a religious festival.

In 'Who's Listening' Victor expresses some of the frustration which the season arouses in many. He orders one garden gnome for the garden and by some quirk of the computer 263 are delivered to his front door and, since it is Christmas, nothing can be done to rectify the mistake until the New Year. 'I've got a bloody population explosion!' growls Victor as they fill every corner of the house, even the bathroom and bedroom. 'It's like sleeping in bloody

Snow White's cottage!' He then turns to Margaret and asks, 'What do you want for Christmas?' And she replies, 'A set of razor blades to slash my wrists!'

In this same episode we also learn that Victor and God are not on speaking terms. But it is when he discovers a letter written by a small boy to Father Christmas saying, 'I want my Dad back for Christmas' that suddenly Victor is confronted by other people's need for faith, especially a child's. What can he *do?* Victor ponders. 'It makes you wonder who's out there listening. How do you make a child like that understand? Some people pray to God, some people write to Father Christmas. Not much difference in the end I suppose. All the good it does.'

Nor does Renwick evade the question of sexuality in the elderly. In spite of the frequent tensions between the Meldrews, Margaret still finds herself capable of sexual jealousy, especially when Victor takes to modelling for a lady artist, stripped to the waist, upside down, posing as St Peter on his inverted cross, and returns home making such comments as, 'Oh, I put my back out at Doreen's. I should have known I wasn't up to it. I was at it for two hours!'

In a later episode, 'Warm Champagne', Margaret decides that she will have an affair. After dining out with her admirer she goes back to his house where he opens a bottle of champagne, apologising that is is insufficiently iced. The implication is that after the champagne the two will go upstairs to bed. Suddenly Margaret realises that it is all a mistake and says, 'No! It's like Christmas presents. They always look so exciting and full of promise under the Christmas tree. We should leave the wrapping paper on, else one of us is going to be rejected. One of the three of us,' she adds. When asked to explain, she continues, 'Victor is the most sensitive person I've ever met and that's why I love him. And that's why also I want to shove his head through a television screen!'

In the highly original 'Dreamland' Margaret does in fact break out and away. The episode opens with the two of them in bed, and Margaret describing a persistent dream she has of battering to death an old man with a bald head. The viewer is led to assume that she is speaking about Victor. 'But always,' she says, 'I am reprieved at the last moment for justifiable homicide. But I don't want to leave prison!' The following day Victor returns from the shoe-mender's with only one shoe. 'They've lost the left shoe so he said he'd only charge me half.' He goes shopping in the supermarket and returns with all the groceries piled on top of a loaf of bread which is now flattened. 'I'll have to get a bicycle pump to it!' exclaims Margaret in exasperation. 'Can't you get the slightest thing right!' It is clear that Victor is more than getting on her nerves.

In the next scene we see Margaret in the drawing room advancing on Victor from behind with a pair of black tights with which to strangle him. The camera moves back and we realise that she and Victor are attempting to entertain their neighbour, Nick Swainey, with charades after dinner, and Margaret is enacting the Boston Strangler. This is typical of the way in which David Renwick builds up the viewer's expectations and then springs a comic surprise. The following day, quite inexplicably, Margaret fails to turn up to work at the florist's shop and the proprietor rings Victor to ask if he knows where she is. By midnight, when there is still no sign of Margaret, not even a phone call, Victor calls in the police. The next day, dredging the canal, the police find her raincoat on the bank and the worst is feared. Victor retires alone to bed for the second night and goes into the bathroom to clean his teeth. As he enters the bedroom he finds, to his surprise, Margaret sitting up calmly in bed, calling out, 'Shut the bathroom door, will you, Victor?' Suddenly he explodes with all the tension and anxiety of the past two days. 'Where the bloody hell have you been? I was dragging the river for you. What happened?'

There follows a long speech from Margaret – unusual in itself on television these days, especially in a sitcom – and is another example of the way in which Renwick expands the mode. 'I just needed to escape,' explains Margaret. 'I saw this sign in the travel agent's window. It said "Two Days in Margate", and I remembered we went there for our third wedding anniversary, and you took me to that place *Dreamland*, a hall of mirrors, and you said you were so happy to see all those reflections of me.' (This remark alone gives us a glimpse of the younger, more romantic Victor.)

'When I was five years old,' continues Margaret, 'we had two budgies that I always felt sorry for, locked up all the while in the same cage. And one day I tried to let them out for a fly round the room. But one of them wouldn't come. And I got hold of its wing and tried to tug it, but it just kept clinging onto the bars and squawking, and just refused to come out of the cage. The other one flew straight out like a rocket, right across the room, crashed into the window and killed itself.

'The next day at school we were asked to write a story about something that had happened to us. I wrote my story about the budgies. And the teacher, Mr Phillips, made me read it out loud in front of the class. And everyone laughed. And I knew he'd done it deliberately, just to be cruel to me. Because basically he was a bastard … and the next day, when Mum tried to take me to school, I refused to go. And she kept smacking me and trying to drag me out, and I kept hanging onto the front door, screaming and kicking, because now I knew how horrible everything is out there and I knew why the other budgie hadn't wanted to leave the cage. Because I suppose he knew he was better off where he was.'

This speech movingly illustrates why some marriages stay together, however incompatible the partners may seem from the outside: better the devil you know than the one you don't know. 'We all make mistakes,' confesses Margaret, 'and I certainly made mine thirty-five years ago.' This remark about their marriage is made at a down moment but, although she frequently expresses her frustration at life with Victor, there is no sign of their marriage falling apart. They provide, in fact, a model of how to accommodate one another's eccentricities within a relationship. Instead of racing to the nearest marriage guidance counsellor or solicitor, they are resigned to their incompatibility, realising that marriages are not made in heaven but on earth.

Such episodes as 'Hearts of Darkness' and 'Dreamland' illustrate how tightly crafted is Renwick's writing, skilfully keeping the viewer in suspense. It is this care which he takes that explains his concern at the way in which earlier press releases had often given away in advance every twist and turn of the plot. On 31 July 1991 he wrote a letter of complaint to the BBC, referring in particular to the episode 'Who Will Buy?', 'when a number of newspapers carried billings that referred to the murder of the blind man and that Victor was suspected of the crime. I can only say that this to me is tantamount to a billing for Miss Marple in which you announce the name of the killer. While it is obviously important to give a flavour of the episode in store, and mention one or two general story areas, I regret the apparent need sometimes to present a shopping list of almost every funny moment in the programme. *What I try to achieve in the writing,* and in harmony with a terrific cast and production team, is a *carefully calculated set of gradations from one interlocking idea to another, springing certain surprises that depend entirely upon their context for their full effect.* Sometimes even to draw attention to certain areas like Victor's decorating the front room is to prime the audience to expect some related disaster which would be far funnier if it came totally out of the blue.'

Some of the episodes have a Feydeau-like quality of farce, and the actors play in the best farce tradition of being utterly real, believing totally in what they are doing, however fantastic may be the events in which they are involved. The merest hint of the actors 'corpsing' or laughing at their jokes, as is sometimes seen on television, would be to destroy the reality on which Renwick builds his superbly inventive and comic plots. The farcical construction can best be illustrated by the episode in which the Meldrews' neighbour, Nick Swainey, returns from holiday bearing a gift for them of a dead scorpion inside a glass paperweight. Roaring with laughter, he tells them, 'It's supposed to be extraordinarily unlucky, according to local superstition!' As he exits, he says, 'I may drop by shortly with some of Mother's drop cakes,' to which Victor mutters in reply, 'We'll build a rockery with them.'

For those not familiar with the series it should be added that Nick's mother is never seen, although frequently referred to: 'Look, Mother's waving to you! Do wave back.' We are left to assume that either she is a batty invention of Nick Swainey's, or he has never

(above) As Uncle Vanya, at the Oxford Playhouse.

(right) With Richard Howard (left) in S. David Wright's *Look at them Smashing all those Lovely Windows,* at the Stables Theatre, Manchester.

(below) Ewen Solon (left) and William Simons in Peter Ransley's *Disabled* at the Stables Theatre, Manchester, Richard's first stage production as a director.

Early television successes: above, in *Only When I Laugh* with Moira Lister, James Bolam, Peter Bowles and Derrick Branche. Below, as Eddie Clockerty in *Tutti Frutti,* with Kate Murphy as Miss Tonar.

In David Lean's film, *Passage to India,* and, below, back on the small screen, in *Hot Metal,* with David Barrass and Robert Hardy.

James Convey (left) with Laurie McCann in wheelchair and Susan Wooldridge (right). In the background, Sandra Voe as the Matron, with Ewan Marshall, Eleanor Bron and Antony Sher.

During the production, three snaps taken
by Richard.

(above) With Lenny Henry at the launch of Comic Relief's Red Nose Day, 1995.

THE
BRIDGEWATER
FOUR

5665 DAYS OF INJUSTICE

Supporting the campaign for the Bridgewater Four.

(above) With Annette Crosbie as Margaret in *One Foot in the Grave,* the series that made Richard and his alter ego Victor Meldrew household names.

(right) In another television series, *Under the Hammer.*

February 29, 1996 and riding in triumph, as the newly elected Rector of Glasgow University.

acknowledged that his mother has died and is perhaps keeping her room exactly as it was in her lifetime, continuing to believe that she is still alive. It is typical of Renwick's writing that this is never explained; to do so would be to undermine the quirky comedy of the character of Nick Swainey, beautifully played by Owen Brenman.

Victor and Margaret decide they must get rid of the glass paperweight as it has already begun to evince evidence of bad luck, so they give it to the Scout jumble sale as a a lottery prize. Needless to say they win it back. In the meantime, Margaret is sent a list of her deceased aunt's will and the contents of her house. She decides that the only thing she really wants is Lot 231 which is listed as 'a cot, back leg damaged'. Some days later they are flabbergasted to discover in their back garden a cow with a bandaged leg and a tag tied to its neck, 'Lot 231'. It is another instance of the bad luck which the dead scorpion is bringing them. When Mrs Skimpson calls, a character worthy of Jane Austen and skilfully played by Hilda Braid, to collect the weekly insurance contributions, the Meldrews give her the paperweight.

After more vicissitudes of the plot it appears that Mrs Skimpson has been mugged and stabbed for the insurance money she was carrying. The Meldrews are appalled, putting it down once more to the influence of the paperweight. At the last minute, however, it transpires that Mrs Skimpson is alive and well, and that when attacked, she had used the paperweight to knock her assailant unconscious. 'There's luck for you!' she exclaims. The intricacy of this plot, the skilful editing of the scenes, the swiftness of the action, make this a fine example of television farce.

Everyone who has travelled on a motorway on Bank Holiday knows what to expect but, in 'The Beast in the Cage', it appears that Victor does not. Stuck in a mile-long queue of cars, Victor grumbles, 'Next Bank Holiday I'll just book a couple of seats in a bread oven.' He blames the car: 'Nothing but trouble with this car from the word go!' He then picks a row with the driver in a car alongside him, after which he shouts at two girls on the other side who are laughing at him, until Margaret cries out in frustration,

'Let it drop, Victor, for God's sake! Are you as happy as a sandboy now? Anybody else you'd like to pick a fight with on the motorway?' Then, quite suddenly, as so often happens in Renwick's writing, the mood switches from comedy to pathos and a moment of real truth when Victor sees driving as a metaphor for life.

This speech is one of the best examples of Richard's playing for truth rather than for effect. 'It's a mirror image of your life really, isn't it?' muses Victor. 'Car journey on a Bank Holiday. The first fifty miles you're on the go all the way, bowling along. Yet past sixty everything slows down to a sudden crawl and you realise you are not getting anywhere, any more. All the things you thought you were going to do that never came to anything. You can't turn the clock back. One-way traffic – just grinding gradually to a complete halt.' There is a pause, and then Margaret adds, 'Same for everyone, I suppose.'

This final scene is one of the most memorable in television sitcom and demonstrates what marks out the series from any other, even *Fawlty Towers* with which it has the closest parallels. No other TV character since Basil Fawlty has so captured the sheer unfairness of modern life, or been led to fly off the handle with such venom. As Gilbert Adair wrote in the *Sunday Times*: 'Meldrew is a veritable Homer of bile.'

Such unrelieved cantankerousness, worse than Scrooge, has none the less captured the imagination and hearts of millions of viewers. 'Every one of us,' wrote Gary Beboff in the *Sun*, 'has suffered the pangs of frustration and then hidden our rage in the name of politeness. But Victor Meldrew can't take any more. Victor has buried his rage too long. Now the worm has turned and is purple with rage. Every time Victor explodes, we explode with him. He may be an impossible, irascible, unreasonable old sod, but we know how he feels because we feel the same. There is a little bit of Victor in us all.'

The classic episode which almost everyone recalls is 'The Trial', in which Victor is at home alone, waiting to be summoned to jury service. The *Daily Mirror* described it as 'the pinnacle of Richard Wilson's career'. Only one other actor has ever had a whole sitcom episode to himself: Tony Hancock, more than thirty years ago, in 'The Bedsitter'. It is a monologue of Meldrew abuse, outrage, self-doubt and self-pity, in which Richard shares Hancock's mixture of pomposity and vulnerability, as well as his sense of outrage and superb comic timing, as he imagines disaster upon horror. Victor's biro leaks all over his face; a crack in the wall makes him fear subsidence; he reads a medical book and convinces himself he has lock-jaw and colon tumour. As he reads: 'Often no symptoms in the early stages,' he cries, 'My God, that's exactly what I've got!' His imagination breeds one disaster after another. Finally, lamenting the futility of his existence, he tries to console himself with the thought, 'Still, I've had a good life.' He pauses and then explodes. 'No, I haven't! I've had a bloody awful life!'

Like Victor, Renwick is often troubled by the many irritations of life today, from struggling to open a packet of biscuits (which gave rise to Victor's 'How are you supposed to open these? With a 500 watt chainsaw?') to waiting in all day for the gas man to put in an appearance, or watching a roofer stroll off to fetch a ladder and not coming back to finish the job. The circumstances that provoke Renwick/Victor are the everyday things we all encounter: telephone answering machines, personal stereos, dog messes in the street, litter louts, and junk mail. 'As a society,' says Renwick, 'I believe that we don't complain enough. People settle for too little, which is why some service industries can get away with the services they provide or, rather, don't provide! Not that complaining does Victor any good, for Victor's battles must be futile if they are to have a ring of authenticity.' Another reason that Renwick decided to make Victor retired was simply as a mechanical device so that he would have more time on his hands, and be more exposed to pressure 'which is, of course, the dilemma in which so many retired people find themselves'.

Victor is often misunderstood, says Renwick. 'He is not a grumpy person; he is a victim of life. He is like the mountain gorilla who won't attack unless provoked. The problems that Victor and I suffer are universal, certainly judging from all the letters I receive. He is not a retired old man but an ordinary chap in his late fifties who has been made redundant. As his skin isn't thick enough to shrug off the things that happen to him, he says the sort of things that many of us think but don't say. We shouldn't laugh at Victor's opinions, rather we should applaud them. Victor, as I see it, is a champion for us all. He is Everyman.'

When Renwick started writing the series he aimed to move away from the tired old formula of gag-writing and the typical British sitcoms about married couples visited by their mother-in-law. 'I wanted to make a comedy about ordinary people. Comedies have been too hidebound by class. I also wanted to extend the boundaries of sitcom into satire. In a way *Fawlty Towers*, with its mix of bite and bile, had done that in the seventies, but there has been nothing much since except the alternative comedies of the *Blackadder* ilk. *Fawlty Towers* would begin with a naturalistic set of circumstances before all hell was let loose and poor Basil was left flummoxed. Like Basil Fawlty, Victor also is unable to cope. Both Victor and Basil are characters who are loved and despised in equal proportion by the audience. The absurdity in comedy, however, should always spin off from a truth somewhere.'

Susan Belbin makes the same point. 'The essence of comedy is failure. Every successful comedy is about people who are failures in society's eyes: *Dad's Army, Hi-de-Hi!* and *Fawlty Towers*. But the characters are all people who are striving. That's why you have sympathy with them.'

Mark Lawson, referring to *One Foot in the Grave* as 'one of the most daring and inventive comedies on the small screen', commented on how its central character is a psychopath whose neighbours need a Neighbourhood Watch because of him. 'He gives off a serious air of danger, chillingly transmitted by Richard Wilson's carefully unsentimental performance. This edge is typical of the way in which the programme treats its large mainstream audience as grown-ups, an intention signalled from the title downwards.' Gilbert Adair in the *Sunday Times* similarly observed, 'We laugh as nervously as we might giggle at a funeral. What the series has invented is the tragic gag. The series encapsulates the dual essence of all true humour: one foot in the comic, one foot in the grave.'

Popular culture, observed Mark Lawson, is a useful guide to

national temperament and spirit, 'so that if I were the British government it would worry me that the two most revered characters of recent British television have been ruined and melancholic failures: Inspector Morse and Victor Meldrew. The green shoots of recovery are a long way off for Victor. British sitcom was famously obsessed with bottoms but this one has found the skull beneath the skin. That so bleak a show should have such a following is at least a reason to be cheerful for television.'

Richard's only regret in playing Victor Meldrew is that he was pitched into the screen role of an older man much earlier than he would have wished. But he doesn't think about his own old age. 'I don't even know when it's going to start. The journey through life is always a learning process and one is still learning, which makes life more enjoyable whatever age you are. But you do become more aware of your mortality the older you get, but because I live in the present that doesn't affect me really. You do realise that certain things are happening in your life that are associated with getting older: for example, when I moved into my new home in 1994 I was thinking that I probably won't be moving again. But I don't fear dying. I know that when I die I won't know anything about it, and if I'm wrong about life after death it will be a great thrill.'

Richard sternly rejects the word 'geriatric', however. 'It is not a word we use any more. Geriatric suggests that someone is past it. The correct term is "older person", with an emphasis on the second word. There are lots of people in their eighties and older whom one would never consider geriatric.'

He abhors the way in which, sometimes, in hospitals and nursing homes, nurses will bellow at a perfectly intelligent and not even deaf elderly person, 'Are you all right, grandad/gran?', assuming that being elderly means senile. He also deplores those doctors who will say to an elderly person who complains of a disability, 'Well, what do you expect at your age?' Such an ageist attitude is what also causes Victor to fume and fret, as he envisages spending the rest of his life having 'people helping me across the road ... forcing me at gunpoint to go on a daytrip to Eastbourne, and listening to *Sing Something Simple*.'

'It is wrong,' says Richard, 'to assume that all elderly people are of declining intelligence, unable to learn or to adapt. It is this ageist attitude which lumps together all people over the age of sixty-five as "the elderly".' Richard is much involved with the charity Age Concern and believes that there is one underlying concern and that is, that the old do not feel themselves to be loved, that too many people treat them with indifference and seek no contact with them. 'There are so many retired people who know that others, be they politicians or social workers, are concerned that they should have "a decent standard of living" but *who know that no personal interest is being taken of them.'* He himself admits that just before he turned fifty he thought he would hate it. 'I suppose I saw fifty as getting older, which is how society expects you to feel. I'm very much for behaving as you want to and *not* applying any rules.' The secret is to grow into old age and to go on growing.

Much of the filming for the series is shot on location in Bournemouth where the cast and crew rehearse for four weeks, doing six episodes, followed by a further six weeks in the studio, finally recording before a live audience. It is a meticulous process designed to create realism. The hours are long and gruelling, for Susan Belbin, like Richard, is a perfectionist, but it is when people tire that accidents are most likely to happen and on one such occasion Richard nearly lost a finger.

They were doing a night shoot, and it was getting late. The sequence involved driving and, inadvertently, Richard was given a wrong cue, so that the man working the car slammed the passenger door while Richard's hand was in the way, and it broke his finger. 'When it happened,' recalls Susan, 'he momentarily deafened the sound recordist, who still had his cans on, with his yell of pain.' Filming was abandoned and Richard rushed to the nearest hospital at one o'clock in the morning. Fortunately a doctor was available to set the bone and stitch up the finger.

In one episode Victor is buried up to his neck in the garden and because of problems with the camera Richard had to be buried three times in the hole. 'What are you doing to me, Miss Belbin!'

he cried out. Filming that sequence, says Richard, was 'deeply uncomfortable. A hole was dug, a box placed in it, and I then crouched in the hole with my head sticking out above a kind of collar covered with earth. I felt rather helpless but I did have a hot water bottle in there to keep me warm. I was in the box for an hour but then we realised the collar didn't look right so we had to do it all again. Then everyone had lunch and after lunch they found there was a fault in the film so I had to clamber back into that bloody hole again! Nightmare. The novelty was that all the film crew found it very funny the first time and a bit boring the next. The third take I was left to myself, sitting in this earthy pit, with my head sticking out just above ground level. Everyone ignored me; they were all having a cosy cup of tea in the corner of the garden, while the wind whipped muck around my face. If I hadn't yelled at them I think I might have been there to this day!'

Renwick almost appears to take a perverse pleasure in not only placing Richard in such bizarre situations but also in exposing his bottom to the camera. The first time it happened was in *Whoops, Apocalypse* and then in *Hot Metal*, in which Richard had to wander naked into the Blue Peter Studio while it was supposedly on the air. In the 'Hearts of Darkness' episode of *One Foot in the Grave* the script called for Richard to do a full strip in the shower. 'We could have fudged something to protect his manhood,' says Susan Belbin, 'but it just makes everyone so self-conscious, so I asked him if he would mind doing it for real, no pouches or anything, and he said of course he didn't mind. We shot him from behind and the only person who saw him naked from the front was Janet Henfrey who played the matron, and the wardrobe gentleman who wrapped him up every time.'

Richard may be no Chippendale, though he has a fine pair of muscular legs, but he was once voted in a national newspaper poll as the third sexiest man on television after Ian McShane and Gary Webster. 'I have started to receive saucy letters,' reveals Richard, 'from women asking me to send pictures of myself stripped to the waist. I've even received a letter asking me to pose in the nude and offering me a fee of £20. Needless to say all they got was a fully clothed picture. But clearly there is no age to being a sex symbol!' Anna Massey describes how, when she and Richard went on holiday together to St Lucia, 'the women *adored* him, wanted to dance with him, and he danced with them all. They were thrilled, and this was way, way before *One Foot in the Grave*, just after he had done *Only When I Laugh*.' As Antony Sher also confirms, 'Women do find him very attractive.'

Before filming, Richard will often ham up a scene which might otherwise verge on the mawkish; 'what I sometimes meet with is Richard's resistance to sentiment,' observes Renwick. As an illustration he describes the episode in which Victor and Margaret agree not to give each other Christmas presents and then, at the last minute, Margaret decides to give Victor a new watch. Renwick had seen this as rather a sad moment but at rehearsals Richard started playing it for laughs, shying away from the pathos, with the result that the studio audience roared with laughter. Eventually they arrived at a compromise.

One of Richard's stocks in trade in comedy is the way he will do a second 'take'. He will walk away, then come back and look at something again, and so get a big laugh. Renwick describes a wonderful double-take in a scene where Victor and Margaret are in bed. Victor is wearing an airline mask over his eyes to blot out the light. He pulls up the mask to look at Margaret. He puts the mask back on, then does another turn and stares at her – but this time with the mask on, so that he can't see her. That, says Renwick, was all Richard's invention.

Although the star of the show, Richard always works as a member of the team and never abuses his star status. Renwick gives a perfect illustration of Richard's innate good manners and democratic spirit when they were filming the episode about a traffic jam on the motorway. The catering waggon was about a half a mile away with the result that Richard ended up behind a queue of extras. 'You could tell inside he was bristling, but he was far too democratic to push his way in, and he quietly took his place at the back of the queue and waited his turn. This is typical of him – not to pull rank.'

Richard finds playing Victor very tiring rather than cathartic

'All that pent-up aggression, the ranting and raving, is very hard work. I find him a very exhausting character.' He would hate the idea, however, of just playing Victor for laughs. Lots of people write to him to say how they have had to cope with the same sort of problems as Victor and that they, too, are frustrated by society's attitude towards the unemployed. 'It's quite humbling,' says Richard, 'when you realise how much the series means to so many people.' He recalls once walking into a north London pub, at a time when he was feeling very low and just wanting to be alone and anonymous, when a man came up to him and started to talk about the programme. Richard groaned inwardly and then, as he listened to the man, he realised how much the series had helped the man to see the funny side of things and view his own circumstances more objectively.

As a result of his success Richard has a huge fan mail, as well as many requests from charities, and endeavours to answer every letter. On 15 January 1995 he received the following letter from a small boy in Lincolnshire:

> Dear Mr Wilson,
>
> I really like your show *One Foot in the Grave* ... You are the best comedian I know ... If you have enough time I would like to invite you to stay at my house for a week, then I could take you on a tour round Lincolnshire ... Perhaps you could teach me to be a comedian like you and I could take over after you? When you have to go back home I will give you five pounds so that you can have something to eat on your way. I hope you are keeping well. Yours sincerely, Rupert White.

Clearly the younger generation is already knocking at the door!

While professors of sociology weigh in with solemn views on the meaning of 'Meldrew' and medical experts from Cambridge pronounce their learned opinions that to rant and rave like Victor is to ensure a longer life, it appears that real-life Meldrews are springing up everywhere. It is almost as though the series has given to the English language a new word or synonym: Meldrew. On 24 March 1994 the press carried such a real-life Meldrew story (and there have been others). The headline in the *Daily Mail* ran: YOU MAKE MELDREW LOOK MERRY, JUDGE TELLS THE GRUMPY GATEKEEPER.

Judge Roger Hunt's scathing verdict came after he ordered Mr Skelton, a 71-year-old pensioner, to dismantle a 22-foot-long steel gate which he had erected across his driveway thereby blocking a shared access, so that Frank and Winifred Reed, his neighbours, could not get out of their bungalow without his permission ...

... Alan Day, a neighbour, described Mr Skelton as 'the most obnoxious person I have ever met', while Mr Skelton, fixing his gaze on several other residents listening at the back of the court, declared they ought to be put on a ship and 'sunk in the bloody Atlantic'. The judge ordered him to pay Mr Reed £1,500 damages and to meet the costs. After the hearing Mr Reed said, 'I'm over the moon but there will be no olive branch, not to a neighbour from hell.'

One is reminded of Richard's own comment that he would not like to have Victor Meldrew for a neighbour. As his friend, the actress Rosemary Martin, has observed of Richard's success as Victor, 'It is because he plays a very real person. He has made no concessions. Most other actors would have wanted to be loved in that part.'

'What I think is so awful,' said William, 'is that I've lived all these years and not *done* anything yet.'

'You've done quite enough,' said his mother. 'You've broken every window in the house at one time or another, you've made the geyser explode twice, you've *ruined* the parquet by sliding on it, and you've got tar all over the hall carpet.' ...

'I bet I'd've been famous by now if I hadn't had to waste all my time at school,' [said William].

'One might almost say you were famous now,' put in Robert, his elder brother. 'At least everyone for miles around knows there's some sort of trouble coming as soon as he sees you. I suppose that's fame in a way.'

It was while rereading the *Just William* books that I encountered the above passage from Richmal Crompton's *William the Rebel* and realised a similarity between William and Victor, a similarity which Alice Thomas Ellis also drew attention to in an article for the *Daily Telegraph* (20 March 1993): 'Observing Victor Meldrew I know at last what sort of person Just William would have matured into. William as a small boy suffers greatly from what he sees as the irrationality of grown-ups and the injustices perpetrated upon him by society. William is given to frequent muttered tirades which remind us of Victor's irritable soliloquies. Both William and Victor share the same sense of chivalry and justice, and the same ability for getting into scrapes.'

It was Wordsworth who wrote, 'The child is father to the man,' and behind Richard's irascible performance as Victor, in his peaked cap, it is easy to see the pout and frustration of a small boy pitting himself against the odds, a twentieth-century Don Quixote tilting at windmills. Alice Thomas Ellis is indeed right: Just William has come of age!

ACT III

12

Changing Step

Nancy Meckler describes how, for several years during the 1970s, Richard would volunteer to work with young disabled people at summer camps, helping to organise games and outings; and Susan Wooldridge recalls how her friendship with him began when she was staying in Paris in July 1986, and received a call from Richard, who was in Paris to attend the Disabled Olympics, suggesting they 'party together'. It is his empathy with those who are disabled, as well as his experience of working in a military hospital in Singapore ('There was one man who had lost both hands in a mine explosion'), and memories of his father talking about the First World War, which had given Richard the idea of making a film about young Scottish amputees of that period returning from the Front, and had resulted in his first exploration of the material in the form of the play *The House* in 1979 for Joint Stock.

During the workshop period for this production he began to formulate the idea that one of the wounded soldiers in the play should be a real amputee, and so he brought in a young stage manager who had lost a leg in a riding accident and who was hoping to become an actor. Rosemary Martin, who had been a regular member of Richard's weekly improvisation group, recalls meeting the young man at Richard's flat and then, after a time, being asked by Richard to go out of the room. 'When I returned, the young man had removed his prosthesis and was sitting there with only one leg. My task was to imagine I was his girl-friend visiting him in hospital for the first time after the operation.' Although he contributed considerably to the workshop process, as Richard and the group were unsure that he could sustain the acting he was not used in the production. However, the experience of working on this production finally decided Richard to use real amputees when it came to making the BBC Television film, *Changing Step*. Able-bodied actors with their legs strapped up behind them no longer seemed appropriate.

It was while Richard was filming *Tutti Frutti* that fellow Greenockian, Bill Bryden, then head of BBC Scotland TV, and a former director at the National Theatre, asked him if there was anything special he wanted to direct. When told of Richard's long-term ambition, he persuaded BBC Scotland to finance the project, including a preliminary two-week workshop, something that was quite new and radical in television. And so, in 1988, at the Limb Fitting Centre in Glasgow, Richard began to interview young men who had recently lost a limb, mainly from cancer, and to set up auditions for those who seemed to show some talent.

James Convey, known to everyone as Jeg, a computer programmer in Glasgow, who eventually played the lead in the film, was one of those who received a letter asking if he would be interested in meeting Richard to talk about the project. Jeg, who had lost his leg to cancer the previous year and was still quite weak, was sufficiently intrigued to go along for a 9 a.m. interview at the hospital. 'I was quite laid back about the whole affair, having rather negative feelings as I did then about actors; I'd only met amateur actors at the University here who thought they were the cat's whiskers!' He was then invited with six other amputees to do some role-playing and simple improvisations. 'I didn't feel competitive at all because, right to the end, I didn't think I was at all cut out to be an actor. I can see now, knowing Richard's thing about minimalism in acting, that this was to my advantage, that I wasn't trying to impress him or prove anything.'

From those auditions two were chosen for the workshop: Convey and Laurie McCann, whose surgeon, Mr McCreath, at the South General Hospital in Glasgow, suggested that Richard should see him. 'For someone of his age, he was only eighteen, knowing as he did that he was facing possible death from cancer, I thought his general attitude remarkable.' Laurie, unlike Jeg, didn't even have a stump as his leg had had to be removed at the joint. In order to have his artificial limb fitted each day he had to sit on a kind of bucket with the artificial limb attached to it, and then be dropped into it and strapped in.

After the two-week workshop Richard invited Laurie to be in the film, but then he developed cancer again, this time in his lung, which necessitated chemotherapy. Richard, however, was not to be daunted. Laurie was thrilled, says his mother Elizabeth, 'and couldn't wait to get his treatment over so that he could start.' Then, just before shooting was due to start in May 1989 Laurie had another tumour, this time on his side, requiring a further operation as well as several weeks of radiotherapy during the time that he was supposed to be filming in Ayrshire. Once more Richard was not to be put off, arranging for a car to take Laurie each day for his treatment at the Belvedere Hospital, as well as to be accompanied by another disabled actor, Ewan Marshall. 'Laurie was amazing,' says Ewan, 'he was riddled with cancer, but because he was a big fellow, although very young, he gave you the impression that he could handle anything. But he knew his time was limited. Radiotherapy is really scary treatment; it's awesome, all those huge machines, like the *Rocky Horror Show*. Obviously Laurie hoped it would finally rid him of the cancer but he was aware that he was getting these recurrences, and they had already taken a bit out of one lung. Until then I hadn't realised how many young people get cancer. Most of the amputees I had met up to then had lost a limb in a car or motor-cycle accident, which is how I lost my arm.'

Laurie was to describe the experience of making the film as the most wonderful time of his life, and when asked by a journalist if it had been fun, replied, 'Has it been fun? Fun isn't the word for it. It's been elation, total elation, every day!'

For the preliminary two-week workshop in January 1989 at the Montgreenan Country House Hotel in Ayrshire, Jeg and Laurie were joined by three other amputees: Ewan Marshall, who has one arm; Jim Brogan, who has one leg; and Peter Howell, an Olympic champion, who has no arms or legs. The other actors were Eleanor Bron, Susan Wooldridge, and Antony Sher who, apart from being asked to write the film script (he had just had his first novel, *Middlepost*, published to much acclaim) was to play the part of a doctor. During the first week there were lectures on the history of the First World War; soldiers and nurses (VADs) who had served in the war were invited to come and speak about their experiences; whilst the psychiatrist Monty Berman, who had worked in an amputee unit during the Second World War, talked about the psychological aspects of disability, and how amputees come to terms with feelings of not being a complete person.

Not only may mobility be impaired, but relationships may be threatened by partners who are unable, or unwilling, to come to terms with such an amputation. Jeg Convey is fortunate that his partner, with whom he had been living, has been able to cope, and they now have a small child. Most of all, perhaps, there is a loss of self-esteem. This is dealt with movingly in the film in a sequence which shows Jeg standing in front of a long mirror, unrolling the trouser leg which is rolled up round his stump, so that, looking at himself in the mirror, he can imagine that once again he has two legs.

Amputees may find that work roles have to be reassessed; indeed, the ability to work may not even be an option, while social and recreational activities may also be severely limited, depending on the back-up of friends, family and neighbours. Although the United Kingdom has 6 million disabled people, how many of us meet them at work, play or on public transport? The fundamental problem with disability in the community is that it is so often kept out of sight. A disabled person in the street is still a sufficiently rare occurrence that people will often remark on it.

As the able-bodied members of the workshop learned, the fitting of an artificial limb, if successful, can help restore a sense of body image and improve both social and work contacts, although there are some amputees, such as Ewan Marshall and Jim Brogan, who never wear a prosthesis and who develop muscular skills that offset their disability. But for those who have poor health, or lack good muscular control, artificial limbs may have to be held on by bulky straps, as in the case of Laurie McCann. For the fitting of any artificial limb clearly the stump has to be in good physical condition, and to use the limb requires energy, perseverance and confidence.

Following an amputation, each individual has to go through a period of mourning which can be very painful, especially for a young person. One of the most telling sequences in *Changing Step* is when Jeg returns home for the first time since being wounded and repatriated. Going out into the back yard he throws himself on the ground, under the line of washing, crying out, 'I want my leg! I want my leg!'

Sometimes an individual may suppress all emotion, or even imagine that the limb is still intact, which is often nature's way of enabling the individual to accept the reality of the situation by degrees, and thus avoid being engulfed by negative emotions. Sexual attitudes have also to be considered. During the Montgreenan workshop it was the lusty humour of the young amputees which often redeemed what might otherwise have been unduly painful. They would cheerfully discuss the difficulty of 'getting a leg over' when making love.

For the first few days of the workshop the professional actors saw the young men with all their clothes on but they knew that at some point they were going to have to see the stumps. Interestingly, Ewan Marshall, who shared a room with Convey, recalls how, on their first night, Jeg said to him, 'You show me your stump and I'll show you mine,' which was something Ewan had not experienced before, not having been among other amputees as Jeg had. 'It's like a dolphin,' he said, referring to the pattern of the scar on Jeg's stump. It was finally about the fourth day that Richard structured an improvisation which involved the unravelling of the bandages as from a new stump following an amputation. Jeg, who was the most recent amputee (two years before), volunteered, feeling it would be good for him, 'like being in an encounter group'. He was, however, worried about taking off his prosthesis for the first time in front of Eleanor Bron, Susan Wooldridge and the others, and whether it would change their attitude towards him, 'but Jim Brogan was a great inspiration. He never wore his artificial limb, never does, and he's one of the fittest men I know. He can do handstands on crutches – there's a sequence in the film where he does this. But when I did finally take my leg off, yes, it was traumatic.'

Susan Wooldridge speaks of the extraordinarily sensitive way in which Richard set up this improvisation, talking to Jeg at some length about it beforehand so that he shouldn't feel like a guinea pig on a slab. For Susan, being confronted with the reality of people who have lost their limbs proved the most frightening moment of her life. 'It took me a long time to recover from that experience but I know I came away from it wiser and humbler. And it certainly changed my ideas about what it must be like to be disabled.'

She was especially made aware of this when, on the middle weekend of the workshop, all the other amputees who were to be in the film, but not playing central roles, arrived for a day, and they went off to a sports centre in Ayr for a game of football (such a game appears in the film). Richard had suggested they leave their artificial limbs at the Montgreenan Hotel so that they wouldn't have to remove their prostheses in the changing room in front of other people. 'There was,' recalls Susan, 'this extraordinary phalanx that went across this enormous bridge over a motorway and down into the sports centre. Tony Sher and I were bringing up the rear and suddenly we realised what it was to be a "you" instead of "us", because as other people walked by they started laughing. They couldn't deal with it at all, because here were twenty or more young men, all on crutches, crossing this bridge.'

Richard himself describes a similar occasion, during the actual shooting of the film, when those with four limbs suddenly found themselves very much in the minority. On a very hot day, during a break in shooting, Richard had returned to the hotel to have a swim in the pool. There were one or two ordinary guests besides himself, and he was swimming up and down, relaxing, when one of the amputees jumped in. Then another dived in. And Richard could see the people in the pool making a note of it: two one-legged chaps, how unusual! But then a third jumped in, then a fourth, and a fifth, and more and more.

'Well, those people just didn't know what to do with themselves', says Richard. Eventually there were about twenty amputees in the pool. And then Peter Howell, the Olympic medallist, waddled in without any arms or legs, 'and those poor people didn't know where they were – some sort of Gustav Doré version of hell, I imagine. They felt outnumbered. *They* were suddenly the odd ones out. And there were all these amputees leaping in and out, jumping in the air, and having a wonderful time. Suddenly it was we, the able-bodied, who were in the minority, and yet we were all equal in the water. I shall always remember that.'

Susan Wooldridge has a very special memory of Peter Howell, 'this incredibly beautiful young man,' who arrived a few days later than the other amputees at Montgreenan Hotel because he had been taking part in the Disabled Olympic Games in Beijing and was flown in specially by the BBC. Susan's call was at half past six in the morning and as she came out of her room she saw him coming down the corridor in his wheelchair. In a panic she thought, oh, God, I've got to talk to him all the way down in the lift! What do I say? Then, as he came level with her, she saw that he had put on a T-shirt with, printed on it, the words: *Drunk? – I'm absolutely legless!* – which was his way of breaking the ice on meeting the whole cast and crew for the first time.

But it wasn't easy for any of them. 'Usually,' remarked Sagir, a twenty-year-old amputee who was in the film, 'you wait to know someone before you tell them you've got a false leg. Here it became the first thing everyone knew.' For them all, not least the amputees themselves, one of the best things about making the film was the chance to share experiences, although for the multi-limbed it was often a shock. As Eleanor Bron has observed, 'It was difficult, though rewarding, to face up to things within ourselves, like our attitudes towards, and understanding of, disablement. And the acceptance, too, that we are all in some way disabled, if not physically then emotionally, psychologically, or as a result of education or our social background.' Antony Sher, who had worked with disabled people before when he was preparing for the role of Richard III for the Royal Shakespeare Company, describes how again he found himself being uplifted by the courage of so many disabled people, especially someone such as Jeg Convey, 'whose amputation was so recent, to put that experience in front of an audience'.

It was in the second week of the workshop that all the actors, both professional and the non-professional (for the purposes of the film all the amputees were made members of Equity), began to build their characters for the story that Richard and Antony Sher were planning. One such improvisation involved Eleanor Bron who, as the commandant of the hospital, was to instruct the newly arrived and totally inexperienced VAD, played by Susan Wooldridge, to go upstairs to Bathroom No. 4 where she would find an amputee whom she was to undress and bathe. Susan was so embarrassed that she left the room and tried to avoid doing the improvisation. Eventually she returned and went to the bathroom where she found Jeg who, in character, said to her, 'I have to tell you, Ma'am, but I don't have any kecks [knickers] on,' and Susan thought, oh, my God! This is awful! What am I doing here? In her nervousness she dropped the plug and everything and started wanting to laugh hysterically, all of which is recorded on video (all improvisations were recorded for Tony Sher's benefit when he came to write the script). Then, when she did pull Jeg's trousers down it was such a relief to find that Jeg had on a pair of swimming trunks.

Of course, when they came to shoot the scene for the film Jeg was completely naked, but by then that was the last thing on their minds. Within the historical period of the film Susan's embarrassment would clearly have been that of her character, Lady Alice Napier, whilst the young soldier would probably never have taken off his clothes with a woman since losing his leg.

Ewan Marshall recalls the occasion when several of the amputees were huddled under sheets in a cellar, by the light of two candles, pretending it was a casualty station in the trenches and that they had just been dragged there, wounded, from the front line. Suddenly Ewan was aware of Laurie retching and spewing up, 'and someone else, too, probably Jeg; but Laurie was being really sick. The white sheets and hospital beds had reminded him of the chemotherapy and all the pipes pumping chemicals into him which used to make him nauseous.' Because Laurie had never done any acting before, it was all very real to him. Bit by bit, says Ewan, Richard and Tony fed in suggestions, 'and you would realise that you were being pushed in certain directions. What I liked was that it was all highly structured, and there was all this input into your character and background, what regiment you had been in, where you had been wounded, and so on. So we were all gradually assembling our individual histories.'

Richard describes one long improvisation which Eleanor Bron did as Lady MacIlvrai, the owner of the house which is commandeered by the government for use as a convalescent hospital, concerning the death of her son at the Front. Susan had to bring her a telegram which she put to one side – 'to have opened it would have been the obvious thing to do,' comments Eleanor. Instead she went to the fire and put on more coal. She then rang the bell for tea and quietly awaited its arrival. She poured and drank her tea – and all this time nothing was said. Finally she opened the telegram and read of her son's death, which she had already intuited but of which she had resisted the telegram's confirmation. There were many such improvisations, including one which involved Susan scrubbing stone flags for a morning (something she does in the film). Not all the improvisations were videoed – or even witnessed by Richard or Tony. Sometimes two actors might go off for a long walk, discussing their characters, and in this way build up shared memories. In all acting, but most especially is this so on film, it is the unspoken thoughts, the unexpressed feelings, which are often the most telling.

The main theme of the film is change. The war is seen to have changed everyone's sense of place at a time when all levels of society were having to learn how to change step. During the First World War hundreds of country houses throughout Britain were commandeered as convalescent hospitals for wounded soldiers, mainly from the working class. They were nursed by a few trained personnel, assisted by members of the VAD who were often daughters of the local aristocracy and who rarely had experience of any kind of manual work, being used to having everything done for them by servants. Many of them, however, like Lady Alice, were longing to break rank and find their freedom as individuals, as is evidenced by Vera Brittain's classic *Testament of Youth*. For them all, soldiers and volunteer nurses, it was a time of huge emotional upheaval.

'I loved the idea of everything being turned upside down,' says Antony Sher. 'A country house into a hospital; the owner of the house into a Red Cross commandant of the hospital but who finds that her title is entirely honorary when confronted by the matron, Sister McCabe [played by Sandra Voe], the one professional among a gaggle of amateurs and novices; and the soldiers recuperating in the chandeliered conditions they would never have experienced in peace-time except as staff.'

While concentrating on the parallel stories of the new VAD, Lady Alice, and the young amputee, Private Ross, the film's main targets are this collision of class, linked to an honest examination of disablement. In addition, there is the relationship of Lady MacIlvrai – 'Eleanor Bron wearing the exhausted manners of an exhausted class' – and the doctor, played by Sher, who is a victim of gassing at the Front. He and Lady MacIlvrai are portrayed listening in secret, behind closed doors, to German music on a gramophone, while taking their drugged solace in Brompton cocktails: a potent mixture of whisky, honey, morphine and cocaine.

The film opens with the arrival of the two protagonists at Sorn Castle (a real place) in Ayrshire, given over for the duration of the war to the care of convalescent soldiers. The year is 1917. Jamie (Jeg) Ross, a private soldier (played by James Convey), hobbles in on his crutches, clattering over the castle's marble floors, while Lady Alice Napier (played by Susan Wooldridge) motors up to the castle to do her bit for 'the most just war since the Crusades', though she would have preferred to be tending officers rather than other ranks. The camera follows Jeg as, painfully and slowly, he negotiates the slippery marble stairs. A little later, when he removes his clothes and is helped into a bath, we see that he really does have only one leg, and that the other ends in a stump. As he lies on a bed, and the doctor probes the stump, he cries out in pain. Mo Haynes, the make-up artist, spent weeks creating stumps out of rubber latex so that in this scene Jeg's own stump should look raw and barely healed. 'It took hours to get it on the poor bugger,' says Richard, 'fitting it over his own stump.'

The film is sometimes harrowing, always moving, often funny. Visually it is beautifully composed, lovingly re-creating the sense of period and place, from the steam tubs and slop pails, the woven cane wheelchairs, and the all-embracing claustrophobic atmosphere of this chandeliered convalescent home, with its Saturday evening entertainment of forced revelry, to the scene of the garden fête in which the young amputees join in an egg-and-spoon race, or play football on their crutches, while others build a mock-up of a Front line trench for the local gentry to visit, with a sign advertising 'A Mug of Front Line Tea'. All is meticulously observed, even to the correctness of period speech and syntax. There are shots of the limbless soldiers on crutches being put through a square bashing drill by a sergeant major with his commands of 'Left! Left! Left!' as though they were being drilled to return to the Front as a one-legged army. Finally there is the idyllic atmosphere of the hazy summer days of 1917, a pastoral quality which Richard deliberately cultivated, far removed from the horror of the French trenches. 'I remember once,' he says, 'when I was in Singapore, there was a concert, and a lot of wounded people around on this spectacularly beautiful evening, and I remember thinking then that wars are also fought in sunshine, though we tend to think of them as being fought in mud and rain as the Flanders battle was. And so I wanted to get the contrast of these men coming back from the Front to this really beautiful house and countryside.'

It is important not to underestimate the impact upon Richard of his experience in Singapore about which he speaks so little. I am reminded of what Joyce Grenfell wrote in her diary in Naples for 20 March 1944: 'Oh, God, the sights I've seen today. We haven't *touched* the war till today. Bed after bed filled with mutilated men, heads, faces, bodies. It's the most inhuman, ghastly, bloody, hellish thing in the world. I couldn't think or work or even feel in the end. It was quite numbing. The first ward was a huge surgical ward full of casts, pulleys and very sick men. All the time we were performing, there were sisters doing dressings, patients feeding from tubes, orderlies bringing in people from the operating theatres, as well as the newly arrived from the line.'

The film demonstrates Richard's belief in minimalist acting: 'You should not be aware that the actor is acting.' It also demonstrates his preference for a slow tempo, allowing events to unfold at a natural pace, rather than imposing directorial changes of tempo. His concern always is with what is going on in the inner recesses of people's minds, and he goes to great trouble to bring this gently to the surface. Richard's fundamental belief is in the importance of the subtext, in what is unspoken, just as in her novel *The Voyage Out*, Virginia Woolf has one of her characters ask a young writer what kind of books he wants to write, and he replies, 'Books about silence ... the things which people do not say.'

Above all in this film he examines disablement in a much more open and frank way than has been previously attempted. As he says: 'We confront the viewer with a cast of amputees who clearly are not pretending. We go beyond the mythical hero to the real person.'

During the actual filming Susan Wooldridge and Tony Sher found Richard to be another person. Susan remembers going for a walk in the rain with Tony, discussing this change, which they decided was first-time nerves as a film director and also the impact of such a painful subject. He was under enormous pressure, not least in arguing with Sher about the direction of the storyline, about what should be kept in and what left out. 'Richard had so brilliantly set up in the workshop period a sort of democratic control of the central idea,' observes Susan, 'that we all felt we owned our characters and our stories. Well, this is a very powerful idea to keep control of, and with hindsight I realise how difficult it was for Richard.'

There were, necessarily, so many conflicting ideas and threads, which had grown out of the improvisations, as well as the fact that the majority of the players were amateur, 'and, of course,' adds Susan, 'the best work he did was with them, especially with Jeg and Laurie. Not just in the workshop but also when it came to performing in front of the camera. That's where his care and generosity lay. We, the professionals, were left to cope on our own because, in a sense, he knew he could trust us. But that wasn't always easy for us and I don't think he fully realised this.'

When Sher was first approached by Richard to write the film script he was both flattered and, at the same time, apprehensive that he was going to be almost ghostwriting it for Richard. In retrospect, he says, his first instinct as a writer was correct. 'Perhaps some authors can take on another person's passion. I couldn't. And so there was a lot of tension, fights even.'

Most of the fights were mainly during the filming, because they worked well together during the workshop process and through the early drafts of the script. It being a first for both friends, his first film script, and Richard's first film as a director, Sher quickly realised that on the set the director has so much more power and creative control, as well as the final say.

'There certainly was a time during the actual filming,' he admits, 'when some of my worries were shared by our producer, Andy Park. I'd been very willing during the writing of it to listen, and I learned a great deal from Richard about the use of minimalism on screen. I mean, he knows a lot more about cinema, he's a great cinema buff, and I was constantly fascinated to learn how a scene can have less and less and yet, paradoxically, more – so I was always keen on that. Then I found that when he was actually shooting the film he was minimalising things even further, to the point where I began to feel actual things were disappearing.'

Sher takes as an example the opening sequence which goes into great detail about Jeg's experience that first day, having been wounded at the Front and then arriving at this grand country house. But it was also important, argued Sher, to see things from Lady Alice's point of view, since hers is a parallel story to that of Jeg. So he had written a little sequence in which Lady Alice had just been told by the matron to scrub the floor, and she doesn't know how to.

'It was,' he says, 'a tragic-comic scene in which she gets

everything wrong, spilling the water, and getting upset because she doesn't know how to do the simplest chores. I was rather proud of this scene. Then Richard ended up shooting the whole scene in long shot, down a corridor, with Susie, going through her routine, as a very small figure at the end, rather like looking through the wrong end of a telescope. As a result the whole sequence went for nothing; and, unlike a film on a large screen, it was even smaller on television.'

Sher felt that Richard had gone for a cinematic effect which just wasn't appropriate for the small screen, rather than for the truth. He remembers bitter arguments about that, imploring anyone who would listen to him – from Andy Parks to the continuity girl – to reshoot it or find some other way of doing it.

This particular incident has an irony about it when one thinks of Richard's complaint that David Lean was often more concerned with visual effects in *A Passage to India* than with the acting. Sher admits that during the filming he wanted to co-direct more than Richard would allow him, finding that, as the writer, there wasn't a lot more to be done once the shooting began. 'I don't think Richard was crazy about me hanging around all the time, saying "Why don't you do this, or that?" – which was really not my business. But we'd been through it all together so much that it was quite difficult to let go and allow him to do his job. Also, because my role in the film as the doctor was quite small, that probably was part of the problem. It would have been much better if I had just come for my few days of filming and then left.' However, when they emerged from the whole thing, they both agreed it was a tribute to their friendship that it had survived, 'because it was the closest we ever came to seriously falling out.'

Richard remembers 'the unending pressures of the work. You shoot all day and then in the evening you watch the rushes and you have production meetings and discuss the next day's shooting schedule.'

Because it was a very big budget for BBC Scotland they had completion guarantors on the set most days, with their stopwatches, timing when they began to turn over and when they stopped. 'I never knew you had to work so hard as a film director!' sighs

Richard. Even though he had worked for David Lean, who was also a perfectionist? 'Well, he *had* directed before, of course! He knew what it was like. Besides, he was surrounded by a team of the highest order, working on a major movie, whereas we were trying to make an epic film with a small crew. I think there was a feeling among the crew, however, and indeed everyone, that what we were doing was a special event in their lives, because so many of them had never met a disabled person before.' And for the boys themselves? 'I don't know whether they enjoyed the acting more, or the fact that they were being paid and could go out drinking every night if they wanted! I used to look at them sometimes on the set in their costumes and make-up, and they were all asleep! They'd been out drinking until four or five in the morning.'

Ewan Marshall remembers once being with Laurie McCann on a beach at six o'clock in the morning after an all-night drinking session in Ayr, when they were supposed to be filming that morning. 'It was terribly important,' remarks Susan, 'to be one of the lads, and if that meant drinking along, and staying up, it was important to do that. Except that you can't altogether, because you've got to be up for your call at half past six in the morning. It was a strange tightrope to walk, but I think it was demanded of us all, Richard too.'

As the other woman, Eleanor Bron was equally popular. 'She is incredibly beautiful,' comments Ewan. 'If she walks into a room everyone notices. She must be used to being the object of every male's attention but she was also very skilful and diplomatic. I think everyone was a fan of hers. Our favourite hobby was talking about Eleanor Bron! She got on very well with people and was very funny. She coped splendidly, as did Susan, with all those guys getting drunk and being raucous.'

Given such a predominantly male gathering, the horseplay was inevitable. Susan recalls one night in the local pub when two of the boys, one of whom had a false arm, were engaged in arm wrestling. Suddenly the artificial arm snapped off and the other boy leaped up, waving the arm, shouting, 'I've won! I've won!' to the consternation of the regulars. She also describes an evening at a nightclub in Ayr, and Jim Brogan, who has one leg and only uses crutches, was with them. 'There were these steps down into the bar, so he handed over his crutches to one of the lads, and somersaulted down the steps, hands over leg, hands over leg, all the way up to the counter. And, of course, it stopped the place dead! He then somersaulted to the top of the bar where he stood, doing a handstand, with his leg in the air, and calling out, "Bring me a glass of champagne!" He drank the glass as he was, upside down, by taking the rim of the glass in his mouth and jerking his head backwards. Then he called for another!'

Ewan, who directs for GRAEAE, the only professional company of disabled actors in Europe, of which he is now artistic director and of which Richard is a patron, asked Richard if he might shadow him for those scenes in which he was not involved, as he was keen to learn more about directing on film, 'and although Richard was often tense, he was perfectly happy for me to be there'. He remembers sitting hunched up in rooms where there wasn't a lot of space and he would just watch. One thing above all he learned: 'Richard's calmness is incredible. But he can also be very chilling when he has to rebuke someone.'

Of the film itself, this long-cherished project, Richard is now very critical. 'What I was trying very much to do, having done all that research, was to capture the pace of life at that time, which was so much slower than life today. And I think now that was perhaps a bit too daring in terms of allowing the film to take its own pace.' In addition, he had not realised how powerful are the producer and the editor on a film, especially if, as in this case, they had worked together before. He also began to sense the closeness between Tony Sher and Andy Park. There was one occasion when Tony announced that he was going up to Glasgow to look at a rough cut of the film with Andy, and Richard said, 'But I can't be there that day,' to which Tony replied, 'Oh, it's only just Andy and me.' Richard almost exploded. 'I'll be there! I'm the director of this damn film!' In the end, when it was all put together, Richard received a very generous letter from Tony, saying how wonderful he thought it was, and how moved he had been by the film.

Given Richard's predilection for minimalism and his respect for the actor, it is curious how often quite delicate scenes are overlaid, even swamped by, lush orchestral music, with the result of softening or romanticising what is happening. One striking example of this is the scene in which Jeg comes to visit Lady Alice who is in bed in the isolation ward thinking she may have to have her finger, which has turned septic, amputated. 'The word *minimalist* was often on our lips,' recalls Susan of this scene, 'and in fact we managed to play it so that all emotion was completely disguised.' This, of course, would have been in keeping with the conventions of the period, which would have inhibited any overt display of emotion by either of them. There is, in any case, a natural frailty and gentleness about James Convey which tends to hide all emotion and which, therefore, was perfect for the character he was playing. In consequence it is a very touching scene.

What shocked Susan when she saw the finished version is that Richard has put so much music over it that it is difficult to hear the dialogue, the more so for those unfamiliar with the Scottish accent and Jeg's natural softness of speech. Richard and she had a terrible row about it, and he was very upset, not only because they were such close friends, but because she was questioning his directorial taste. 'My father composed a lot of film music,' adds Susan, 'and it was from him that I learned that in a movie the music is there to aid and abet a scene but that you shouldn't really be aware of it until it is over. I found so much of the music in *Changing Step* distressing.'

Susan Wooldridge is not alone in this criticism. So very often in the film Richard does not allow the delicacy of emotion which he has so skilfully evoked from the actors to work for itself but, instead, reveals this contradictory, almost perverse, need to embellish it with a musical commentary. In the scene referred to above, Susan recalls that on the day of shooting, a bluebottle fly buzzed against the window – a sound, which more than any other, evokes the atmosphere of a hot summer's afternoon; yet Richard failed to observe this detail or even to utilise it. Given two such shy and inhibited characters as Lady Alice and Jeg, it is the *silences* between them which should convey so much of what is unspoken. Watching the film several times, as I have done, it appears almost as though, at the last count, Richard failed to learn from the silences which he so admired in David Lean's direction of *A Passage to India*. Or it may be, as Ewan Marshall has observed, that 'there were possibly too many strands going through the film, with the result that some of the things didn't engage, didn't quite have the punch that was needed,' which may have made Richard feel the need to pull the whole thing together with Michael Gibb's music.

After the film was completed, Richard continued to keep in touch with Laurie McCann, telephoning to enquire after him, and sending postcards from wherever he happened to be. Susan and Eleanor also kept in touch with him, 'all of which,' comments his mother, 'was very good therapy for him, for he knew without doubt that the cancer would come back'. Which it did. By the time the film had been given a second showing on television, the cancer returned to his lung but, with his usual strength, and amazing resilience, he seemed once more to recover. During this period of remission Richard invited him to stay in London to see a recording of *One Foot in the Grave* and meet the cast. Then, from July to November 1993, Laurie was again very ill with a recurrence of the lung cancer, followed by other tumours on his brain and behind his stomach. By Friday 5 November (the anniversary of Jeg's amputation) Laurie was just finishing his chemotherapy when Richard telephoned his mother. He was in Glasgow, he told her, for the BAFTA Awards, to receive BAFTA Scotland's award for the Best TV Actor, and was hoping to take Laurie out for a meal. Learning that Laurie was in the Western Infirmary, Richard went to visit him there. 'It caused quite a stir,' says his mother. 'Everyone was so thrilled that he was there, none more so than Laurie.'

Richard told Laurie, 'Whenever you finish your treatment, phone me and I'll send you a plane ticket so that you can have a holiday at my new home in Hampstead, and we'll have all the old gang there for a party.' Once again Laurie appeared to recover and went home.

'We had him out every day,' says Laurie's mother. 'He wanted to go here, there, everywhere. We were so thrilled. It looked like the cancer was gone. He had had radiotherapy, and five days of cobalt treatment, all in four and a half months. He was brilliant for the next weeks. He even went fishing on the last Saturday. And then, on Monday 15 November he closed his beautiful eyes at 3 p.m. in a coma and died peacefully at 11 o'clock that evening.' Richard sent carnations and, more recently, a donation for Laurie's ward at the hospital.

Changing Step is a rare film, not only in its subject matter, but in its fusion of professional and amateur actors, being part-fiction, part-documentary; while for Richard, quite clearly, it was and remains a deeply fulfilling experience.

13

Working from the Centre

It is a quarter to eleven on 10 March 1995, at the Actors' Centre in the heart of London's theatreland, just off Upper St Martin's Lane. Richard is changing into sneakers as actors who have signed up for a day's workshop with him begin to arrive. We are in the Media Room, high-ceilinged, with no windows, and red-painted heating pipes overhead. From adjoining studios can be heard the muffled sounds of other workshops in progress, while from the canteen in the basement drifts the aroma of coffee.

The centre, of which Richard is a patron and to which he has made generous donations, provides an important focal point for professional actors, offering a wide range of classes in singing, dancing, speech, acting techniques for film, television, radio and stage, as well as a small theatre, a canteen and a gymnasium. Like musicians and dancers, actors need constantly to work at their craft and, because there is a high level of unemployment in the field of entertainment, the centre enables actors to keep in touch with one another, sharing news of forthcoming auditions.

'I've called this particular workshop,' explains Richard when all the actors are assembled, ' "Working from the Centre" – which doesn't mean the Actors' Centre! What I want is to encourage you to work from your own centre. I call this a *minimalist* approach. I want to stress the importance of believing in the idea that the *thinking* of a character is more important than the words. The text of a play tends to be regarded as the Bible, but I say the text is an ingredient with which you, the actor, make a character. Too many actors are too busy trying to demonstrate how good they are, rather than showing who the character is, and so they do not let the audience in. So much "acting" only keeps the audience out. It is, however, by doing less that you achieve more; when you are not telling, or dictating to an audience, then you are saying to them, "Come in! Watch what I am thinking and feeling." An audience should feel as though it is eavesdropping on real people. And I am not just talking about acting for television or film, but acting in general. If I speak about *minimalist* acting, there still has to be *energy* there, whether it is for the stage or the screen; if for the stage, you simply have to increase the amount of energy in order to project the performance into a bigger space.'

He describes sitting opposite a woman at the National Theatre restaurant, who was wearing a loose cashmere sweater. 'She was drinking and rolling cigarettes, twitching at this sweater, crossing and recrossing her legs, touching her hat, her hair – never still for a moment. Now here was a very real person who was being very active, very busy indeed, and I'm not saying you can't create a character like that, someone who is constantly drawing attention to herself, but you, the actor, would still have to find a centre for her, in order to make her believable – even if the point was that she had no centre. So often, as a director, I find myself saying to an actor, "I don't believe you."'

One of the actors present asks whether such non-acting isn't likely to come over as lifeless, to which Richard responds, 'In the theatre even doing nothing has to have energy and be emotionally charged.'

'As a director,' he continues, 'I find that one of the hardest tasks is to get actors to trust the fact that doing less, rather than more, really works. If you have a part where a character has to break down I wouldn't expect that actor to break down in rehearsal until much later on, when he will have found a centre for that character. Too often an actor will say, "Let me try that scene; I can always take it down later," but no, that is to force what should be an organic growth. All too easily it can result in acting-acting. Often in rehearsal I use the expression "open" – "That needs to be more open," I may say. *Open* means allowing people in. I find quite a lot of actors struggling to tell me what they are about, like that woman in the restaurant at the National Theatre, instead of *being* their character.'

Richard pauses to sip from a bottle of mineral water and then invites everyone to stand in a circle. 'Now, in order to learn each other's names and find out a little about each other, we are going to play a few games. These are games which I always use at the start of rehearsals when I am directing.' Moving clockwise round the circle (which includes Richard) everyone speaks their name, then a second time but more loudly. Next, one person names someone else in the circle and, keeping eye contact with them, walks quietly towards that individual and then, 'just before you are on top of that person, he, or she, will look at someone else and speak their name and start to move towards them, while you take the place of the person you named.'

To anyone unfamiliar with the working practices of actors these and similar exercises might appear childish, but what they do is to enable the actors to focus upon each other as individuals as well as on the group, keeping everyone alert, almost telepathically attuned, and with a heightened concentration. Acting is part technique, and part intuition. In rehearsal an actor may suddenly do something – it may be a gesture or a change of tone of voice – which can then trigger off a response in the other performer, resulting in something quite unexpected, and which could not have been arrived at by a rational or cerebral process. The more focused the actors, the more subtle will be the interplay between them.

Richard now divides the room by placing a line of chairs down the middle, and splits the actors into two groups. On one side the first group is to observe the actors on the other side, who are to imagine that the space is the waiting room of a cancer hospital. To one actor he says, 'You can choose whether or not you are a patient.' To two actors he says, 'You are a pair and are allowed to talk, but quietly.' To another he gives the instruction, 'You are a patient and at one stage you will succumb to real pain, while you,' turning to another, 'can read.' Finally, one of the actors is told that he can use the telephone that is in the room, but not until Richard calls out, 'The phone rings,' and then he has to answer it. The observers are asked to turn their backs for a minute to allow the other actors to get started without the feeling of being watched. 'You must carry on,' says Richard, 'until I tell you to stop. If nothing happens, don't worry. We are not here for results. What we, the observers, are looking for is simply: can we believe what they are doing? Are they working from the centre?'

When the improvisation comes to an end, he comments how the conversation of the couple who were allowed to talk was 'so much more effective when we could only half-hear what they were saying. The moment, however, when they started saying things like, "Why me? Why now?" we feel they are trying to say too much, and in any case all that would have been talked through endlessly at home, not in a public waiting room. How does one, in fact, behave in a public place? Don't try and tell us too much!'

The second group is now given its instructions. 'You are in the waiting room of a law court. You are relatives or something to do with criminals. You could be waiting for a relative who is being tried in one of the courts, but you are not witnesses. You are either a relative, friend or associate. Again, one of you will have access to a telephone.' To each actor he then gives specific instructions. 'You will slowly fall asleep. You can talk, but you can't. Nor you! You can. You three are inside already, while you two come in from outside.'

Throughout both exercises Richard prowls restlessly up and down, like a schoolmaster during an examination, keeping an eagle eye on the proceedings. When he sits to comment he crosses both legs, pushes his glasses to the top of his head, and folds both hands over his knee. 'Did you observe how Leigh, although she was allowed to speak, chose not to, but just sat very still, without any expression, and yet clearly was thinking and feeling very deeply, and was involved with someone beyond that door? Think of the interminable hours people have to spend sitting in such places.'

He then invites each actor to comment on what was happening. Vernon Thompson, whose task was slowly to fall asleep, describes how he had been up all night with a friend who had been arrested on a drunk-driving charge, 'and I was trying to be strong in order to compensate for his worries. Then I tried to stay awake by doing the crossword but eventually I nodded off.' Richard listens to each in turn and comments how, when the telephone rang, had everyone turned towards it (which they didn't), that would have been too theatrical, too obvious. 'It is when actors trust being still, even when so little is happening, that we see how our interest is held.'

During the lunch break one of the actors brings Richard a bowl of soup and a roll from the canteen while he sits chatting with Sheila Gish who has taken a break from working out in the gym. Like Richard she is performing at the National Theatre – in Sean Mathias's production of Cocteau's *Les Parents Terribles*, while he is playing in the revival of Joe Orton's *What The Butler Saw*. There is the murmur of conversations from the canteen, punctuated by bursts of laughter, and the purr of the coffee machine.

At the beginning of the afternoon session Richard clarifies certain points before setting up some new exercises. 'Remember, it helps if we can hear what you are saying. Don't become so self-centred that you forget the audience! Try and keep the reality so that we, the audience, feel we are eavesdropping. If there is dialogue, then we need to hear it – either the rhythm of the words or the words themselves, but don't get locked into words and an endless narrative. Be sparing of any dialogue. Find the centre, the existential moment, of any encounter. And when entering from outside, remember to ask yourself: *where* have I come from? And *why* am I entering this room? Try also to be aware of spatiality. Remember that as soon as you are in the doorway you are in the picture, you are *on stage*. How do you use the door? It may be a familiar room you are entering or it may be an unknown space. How you use the room spatially becomes visually very telling. If you make it true and believable it can be whatever you want it to be – within the limitations of this particular space we are in. Finally, you are not allowed to mime anything. You may use only what is actually here.

'Above all, remember that theatre is not naturalism but heightened realism. But use your imagination. Try to see how the situation can develop. Even the accidental sound of footsteps outside this door, or voices heard afar off from another studio, can be used. But don't be afraid to risk boredom. I am not, I repeat, looking for wonderful but for *believable* things.'

For a moment he pauses, circling his head like a tortoise, relaxing the neck muscles. Then he continues. 'Beware of looking-at-your-watch acting, tea-drinking acting, cigarette acting, all the usual acting clichés. Something terrible can have happened and yet you do not need to *demonstrate* this. And since some of these exercises we are going to do now are solos, in which one person enters a room, remember that what someone does alone in a room is always fascinating. You must resist the temptation as an actor of feeling that you have to start "acting". Of course most acting comes from being able to interact and react with one's fellow actors, but when you are on your own you don't have that to help you. But the fact that you do have in this room a telephone and a piano could be very important. Lastly, remember that an improvisation has to develop. You have to build it. A part of you as a performer is thinking: where is this going next?'

One of the younger actors, Alexander McConnell from Cardiff, now attempts the solo exercise. He goes out of the room and we wait. Suddenly he enters in a rush, carrying a bag. Closing the door he stands by it, listening. Then he opens the door a crack to peer out. It seems that no one has followed him. He now closes and locks the door, turning to look at the room, clearly thinking: what is this space? He observes the telephone but resists going to it. He waits, listening with great concentration. There is a sense of danger. He puts down the bag against a wall and goes to lean against the wall but resists the impulse. He is thinking he must not relax, he cannot afford to be off guard. He must remain on the alert, not knowing what he is meant to do next. He returns to the door, unlocks it and slowly opens it, but there is no one outside. Closing the door he comes back into the room. He looks at the bag but doesn't go near it. Clearly what is in the bag is important. His attention returns to the telephone and he now goes over to it and dials a number. Speaking into the phone he says, 'I've got the bag, but there's no one here.'

That was all, but the whole exercise was compelling to watch because he was following throughout the line of thought of his own subtext so that, although nothing was said until the last moment, we always knew what he was thinking and feeling. He then explains to us his subtext. 'I had stolen the bag from a bank, as I had been instructed to do by my bosses, and I had been told to come to this room with it and wait for someone to whom I would hand it over.'

Richard compliments him, and suggests that he might have developed the situation further by shoving the bag centre stage, circling it out of curiosity, and in this way built up the tension even more. He might even have opened the bag. Turning to the rest of us, he adds, 'What you need, as you can all see, is enough subtext to carry you on, and of course it is much more difficult in a solo. People in a solo often tend to do too much, something Alex avoided, because they think they are not interesting. The value of this exercise, and what makes it so challenging, is that it is not often that an actor is alone on a stage.'

More exercises follow and always, like the skilled teacher he is, Richard finds something to praise even with the least talented. Finally the afternoon draws to an end. 'In ordinary situations let your imaginations free, so that when you are given a text you don't take it at its face value. Your task is to get *inside* the text, so that very often you will then find yourself working against the line of the text. Someone may ask you, "How are you feeling?" and your reply is "Fine!" But that does not necessarily mean you reply in bright cheerful tones. You might in fact be feeling lousy! Once you have found your subtext you may well find yourself playing against the line of the text.'

He pauses to look at the clock. 'Now, any questions? It will have to be a minimal question time as I have to be at the National!' Rita Shaer asks, ' In real theatre you couldn't hold pauses as long as that, surely?' to which Richard replies, 'No, but in rehearsal you should allow each other the freedom to pause, and although in a production you have to be aware of the overall pace and tempo, none the less, a long pause can be held – provided it is *filled*.' For a moment he is silent, stroking his jaw, and then adds as his final comment, 'Remember there is no such thing as a cliché line, only cliché acting. If you are given a terrible line, *think* it through and make it work.'

Richard's meticulous and microscopic way of working, paring down to the truth of each situation, works ideally in the extended rehearsal period that is possible in subsidised companies such as the National and the Royal Shakespeare Company, but it can create problems within the more usual span of only four weeks' rehearsal. It is a process that takes time. Richard himself admits, 'The problem I have as a director is when I get to the stage of moving the play from the rehearsal room to the stage, that's always my stumbling block. Because of my minimalist approach in rehearsal it's almost as though the actors don't want to share it with the audience, as though they feel, "We're quite happy where we are, thank you very much!" So the process of opening up a production to a larger space does take longer with my way of working and calls for as many previews as possible before the critics come in. Otherwise it's like bringing plants out into the light before they are ready.'

The general public pays little heed to the work of directors, especially in the theatre; people go to see stars or individual actors, and so the millions who watch *One Foot in the Grave* will have no idea of Richard's work as a director nor what this entails. One of the things he most enjoys about directing is being in at the beginning of a new script and working closely with the author. As the innovative Russian director, Meyerhold, once remarked, 'In every good director there potentially sits a dramatist'; and so it is in the early sessions with an author, before a play is even cast, that Richard's work as a director often begins.

Kevin Elyot, the award-winning author of the play *My Night with Reg*, describes working with Richard on one of his earliest plays, *Coming Clean*, which was produced at the Bush Theatre and which it was suggested Richard might direct. 'We worked on the script over several months. Richard would say, "Well, maybe I will direct it but, if I do, I would want this or that altered," and undoubtedly he improved the text with his suggestions. Then he decided not to direct it and it was very disappointing at the time. But he was great to work with on the text. I will always remember one thing he said: "You should never have a character say what he means, such as "I love you" or "I hate you", but rather "I'll go and put the kettle on" or "Will you have another drink?" In real life it is often what is not said that is important. It is the tone of voice used with such ordinary statements which tells us what is really going on between people.' Elyot says that when he was working on *My Night with Reg*, whenever he was in doubt, he recalled Richard's advice and so he'd never have his characters say what they meant but 'Will you have another drink?' 'There's a lot of that in the play!' laughs Elyot.

The task of a director is to understand the author's intention and, like a sculptor faced with a block of stone, to unearth the form within. A director seeks the heart of a play, the reason for its having been written. The search should always be for what the American critic Stark Young once described as 'the original design', rather than for what a 'clever' director thinks he can impose on a text.

On the surface Richard studies the narrative, for theatre is a form of storytelling; but then he begins to go deeper, exploring the subtext. On one level there is the storyline, the plot, which carries the action forwards, and on another level there is an inner storyline for each character as well as for the play itself. Of necessity any play will also require the director to do a good deal of preliminary research, as we have seen Richard do for such productions as *Changing Step*, and *An Inspector Calls*. This information the director then has to feed to the actors. A play about a hospital, or a major auction house, will require that the actors be familiar with the history, the practice, the jargon and the attitudes of such a milieu.

During the first week of rehearsals Richard always has the actors read and discuss the play. If people start to act he will say quietly, 'Please don't *act*. You don't yet know who this person is so how can you put colour into the words?' He will persistently ask such questions as, 'What does it *mean* ? What do you want out of this?' Sometimes the discussions will go on for ages and he will just sit there, listening. Every now and then he will invite the actors to work out the clues from the text, saying, 'It's what comes between the lines that interests me.'

At intervals he will ask the actors to improvise upon a situation in or arising from the text. Sheila Hancock has a very vivid memory of such an occasion when she was rehearsing *The Remainder Man*, a television play by Philip Martin that Richard was directing. 'He made us do this improvisation down a nuclear shelter somewhere in Surrey and he shut us down there for several hours. He sat in a corner taking notes while we did this improvisation of what it felt like to be trapped in this bloody shelter! It was really a long time and we did get rather hysterical. We had food down there, corned beef and baked beans, and I had to prepare a meal, and I wouldn't give any to Richard. I said he was the cat and that we weren't going to give any food to the cat. And he was livid! And there wasn't anything to drink. I was so angry with him for making us do that, stuck down in that horrible hole. I remember the relief and the feeling of release when we were let out, and were able to come up out of that claustrophobic hole he had forced us to go down. But it did help us when we came to do the television.'

The result of Richard's democratic and collaborative way of working in the beginning of rehearsals is that when, in the second week, the actors start to block a scene, the moves and the business begin to unfold quite naturally since the actors now know their characters and what they would be doing. There is none of the old-fashioned director's 'Now move downstage left, darling!'

At the same time Richard is quite tough, quite steely, as a director, as he himself admits. 'The actors know what I want or they don't get cast.' Jenny Topper, the artistic director of the Hampstead Theatre, who has known Richard a long time, comments on the extremes between his democratic way of holding rehearsals 'which can become almost anarchic if it is a cast of strong egos' and being quite autocratic about the way he wants performances. It means that those whom Richard has cast have to be prepared to go through *his* method, just as they would if they were to work for

Max Stafford-Clark, Mike Alfreds, or Peter Brook, each of whom has a very distinctive method of working. Clearly Richard's minimalist approach is inspired by such films as *Tokyo Story*, and is a method very much at variance to the high-energy performances of an actor like Antony Sher. Sher does indeed wonder whether Richard's austere approach is not ultimately limiting. 'I'm always worried,' he comments, 'about people who have a *method*. For example, Peter Hall believes that there is only one way to speak Shakespeare and that is his way, but Shakespeare is far greater than that. Max Stafford-Clark is another who has a very solid system. Both he and Richard train the company they are about to work with in their method, so that they can then have that as their common language. Perhaps that gives such directors a kind of security; you map out your way of doing it and then stick to that.'

Of course there is no one 'salvationist' way of working for the actor. Each play may call for a different approach and style, and actors have to learn how to be flexible so that they can move from one method to another, although Richard would argue, and rightly, that the search for truth must remain at the heart of all good acting. It was this search which led to his leading, for several years from 1970 onwards, a weekly acting workshop. Among those who regularly attended was Bridget Turner, who recalls one exercise in particular. 'Without explaining why, Richard asked us who our favourite film star was, and I replied, "Paul Newman." He then set up an exercise in which he and I were husband and wife. He had just lost his job and I, as his wife, had to behave as though I were Paul Newman. It was amazing because, suddenly, I *was* Paul Newman, very cool and confident, which was so unlike the person I was in those days, and I rang up my husband's boss to demand why he had been sacked. That one exercise taught me so much about myself and gave me greater confidence than I could have imagined.'

'I try to make the characters believable,' is how Richard sums up his task as a director. 'It's an actor's job not to show he is acting.' Similarly Samuel Beckett, when directing Billie Whitelaw, would say, 'Don't act out the story!' She describes in her autobiography *Billie Whitelaw ... Who He?* how, when they worked on other plays, Beckett would reiterate over and over again, 'No, no! That's too much colour!' – clearly, she comments, a euphemism for 'Please don't *act*!' And so Richard will spend a lot of time in rehearsal getting the actors to behave rather than *act*.

Sheila Hancock describes Richard as her ideal director, along with Trevor Nunn and Mike Alfreds. 'Because he is also an actor he knows what you are talking about, and how you can cheat. He can be quite brutal in his honesty, and I can imagine some people being quite scared of him. Some need the truth wrapping up a bit but Richard will never do that. He is also very good at detecting when you think you are showing emotion but in fact you are merely being self-indulgent.'

She gives as an example the final scene of Andrew Davies' play *Prin*, which Richard directed in the West End in 1990, after opening at the Lyric Hammersmith. 'I found the last scene unbearably moving and I couldn't stop crying, but Richard pointed out that what I was moved by was Sheila Hancock thinking how sad it was for this woman to see her whole world fall apart, whereas Prin would not have been thinking, oh, how tragic! but quite simply, What am I going to do next? Very often tears can impress an audience but Richard won't let you do it, especially if you have an affinity for it, as I have!'

Among members of his profession Richard's opinion is very much respected. 'If you're having a bad time in a production,' says Sheila Hancock, 'and ask him to come in to give you his opinion, he'll secretly put you on course. What he has to say when he comes backstage is always very helpful. He's an amazingly shrewd critic and very honest which, in this business, is particularly valuable, especially when you know it is based on love and respect.'

Richard's thoroughness as a director is perhaps best illustrated by a story told by the actor, and former President of Equity, Hugh Manning, who had been invited to play Uncle Vanya for the Welsh Theatre Company, and who had asked Richard if he could help him. 'He came to my house on three separate occasions and what I remember most is his saying that one gets the whole tenor of the play with Vanya's first utterance, that if one gets this right, then all the rest falls into place. The play opens with Vanya lying on the grass, a handkerchief over his face, and the first word he utters is "Yes". Well, we spent the whole of the first evening just rehearsing that one word! He would stop me and say things like, "You need more world weariness," and then we would go on. Over and over again, just that one word, for a whole evening. That was all he concentrated on, which is incredible in a director to spend so much time on detail, and that is typical of him.'

Perhaps the best summing up of the way Richard works as a director comes from John Michie, who has worked for Richard twice. 'I have this analogy about working with Richard. People often say to me: well, what's his system? And I reply: if you imagine a baby in the womb – and I've had a few recently! – you let that baby grow. You don't, in the first few weeks of its life, try and put your arms on it, because the body is not yet grown. It's a gradual, slow process. In the same way your character has to be born and then develop, and in this ridiculously short time of rehearsal, usually four weeks, you must start from nothing and gradually, gradually, build it up. *Gradualism* – that's one of his words. And then, within this growth, you draw upon the only truth that you know, which is the truth of your own life experience, everything that has ever happened to you, and out of that and the role the author has written, you begin to develop the character.'

It is Richard's fundamental belief that if an actor has one foot on the stage, the other foot must be firmly in everyday life. As Isadora Duncan remarked, 'Life is the root and art is the flower.' For Richard theatre has a social purpose, which explains why he prefers new plays to revivals, believing, as we have seen, that theatre 'should be about what we are now and reflect the society we live in.' For Richard, to be able to direct at least one new play a year is essential to his well-being, because it is an activity which involves other sides of his personality, as well as drawing upon his natural qualities as a leader and organiser. Also, aware of his own limitations as an actor, he is able, through other actors, to explore a variety of emotions and experiences that are outside his own skills, seeking, like an analyst, to understand more profoundly the human condition so that we, the audience, may be moved and illuminated.

'Theatre,' says Peter Brook, 'only exists at the precise moment when the two worlds of the actors and the audience meet: a society in miniature, a microcosm brought together every evening within a space. Theatre's role is to give this microcosm a burning and fleeting taste of another world, in which our present world is integrated and transformed.'

For Richard, also, art is not about being aesthetically pleasing, but about touching us at our deepest level and inviting us, even inciting us, to change. And because theatre, unlike the cinema or television, is so immediate in its impact, a living relationship between actors and audience, happening *now*, 'it is also,' says Richard, 'a revolutionary art.'

14

Life at the Top

'If I were asked who I would most like to meet of all the people in the world,' says Richard, 'it would be Marlon Brando. As a screen actor no one else can touch him for his sheer inner integrity, and his metamorphic ability.'

When, therefore, in 1990 Richard received a call from his agent Jeremy Conway saying, 'Would you like to be in a film with Marlon Brando?' it seemed like the fulfilment of another of his life's ambitions. 'Repeat that!' he replied

The film was *A Dry White Season* and when Richard went to meet Euzhan Palcy, the director, it was to find he was being considered for two roles. Finally they decided he would be best as the headmaster. 'Does his character come into contact with Brando?' asked Richard. No, was the reply, but it is a better part. The film was shot mainly in Zimbabwe but Richard seemed fated not to even meet his hero, whose scenes were all shot in London. After completion of filming, and back in England, Richard had to go to the studios for some post-synching. While doing this he was asked if he would like to go on the studio floor to say hello to Euzhan Palcy. 'I thought they had finished filming,' remarked Richard, only to learn that they were shooting one final scene with Brando.

Richard found his hero doing a court scene in which he had to leave the room. 'He walked out of the set until he came to a wall and he stood against this, very still, the way actors do when they leave a set, so as not to make any noise. And I thought, gosh! even Marlon Brando obeys the rules.' He then asked the director whether he might meet Brando and she said, 'Oh, yes, sure,

Richard!' but when Euzhan Palcy returned it was to tell him that Brando was learning his lines and not to be disturbed. Richard knew this wasn't true because Brando has his lines fed through an earpiece. Knowing, also, that he is a very private man, and was also probably getting into the mood for the next scene, he decided to leave. At that moment Palcy reappeared, saying, 'Come now!' and took him to Brando.

Richard recalls the scene. 'I managed to stammer out something about how much I had always appreciated his work, that he had been such a hero to me in my early years, and how, initially, I had been up for a part which would have meant acting with him, to which he replied, "Ah, well, we can't have it every way always." We shook hands and then I walked away. He was utterly charming, as though he had all the time in the world. Although Brando is now physically very large, his face still has this wonderful expressiveness.'

The following year Richard won the BAFTA award for Best Actor in Light Entertainment for his performance as Victor Meldrew in *One Foot in the Grave*. (Two years later, in 1993, he was to win a BAFTA award for the second time, for Best Actor.)

In 1991 he directed a new play by Terry Johnson, *Imagine Drowning*, at the Hampstead Theatre, with the disabled actor and cofounder of GRAEAE, Nabil Shaban, Frances Barber, Sylvester Le Touzel, and Douglas Hodge. The cast also included animals: mice, a hamster, countless fish, and a parrot which was supposed to speak on cue. A tall order this last, remarks Jenny Topper, the theatre's artistic director, so they settled for a silent cockatoo whose cage had a small speaker outlet. For the first two weeks of rehearsal the cockatoo was silent but, like the actors, it grew in confidence, becoming affectionate and greedy. Then one day it stunned them all when, returning from lunch, Richard was greeted, in an accent that was a perfect imitation of his own, with a 'Hello, everybody!' Things began to go from bad to worse with the bird rarely shutting up until, finally, Richard rounded on it in the technical rehearsal, saying, 'That's it! You're fired!' And it was.

In 1992 Richard joined a group of actors, writers and directors, which included Kirsty MacColl, Julie Christie, Simon Fanshawe, Andy de la Tour, Susan Wooldridge, Charlotte Cornwell and John Gillett on a fact-finding mission to the Occupied Territories of the West Bank and the Gaza strip, which had been organised by de la Tour and John Bevan who was former general secretary of the World University Service. Up to that time they felt that the western press had been very pro-Israel and that it had been difficult to glean much information about what was happening in Palestine. The presence in the group of names such as Julie Christie and Kirsty MacColl would, they hoped, create some media interest on the group's return.

The expedition was headed by Albert Aghazarian, External Relations Officer of Bir Zeit University (closed under Israel military orders at the time), who was able to take them to places which no tourist would have been allowed to visit, such as the Deishe Camp on the road from Jerusalem to Bethlehem. In a First World country they found themselves plunged into Third World despair and brutality, dirt, rubble, and no flowers, all encased in barbed wire. They visited other camps as well as hospitals, meeting people who had been the victims of the *Intifada*. This word, translated from the Arabic, means the shivering caused by fever and so, in political terms: an explosion. The *Intifada* had erupted in Gaza in December 1987 after twenty years of Israeli occupation. What many in the group had not realised was that when the State of Israel was formed, the Israelis had ignored the fact that the Palestinians had already been there for hundreds of years. As a result of the *Intifada* Gaza was placed under a curfew every night. They were also told by a physician that internationally outlawed dum-dum bullets, which explode once they are inside a person, had been used by the Israeli army.

At Bethlehem they found Manger Square, the birthplace of the Prince of Peace, covered in razor wire and gun turrets which would only be removed on Christmas Eve for the benefit of television cameras. But the climax of their visit was their trip to Gaza, 'which by any other name is Hades,' observes Susan Wooldridge. 'It was appalling.' They were all quite traumatised. 'Nothing had prepared us for Gaza,' says Richard, 'which must be one of the most densely populated areas of the world, a desolate concrete jungle, a man-made nightmare, set on the edge of the Mediterranean.' On the beach lay a great white horse – dead; while above a barricade in the street (to stop people running away) was the ironic sign 'Welcome to Gaza'.

In Gaza they were joined by Dr Eyad Al-Surraj, a children's doctor who was working on the Gaza Mental Health Programme. He told them how ninety-seven per cent of the children in Gaza had had their homes raided and seen their parents taken away and beaten by Israeli soldiers; while fifty-five per cent had experienced being beaten themselves, and nine per cent had had bones broken as a result. He revealed that the Israeli soldiers would systematically beat the children's parents in front of them, the effect of which upon the children had been, needless to say, deeply traumatic.

The whole expedition was, as Susan describes it, 'an horrific experience' and one that revealed Richard in all his powers of leadership, humanity and humour. At the end there was a press conference which was extremely gruelling, and entailed being very honest about what they had seen. Richard read out the statement which they had agreed and chaired the meeting with great diplomacy and an enormous amount of humour.

On the afternoon that they were due to leave Gaza, they were sitting in the courtyard of the Marna Hotel (used by visiting journalists and representatives of the United Nations) when Richard, looking around at the group and sensing the mood of everyone, suggested they should all play Grandmother's Footsteps. 'It was,' says Susan, 'the most extraordinary thing, something only Richard would have thought of.' And so the game which he had used to play at school now fulfilled a therapeutic role at a crucial moment, helping to release the tension and emotion which everyone had been experiencing.

On the return journey, such was Richard's growing celebrity, that it was not Julie Christie or Kirsty MacColl who attracted attention but Richard, now recognisable from his new series *One Foot in the Grave,* with the result that he was invited by the stewardess to move up into First Class.

On 24 August of that year Richard and other members of the team wrote a letter to the *Guardian,* drawing attention to the death in suspicious circumstances of a young Palestinian whom they had met earlier in the year. Hazem Id, aged twenty-three, from Ramallah in the occupied West Bank, and a student at Bir Zeit University, was arrested on 22 June and remained in the custody of the Israeli General Security Services until his death on 9 July. Neither Hazem's family nor the Bir Zeit University authorities were satisfied with the Israeli assertion that his death was suicide. It was clear, the letter stated, that the authorities were withholding vital information that would enable a proper investigation to be made. They urged the Israeli authorities to submit to Hazem's lawyer a detailed, written police report and all material evidence relating to the case, and to allow for an independent investigation. 'We believe,' the letter concluded, 'that Israel must not be allowed to continue to ignore UN resolutions and flout international law, and Hazem's death must serve as a reminder that for as long as the illegal occupation of the West Bank and Gaza is allowed to continue there can be neither peace nor justice.'

Four years on, Richard and the other members of that expedition continue to maintain a close interest in developments in the Middle East situation. Actors, like everyone else, have political views, but those among them who have a high profile are often able to use this to promote their views more effectively, especially if, like Richard, they are known only to support causes in which they believe.

The Bridgewater Four is one such cause which Richard champions. The Bridgewater Four Support Group was set up to fight for justice for the four men wrongfully convicted of the murder of newspaper boy Carl Bridgewater in 1978, and who have been in prison now for eighteen years for a crime which, their supporters believe, they did not commit, and for which there is no forensic evidence, the judgement being based solely, they claim, on unreliable witness hearsay and police malpractice. Although there are now over one hundred items of new evidence, the present Home Secretary, Michael Howard, is 'not minded' to refer the case back to a court of appeal.

Together with Victoria Wood, Alan Bennett, Ben Elton and others, Richard is one of the principal supporters of this cause. His presence has brought a public face to the campaign which was very much needed. He is widely known for his integrity, and for not allowing his name to be linked to anything in which he does not believe. When he joined the first all-night vigil outside the Home Office in June 1994, a photograph of him attending the event was published the next day in the *Birmingham Post*. A woman came up to Ann Whelan, the mother of Michael Hickey, the youngest of the convicted men, in the local supermarket and said to her, 'If that nice Richard Wilson is a supporter then they must be innocent.'

In April 1992 Richard appeared in a different political guise: chairing a public meeting at Blackburn Town Hall, two nights before the General Election, in support of the local candidate, Jack Straw, MP. According to those present he made a brilliant speech but he himself was nervous. 'I hadn't done anything like that before and certainly not to that size audience. I thought I was just supposed to go on stage and announce, "Ladies and gentlemen, your future Prime Minister – Neil Kinnock!" but the organisers said, "You've got seven minutes to fill, Richard," and I had to fill them.' Although he has been a member of the Labour Party for many years he was shattered by the eventual result of the Election. The state of the subsequent Tory administration, he says, showed what a mistake the electorate made. The following year, on 21 November 1993, he joined thousands of health workers at a rally in Trafalgar Square to protest against the decimation of the National Health Service, telling the crowds, 'This government is determined to destroy the NHS.' Of Margaret Thatcher he says, 'She annoys me still even though she has been gone a while. I hated her so much. I hated her politics. Selfishness annoys me and I think she was selfish. Had I been directing her I would have said, "Come on, Margaret, let's try harder. *I don't believe you*, Margaret!"

I never understood why so many people did believe her. I can't understand that at all.'

On his return from Gaza Richard directed, at the Royal Exchange in Manchester, the 1993 winner of the Mobil Playwriting Competition, *Women Laughing*, by Michael Wall who had previously won the Mobil Prize in 1989 for his play, *Amongst Barbarians*, which subsequently transferred to the Hampstead Theatre. *Women Laughing* is a disturbing analysis of misogyny, marriage and mental breakdown, examining with great precision the atavistic antagonisms between the sexes. The play opens with the two women off-stage, laughing at the coincidence that both their husbands are in psychotherapy although, in the first act, neither of the men is aware of this. In the second act we see the men in a mental hospital being visited by their wives. The question which Michael Wall raises is: are the women, who are shown as being hostile towards therapy and intolerant of the mentally ill, responsible for their husbands' condition? Of the production of this very moving and also funny play, James Christopher wrote in *Time Out*: 'Richard Wilson imbues the play with endless disturbing innuendoes, registering subtle twists of mood and tone with Pinter-like beats.'

Once again it was the fact that it was a play about outsiders which attracted Richard and significantly he quoted in the programme the following sentences from an essay by Jonathan Miller: 'I am oversimplifying it now, but this is the central problem of psychiatry: people in society who somehow can't make it; who don't make it; who are, or who have become, outsiders.' As John Michie, who was in the production, comments: 'One of the things that I think drew Richard to the play is that he has a real affinity with people who aren't successful in their lives. He seems to understand them very well.'

Typical of Richard's approach to such a text is that the actors were not only required to have individual therapy sessions with a psychotherapist, who also talked to them about schizophrenia, but they were taken to the north London mental hospital at Friern Barnet to meet some of the schizophrenic patients. Michie describes talking with one who was very twitchy and nervous, asking him what it felt like taking so many drugs, and the man replied, 'I feel as if I am full of water. I'm walking around but I feel the walking is not going to take me anywhere.'

Richard returned to acting in a new seven-part series for ITV, *Under the Hammer*, by John Mortimer, about the international art market, in which he played Ben Glazier, an art expert at a major auction house, opposite Jan Francis who played Maggie Perowne, Head of Old Masters.

ITV felt that it had scored a triumph by luring Richard away from the BBC, and the tabloid newspapers made much of this, but, as Richard says, he had never been under contract to the BBC so there was no question of his swopping sides.

At the press conference to launch the series, Richard and Jan (who had starred in such series as *Just Good Friends* and *Stay Lucky*), never having met before, were thrust into a room on their own for half an hour – as Jan recalls, 'to see if we got on.' Meridian, who made the series, clearly thought that the combination of Mortimer, Wilson and Francis was a guarantee of success and Richard was paid a very high fee. However, *Under the Hammer* proved an uneasy mix of thriller, romance ('A slow burning romance between Wilson and Jan Francis, I will try to believe it,' wrote Nancy Banks-Smith in the *Guardian*) and documentary about the international art market.

In the same week as the first episode went out on ITV, the BBC started a new documentary series, *Auction*, set in an auction house. Brian Sewell, in the *Evening Standard*, criticised John Mortimer's script for having 'no intimate knowledge, no critical foundation, and scant real interest in the art market'; while of the auction house depicted in the series, he added, 'Mortimer constructs only a cardboard caricature, its staff and clients grotesque and unconvincing ... the intellectual level of *Under the Hammer* is that of a situation comedy, not the drama that it pretends to be ... Far better drama is seen in *The Bill* and *Casualty*, far better humour in *One Foot in the Grave*, and far better caricature in *Keeping Up Appearances*.'

Viewers agreed with Sewell's judgement and switched off in droves, with 3 million viewers tuning in to the last episode, 2 million fewer than the previous week. Not surprisingly, plans for a second series were dropped.

That Victor Meldrew's 18.5 million viewers failed to follow Richard in the new series was articulated by John Naughton in the *Observer*: 'Now, with the possible exception of David Jason, Richard Wilson is the most "bankable" star in television ... all of which must be very gratifying for him, but carries with it the risk of type-casting. The Meldrew persona is a powerful one which will be hard to escape ... a terrible future beckons in which, like John Thaw, he is locked forever into the fictional stereotype which he has created.'

Although it was considered by ITV a prestigious production there was neither time nor money, says Jan Francis, for adequate rehearsal. 'Hopefully you met the actor with whom you were doing a scene in the make-up caravan and so could go over your lines, otherwise it was straight in front of the camera.' The great treat to which Richard and Jan looked forward was a trip to New York, though only for three days, to make one episode. They were both very excited until they arrived at their hotel, a huge blank edifice with a lot of dirty windows. They had been told they had two pent-house suites, which turned out to be horrendous. It being August and a heatwave, the air-conditioning had been switched on, but pumping out water as well as air, so that the carpet in Richard's suite was completely sodden and he had to squelch his way around. 'It was the worst hotel either of us had ever been in,' recalls Jan, whilst Richard adds, 'It was appalling, we managed to cope because we were working so hard, but all fantasizes of *Breakfast at Tiffany's* were swiftly dispelled!'

They also quickly learned the difference between American and British film crews. As Richard and Jan waited on Fifth Avenue to do a shot, scores of young assistants suddenly bounded forward, wearing baseball caps and carrying loudhailers, to position themselves around the area, bellowing through the loudhailer, 'OK! We're making movies here! Everyone shut up!' The traffic and noise ground to a halt while Richard and Jan began their scene with everyone on the sidewalks watching. They also discovered that because New York is used so frequently as a film location, there is even a special police department for film making, with cops on full-time duty to redirect traffic or remove unwanted pedestrians. But once again rehearsal time was insufficient: straight in front of the cameras and then back to London to start the next episode.

Three weeks later Richard and Jan were in Russia for five days, staying in another Kafka-esque hotel, the Osmos in Moscow, a slab of concrete resembling a fifth-rate airport, and with a staff who had no idea of service. For Richard and the other male members of the cast and crew there was an additional hazard: to use the hotel halls was to invite persistent overtures from micro-skirted prostitutes competing forcefully for custom and who, in the small hours, often outnumbered the men by two to one. Richard, who was very low and tired at this point, was afraid of expressing his anger lest there be headlines: 'Grumpy Meldrew Does It Again In Moscow'. He found the noise tiring, and the film schedule particularly punishing. He was also deeply disturbed by the evidence of so much poverty and found it extraordinary to see people walking about the streets selling even the clothes they were wearing. Jan, having been warned in advance, had packed her bags with toilet rolls, plugs for the bath, teabags, biscuits, and an electric kettle. One night, having missed supper because of working late, Jan found herself hurrying along the corridor of the hotel, carrying cups of instant soup which she had made for Richard 'who looked really ill'.

Ironically their characters were supposed to be in the most luxurious hotel in Moscow (where only foreigners can afford to stay). Although allowed to shoot certain scenes there, the filming took longer than planned and they were thrown out, even though they had not finished.

'It was then about eight o'clock in the evening, and we had already been going since seven o'clock that morning. Finally we had to shoot the remaining scenes outside on the pavement rather than inside the hotel.' By ten o'clock Richard and Jan were famished and protested that they must have something to eat. About half an hour later they were each presented with a Big Mac from

Moscow's McDonalds! There they stood, outside this grand hotel, munching their Big Macs, with their noses pressed up against the windows, watching all the wealthy guests sweep in through the revolving doors and up the marble staircase. It was the time of the film of John le Carré's *The Russia House*. 'I don't think Michelle Pfeiffer and Sean Connery would be doing this, do you?' said Jan to Richard.

On the Sunday they were shooting a scene in a graveyard, where Jan to her excitement found Chekhov's grave, when they were told that lunch had been laid on at a restaurant, paid for in advance, as a special treat for the actors and crew. But on arrival they found that the restaurant had been shut down, its owners having decamped to Armenia with the money. Another restaurateur was found who agreed to open up his place and serve a meal, the price being agreed in advance. After the meal the actors and crew departed to set up the next scene, leaving the location manager to settle the bill. Suddenly four men appeared with guns, and he was told to double the amount on the bill. He had no option but to pay up. As Jan remarks, 'We were all aware of the violence around us. Nobody knows whom to trust anymore.'

Although Jan and Richard got on socially and shared a similar sense of humour, the lack of adequate rehearsal troubled her. 'I felt that Richard and I needed longer to establish our relationship within the story, but we never really had a chance. It had all been written and put together in a hurry; and it was being shot in a hurry. Richard and I needed time to make those characters fit us.' The situation was not helped by John Mortimer's reluctance to rewrite; nor was he with them in America or Russia. Jan even asked Richard to help her, saying, 'I don't know how to play this.' But he replied, 'I can't. I've got to keep the two roles separate. Because if I once start thinking about directing it is going to confuse me, and then I would want to change so much.' There were times, says Jan, when she could see he was itching to change things, and sometimes he would say, 'Oh, if only ...' but he would never take it any further. He knew, and knows, that if ever he were to cross that boundary he would not be able to stop himself. He is meticulous for his own sake and for everybody else's about keeping the two roles of acting and directing separate. None the less, having watched his direction of the earlier *Under the Hammer* by Stephen Fagan it is apparent to me how vastly superior the Mortimer series would have been had Richard directed it.

Richard admits to coming out of the series feeling like a zombie. 'The difficulty now,' he says, 'is that the whole trend for independent television companies is to get things done quickly. I did go into it knowing what the schedule was going to be, but I know now that doing two episodes back to back, for example, is absolutely exhausting. To do good work one needs more time, and on that series there was very little. Now that I know what it costs in energy I can begin to make more demands.'

Part of Richard's tiredness stemmed from the realisation that he had taken on too many things for 1994. He directed a new play, Simon Burke's *The Lodger*, at the Royal Exchange in Manchester, which then transferred to the Hampstead Theatre; he was filming more episodes of *One Foot in the Grave*; rehearsing for a new play in the West End; moving to a new flat in Hampstead; as well as being committed to making a travel film for the BBC in Australia, and another in Kenya for Comic Relief. As Jan says, 'It was a difficult time for him because suddenly he was being offered everything and it was very difficult for him to turn anything down. He admitted to me on a couple of occasions that he had taken on too much by having booked himself so far in advance.'

Not surprisingly many of his friends began to express concern about his increasingly pressurised life. 'I think he has always found it difficult to say no,' observes Maggie Ollerenshaw. 'Considering his status and reputation I find it quite extraordinary that he's almost never said no. Lots of times he is tired, going from one job to the next, and I say to him, "Why don't you say no?" I suppose it is the old actor's fear that it may suddenly all dry up. I think it's a pity he doesn't do more teaching, he's such an inspirational teacher, rather than all these public appearances. I think he has always put his career first. I remember his saying to me once, "I mean, what is more important than work?" And, of course, if you live alone, then all your energy can go into your work.'

Early in 1994 Richard was invited to play the title role in Peter Luke's play *Hadrian VII*, based upon the novel by Frederick Rolfe, alias Baron Corvo; an extraordinary study of a psychotic who dreams that he becomes Pope. It was a role which brought Alec McCowen to stardom in the original production thirty years before, and one which Richard would have played with a devastating acerbity, wit and vulnerability, revealing new layers of himself as an actor. At a luncheon with Patrick Garland, then artistic director of the Festival Theatre, Chichester (where the production was to be mounted), and myself, Richard remarked, 'It is a wonderful role. And so funny!' He and I planned to go to the Vatican to research the background to the play if he finally decided to do it. Then, quite suddenly, he announced that instead he was going to do a new play by Michael Palin, *The Weekend*, playing a role which broke no fresh ground for him as an actor. As Patrick Garland remarked recently, 'One of the saddest blows of my last year at Chichester was to see Richard Wilson's *Hadrian VII* go to ground.'

David Pugh, the producer, was initially hesitant about sending the Palin play to Richard, knowing that the central role was very much a Victor Meldrew type, and that repeatedly in interviews Richard had been reported as saying, 'Anything that is similar to Victor Meldrew I reject.' So what made him change his mind? Was he tempted by the thought of being in the West End, which he'd never been, and being the star of the show? Did he think it a better career move than going to Chichester?

At his first meeting with David Pugh and his partner Billy Russo, Michael Palin and Jeremy Conway, Richard suddenly announced that he did have what might be a deal breaker, one which was in no way negotiable – he would not do matinées, feeling that to carry the main burden of a play which rested on him, for eight performances a week, was too much. 'To ask anyone to play Hamlet twice a day is an insult of the highest order. I'm not comparing Palin's play to Hamlet but I refused, not because I'm lazy, but because I want the work to be good.' Yet in 1995 Ralph Fiennes thought nothing of playing Hamlet for seven performances a week, which meant a matinée on Saturdays, in the huge packed auditorium of the Hackney Empire, and then went on to give eight performances a week on Broadway.

The demands of a role such as Stephen Febble are in no way comparable to Hamlet, or a role such as that of Willy Loman in *Death of a Salesman*. There is no doubt that Richard's decision has created an uncomfortable precedent in the theatre. Previous to this Elaine Page had refused to do matinées of *Piaf* but that is more understandable in a singer. When I directed John Gielgud in Hugh Whitemore's *The Best of Friends*, our producer, Michael Redington, proposed that Sir John need not play Mondays, so that the production ran from Tuesdays to Saturdays, with a matinée on the Saturday. Given Sir John's age, he was then eighty-three, and that he had been away from the stage for ten years, these were exceptional circumstances; but for a younger actor to refuse to do matinées of a lightweight play is more questionable.

As David Pugh observed, 'Richard has a large following of elderly people, many of whom don't like coming into the West End at night, and so they were deprived of the pleasure of seeing him. Also, as theatre owners heard that we had agreed to only six performances, a week, some of them were saying that we were being irresponsible, that we were creating a precedent, and we were none too sure that we were even going to get a West End theatre.' From the start, however, Richard had asked to do a Sunday matinée, an idea which was not pursued by the management.

Richard is also set against long runs and refuses to do more than three months; yet for a management to break even, let alone show a profit, a star needs to stay with a show for six months. Richard once had a fierce row with the late Robert Stephens about long runs, saying how dangerous he thought they were. Stephens shouted at him how pathetic he was, saying, 'I used to do three years in a run and never thought anything about it. Wonderful! That's our job! That's what we're supposed to do!'

Part of the difficulty lies in a new generation of actors who have not had the grounding and experience that so many once had in weekly or fortnightly repertory, as well as performing in large theatres. There is a whole generation now of actors whose work has been primarily, if not solely, in small fringe theatres or in television. As Adrian Noble, artistic director of the Royal Shakespeare Company, recently observed, 'Most actors are trained as television actors, where the work is, and they lack the ability to dominate a packed auditorium by sheer will. That's the magic. I despair at the quality of actors arriving at the RSC from repertory,' while Cicely Berry, who has taught voice at the RSC since 1970, and trained most of Britain's recent stars, agrees, blaming the decline on stage education standards in drama schools.

Richard had to admit that he had never played as big a role as this, and also that he was not used to playing in front of full houses. 'When you find yourself faced with an enormous space like the Strand Theatre (where *The Weekend* played), filled with people, there is a colossal sense of expectation there and you feel you have to give a great big performance. The bigger the audience the more points of view you have to cover, which is why I prefer playing to smaller houses.'

From the start Richard wanted to be involved with the casting and the management was very happy for him to do this. 'There were certain people he wouldn't have,' recalls David Pugh. 'He really does have his strong likes and dislikes. And so some actors got short shrift.'

For the tour, which was sold out, Richard had been promised a chauffeured car. 'Then, when we were in rehearsal, he suddenly wanted to know where his driver was. And we said, "Yes, yes, of course you can have a driver." No, no, he replied, I want to meet the driver. It was rather like auditioning an actor. Once he had met the driver and OK'd him, he was happy.'

When the production was at Crawley, David Pugh suggested that Richard should travel by train because of the traffic crossing London, but Richard said, 'No, no, I'll use the driver, so that I can do some work in the back on my way to the theatre [he was by now directing the Simon Burke play at the Hampstead Theatre] and then on the return journey I can sleep.'

David Pugh takes up the story. 'On the second night in Crawley he gets stuck in a traffic jam, as I had feared. Michael Medwin, who was understudying him, was in a state of shock at having to go on, not having had time to learn the whole part, as he was already playing another role in the production. The "half" had already gone and still there was no sign of Richard, and Michael was struggling into Richard's costume.'

In the meantime Richard, from the car, telephoned the stage door on his mobile phone to find that at Crawley there is no stage door number, only the administration office which was by then closed, and the box office. He rang the box office but all he got was a recorded message saying, 'Tonight's performance of Michael Palin's *The Weekend*, starring Richard Wilson, is sold out [it was, in fact, sold out for the entire week]. If you would like to leave a message, please do so after the bleep.' So Richard left a message, saying, 'This is Richard Wilson speaking, and I'm stuck in a bloody traffic jam and won't be there!' In the end he managed to arrive a few minutes before the curtain was due to rise.

Because it was the first time Richard had starred in the West End he was, says Billy Russo, 'very concerned as to the right way of dealing with this, from tipping the stage doorman to all the other responsibilities of a leading man. He hadn't expected the No. 1 dressing room at the Strand Theatre but when he got it enjoyed it enormously, holding court there each evening after the performance. He insisted on having his fridge moved three times. The first wasn't right because it wasn't big enough to contain those odd shaped bottles of pink champagne which he insists on having for entertaining; we brought in another which he said was too noisy and sounded like an airport, so then we got him a quieter one.'

Outside the Strand Theatre was a huge poster showing the scowling face of Victor Meldrew. As Charles Spencer wrote in the *Daily Telegraph*, 'The size of his fame can be gauged by the size of his picture which adorns the façade of the Strand Theatre. It is almost obscenely huge, his livid and disapproving face blown up to a height of some twenty feet. Not bad for a man belatedly making his West End debut, though Wilson had the grace to look faintly embarrassed about it. "It's a bit of a shock," he admitted, "though I expect my sister will like it when she comes down to see the show."'

After the first night on 4 May there was a grand party at the Waldorf Hotel next door with hundreds of people circling and Richard caught in a spotlight as he entered. The following day proved, however, a rude awakening. In the *Evening Standard* Nicholas de Jongh wrote, 'If there were awards for theatrical heroism Richard Wilson would today be wearing a DSO for heroism beyond the call of duty. The citation would record how he, protected only by his comic reputation, gallantly rode out, risking critics' gunfire, to try to save a boring little comedy which could never have survived without him. It would also commend his valour in giving his comic all to such a losing cause. But in harsh reality not even Richard Wilson can save Michael Palin's play from death in the field.

'Mr Wilson is one of those rare actors who suddenly achieve extreme fame because they take a role which catches the mood of the time, a disgruntled old codger who cannot believe the world has sunk so low and bad, captures today's bad spirit. And Palin has provided Mr Wilson with a role capitalising upon this actor's unrivalled capacity for complaint. Here he is, Stephen Febble, a cantankerous grumbler, forever outraged ... Stephen has only one voice – the long-distance moan of the disappointed. In the confessional finale we gather he is a failed salesman. He rages for a wasted life. Here he practises his line in lofty, vituperative sarcasm. No one else can manage that pouting snarl, that brand of prickly pompousness, head craned forward like a resentful tortoise. What a comic actor and how wasted here.'

Benedict Nightingale in *The Times* described *The Weekend* as often looking and sounding 'like the first stage play it reportedly is. It lacks economy, tension, momentum, control of mood, sureness of tone.' All the other critics followed suit, while even the usually sympathetic Tom Aitken in *The Tablet* was forced to acknowledge that '*The Weekend* is a broken-backed, unintegrated, rather shallow piece. The script appears to have been improvised from sitcom leftovers.'

In the face of such a battering from the critics it was Richard who, as leading man, held the company together. 'It was a tribute to him,' says David Pugh, 'that the mood in the company never changed one iota. On tour, houses had been packed and then, suddenly, in London, after the reviews, they were half full, but the mood never changed; it remained good fun.'

Almost every night Richard made a round of the dressing rooms, not waiting to be visited in his, as some stars would, climbing to the top and then working his way down to say hello to everyone. Billy Russo also remembers sitting with Richard and David Pugh, in Richard's dressing room, before the second performance, when suddenly Michael Palin walked in. Turning to David Pugh, Richard said, 'I thought you said you were getting me a real writer! I don't want to work with him any more. Can't you get me another, one that has won an award?!' Billy bubbles with laughter as he recalls this moment. 'It was wonderful the way Richard took the piss out of the situation, and you could see it was such a relief for Michael, because up to that point everyone had been tiptoeing around the subject of the reviews, or clapping him on the back, pretending everything was OK. Richard, by making a joke, helped to defuse the embarrassment.'

Richard was also tireless in doing press interviews, even the very early morning ones. Pebble Mill was the only one he vehemently refused. 'I'd never seen him lose his temper before,' remarks Billy Russo, 'and when he loses his temper all humour goes. When he gets angry, then step out of the way! Apparently he'd done Pebble Mill once before and had a very bad experience and swore he would never do another. He was absolutely adamant about not going. He changes suddenly, just like that, and you don't necessarily know whether he is being angry or whether he is just doing a Victor Meldrew on you.'

Three weeks after *The Weekend*, Richard had another first night – his production of Simon Burke's play *The Lodger* – at the Hampstead Theatre. The play had won the Mobil Playwriting Competition in the previous year and Richard, as one of the judges, says, '*The Lodger* was the last I read. It was certainly the most assured. Simon Burke has a very strong sense of dialogue and it resonates in terms of getting these characters, at the lower depths of society, with simple dialogue, to become very rich.' It is indeed a play of astonishing vigour in the writing, exploring the loneliness and also the lovelessness of urban lives today, especially of those on its fringes.

In the honours list that summer Richard was awarded the OBE along with honours to Sir Alec Guinness, Diana Rigg, Angela Lansbury and Simon Rattle. Earlier, Richard had taken David Pugh and Billy Russo to a meal at the Ivy restaurant, to ask them whether they thought he should accept it. 'We were sworn to secrecy,' remembers David Pugh. Richard then arranged a special drinks party to which he invited the casts of *The Weekend* and *The Lodger* on stage at the Strand Theatre after the show. Just after midnight on 1 June he got up on a chair and made an announcement that he had been awarded the OBE for his services as an actor and as a director. He wanted people to hear it direct from him, he said, rather than discover it on their own on the radio or in the newspapers the next day. It seems a curious gesture to announce publicly one's own honours, though Billy Russo suggests that one of the reasons Richard wanted to tell people himself 'is that he was still in two minds about accepting it', whilst David Pugh adds, 'I wonder whether the underlying thing here is that he is always concerned to protect his privacy and he worried therefore whether by accepting an honour he would in any way have that privacy encroached upon.'

Curiously, also, after the award, Richard launched into an attack upon the Queen, saying, 'I'm not a Royalist. I don't see why the Queen needs five large houses. I'm not sure the Royal Family is an institution I support. There are too many people who are not doing their job, or justifying their insulated positions.' Like the writer, P.D. James, he would like to see a more modest, scaled down royalty, supporting the monarch of the day, but getting rid of all the palaces and ceremonials, and in this way losing all the troublesome hangers-on.

It was during the run of *The Weekend* that Richard, having sold

Tudor Close, moved up the hill to Hampstead, to a handsome new flat, with a garage for his car. Opening off his dining room-cum-kitchen is a terrace surrounded by terracotta pots filled with camellias, lavender, honeysuckle, and japonica, with banks of clipped box and cotoneaster, a topiary silver pear tree, and two ornamental maples. Gardeners come one day a week to tend the gardens for the whole house: each apartment having its own area, one flowing into another, like a series of small gardens within a larger, but without boundaries. It is all manicured and shaped like a public garden. Although he has not inherited his father's passion for gardening, Richard appreciates the well-kept order of a garden which echoes the immaculate tidiness of his home. One cannot help feeling that the garden, like the flat, is too controlled, too much a public image.

As John Collee observes, 'For someone who is so generous and expansive, he is obsessively neat. There's none of the untidiness of home, no books or papers lying around. It's more like living in a very smart hotel.' Yet this is also the essential Richard, reflecting his need to exercise control over every aspect of his life. His home is no longer the monastic cell of Tudor Close. Large paintings, brilliant in colour, bold in style, hang on the walls, while flowers in vases, toys on shelves, even a newspaper! reveal that he is at last relaxing into his home. As much as anything it is all a matter of having enough time. It is little wonder that his office remains the centre of his home, with pictures on his pinboard of his parents, a small African child, the horse that he and Dinah share.

With the closure of *The Weekend*, at the end of its specified three-month run, Richard went off to Australia to make a film for the BBC *Holiday* programme. The Palin play, which had been capitalised at £180,000, lost about £140,000. There were many reasons it didn't work, admits David Pugh. Mainly it was because of the savage reviews for the author, although Richard himself emerged with honour, but 'basically the play just didn't work and that was it'.

While in Australia Richard decided to visit John Collee who, after four years of writing a medical column for the *Observer*, had felt the need to get back to practical medicine and so, with his wife and small baby, had gone out for a year to work as a doctor in the Solomon Islands, one of the few places in the world that is almost unspoiled as an environment. During his stay Richard accompanied him on a medical trip to two of the outlying islands, Simbo and Ianongga. This turned out to be an endurance test, especially on the crossing between the two islands when they were continually swamped by high waves in the narrow channels. Collee was at the back of the small boat, where the water was deepest, busy bailing out, while Richard, whose main task was to stay as steady as he could, sat in the middle, lugubriously watching it all. 'It was,' he admits, 'a bit nasty for my liking – especially knowing there were only two lifebelts among five of us.'

When the doctor lands on one of these islands the people lay on what is for them a huge feast but for Richard, who loves good food, it was quite a shock when he was served with scraggy chicken and wet cabbage. 'The whole week was very tough for him,' says Collee, 'but he gritted his teeth and plodded on through the steaming jungle-like vegetation, and his natural dry humour saw him through it.'

Because it was raining almost all the time, and he could not explore, Richard sat in on Collee's surgeries, watching the patients, 'and then afterwards, at the end of each day, he would talk about how I had dealt with them, their body language and mine. For example, he observed how as the day wore on I became increasingly less sympathetic, having, earlier in the day, given endless time to people with small complaints. He also asked searching questions about what was wrong with individual patients, what was their diet and so on.'

Here one can see the observing and analytical eye of the actor and director at work, storing up information for future use. After a week of sitting in on these clinics Richard remarked one evening how glad he was he had given up medicine, that he wouldn't have the patience now for it. 'Of course, when Richard was practising medicine,' comments John Collee, 'he was working as a technician in a laboratory, whereas a doctor has much more variety in his work. The symptoms and ailments may be repetitive but each patient is different.'

'I think,' says Collee, 'that trip was memorable for Richard, partly because being wealthy is a kind of ghetto and you can easily find yourself cut off from real life. On those islands he was up against the elements and the stark simplicities of life which is something none of us should ever forget.' For Richard indeed it was, as he admits, a novelty to be tossed about in a fragile boat on heavy seas; to eat tuna fish by candlelight out of tins which Collee had brought with him for their improvised suppers; to lie on roll-up beds inside a mosquito net, talking for hours, in thatched huts made out of palm leaves, with the rain incessantly drumming down.

One of the things they talked about in those late hours was the question of Scottish roots. Collee, himself a Scot, suggests that 'there is a peculiar Scottish guilt in being attracted towards the upwardly mobile and successful English way of life. The Scots come to England to prove themselves equal to the English. But although Richard has outgrown his roots, like so many of us, his family and his friends continue to treat him as the Iain he was then, and do not make enough allowance for the Richard he has become. We talked about that a lot.'

Towards the end of that year Richard and I had dinner in Hampstead. Once again he had been asked to do *Hadrian VII* at Chichester, this time by Duncan Weldon who had succeeded Patrick Garland. At the same time he had been invited to play Dr Rank (the part created by Ralph Richardson) in a revival of Joe Orton's *What the Butler Saw* at the National Theatre, to be directed by Phyllida Lloyd. He asked me what I thought, since we had talked several times of his doing Hadrian. It was clear, however, that he felt honoured by being asked to play at the National. Like his OBE it was all part of an onward and upward curve. As Alan Rickman remarked to me, 'I hadn't realised how important a label in the sky it was for Richard that he was going to play a lead at the National. I just thought: well, that's a nice part, he'll enjoy that; rather than – oh, Richard's at the National, playing a lead! In this there is a kind of innocence about him.'

My response to Richard was to urge him to accept the National's offer as it was clear this was the direction in which he wanted to go. It would be, to use a frequent expression of his, *prestigious*.

Richard ended the year by flying to the borders of Northern Uganda and the Sudan to make a film for Comic Relief, appearing on behalf of the refugees fleeing from the Sudan. With several days' growth of beard, tired and shaken by what he saw, wearing shorts, a T-shirt, and a baseball cap turned backwards, he spoke into the camera words that clearly had not been scripted for him: 'These people have just got the wrong end of the lottery of life. They've left everything they own just to try and stay alive. These refugee camps are their last chance to do that. Comic Relief provides at the least the very basics of life. I'm not going to say "I don't believe it", but there are some things that are hard to believe. It's hard to believe that these people are left here with so little. It's hard to believe their lives will ever be right again. But there's something else that's hard to believe: clean water, shelter and medicine are needed if these refugees are to stay out of the headlines.' Then, as the camera panned around the camp, he continued, 'Thousands and thousands of Sudanese have made this journey and for many of the children and elderly it was too much. These are the survivors. Please remember that more and more are arriving every day. Most of the children suffer from malnutrition.'

At this point the camera moved in on Richard holding in his arms a tiny black baby, its face covered with flies. 'This is probably one of the first babies born in this camp. There are 125,000 refugees here and there are not enough bore holes for clean water, so that they are drinking water from the latrines. Many thousands from Rwanda have died of cholera. More bore holes are urgently needed. These people have the determination to rebuild their lives out of nothing. It costs only £2 for a blanket, 75 pence for a bucket. These things are cheap and you can give them.'

It was a scene that many an actor would have sentimentalised, with tears in his eyes, but Richard was speaking with *gravitas*, from his own centre, a world away from the showbiz jocularity of Billy Connolly in the same programme.

Disturbingly, just over a year later, in January 1996, reports from Zaire are of a population explosion in the Rwandan refugee camps, with more and more overcrowding, increasing incidents of violence, rape and abortions, with newborn babies thrown into the cesspits. The millions of refugees are entirely dependent upon aid, costing the international community $1m. a day.

Before Richard flew off to the Sudan he was already very tired and I urged him to take a proper holiday before starting rehearsals at the National in January 1995. He agreed and decided to spend Christmas in the Masai Mara after completing the film for Comic Relief.

After Christmas, Susie Figgis and her husband and small daughter were waiting in a tiny airport in Africa, 'when the doors opened and in walked Richard! He looked terribly grumpy, and didn't seem at all pleased to see us. We found out subsequently that he was suffering from a terrible infection. We said to him, "Come and join us for New Year," because we'd always spent New Year's Eve at his place for as long as we could remember. We said to him, "All you have to do is to take an internal flight, then you take a dhow and sail across to Lamu, the island where we are staying, and when you get to the beach just ask for the Mitchells' house, and we'll be there."'

They never thought that he would make it, but he turned up on New Year's Eve, loaded with bottles of wine. 'And he stayed for three days. Which is really a lovely story because, although he travels a lot, he is not really a brave traveller. I don't think he enjoys it. So there we were, on New Year's Eve, sitting on this balcony, wearing sarongs, eating shepherd's pie and drinking Richard's expensive wines! He spent hours playing on the sands with our small daughter. He loves children and seems so much more relaxed in their company. Amazingly, even on that remote island, someone came up to him on the beach and said, "Is it? Are you?"'

'If I think about Richard,' continues Susie, 'it is about the fronts of his social life, a very highly evolved social life, with very ritzy people in very ritzy places: the Christmas party that he throws in the most expensive suite at Claridges, or holidaying in a castle in Tuscany with other high fliers: other stars, script writers, directors, that kind of crowd. I think he finds that kind of world a secure place to be. If you're in that kind of world you don't have to look too deep. I'm sure that if we had telephoned beforehand and said, "Look, you're coming to Kenya, and we're going to be there on our own, for God's sake come and spend a week with us on Lamu," I bet you anything he wouldn't have come.'

Richard returned from Kenya for Joe Orton's *What the Butler Saw* at the National Theatre. The role of Dr Rank, the mad psychiatrist, did not extend him as an actor, and led the critic, Nicholas de Jongh, to reflect: 'Here is a man who would be stretched, challenged, and would interest us hugely, if he were to do a certain line of Shakespeare roles, beginning with Malvolio. Malvolio is a preposterous man, stuffed with vanity, with a dominant sense of insecurity, which he has to mask by putting on the swagger of the essentially little and unconfident man, "dressed in a little brief authority". And, of course, when we see the real Malvolio, it is as a man overwhelmed with the idea that some woman could be in love with him, and who responds with a rich sense of pompous absurdity. Richard would do this quite brilliantly.'

He was, in fact, offered the role of Malvolio by the Royal Shakespeare Company and turned it down on the grounds that he would be bored 'having to spend so much time in the dressing room between scenes'. When one thinks of the memorable performances by Olivier, at the height of his powers, in such small roles as Justice Shallow in *Henry IV* and the Button-moulder in *Peer Gynt*, it is even more puzzling that Richard should choose, for his West End debut, a play like Michael Palin's *The Weekend*.

Richard often refers to the experience of playing Vanya and Vladimir at the old Traverse Theatre in Edinburgh as the high water mark of his acting career. The mystery, and to many the sadness, is that he appears now to eschew all such roles. 'I think he is capable of taking on new challenges,' remarks Maggie Ollerenshaw, 'I just don't know if he will. I think actually he's quite insecure.' Susie Figgis agrees. 'My instinctive response is that he will stay safe as an actor. It would be very hard to stretch Richard as an actor. I think he's capable of it, but it would be hard, hard work for him, and hard work for his director.'

Deep down, there is a discrepancy between Richard as actor and as director. As Max Stafford-Clark observes, 'There's a bit of schizophrenia in him about the two roles. He has always been a comic actor with a wonderful sense of timing and presence. There's a kind of richness and fruitiness about him as an actor; he never misses a comic moment and he guards his laughs jealously. Whereas, as a director, he is very puritanical and probing, focusing on getting the actor to do the absolute minimum, and so you do wonder how, as a director, he would deal with himself as an actor.'

Richard's own response to all this is that he has always been a comic actor, from the moment when, at school, he found he could make people laugh and realised he had a special gift which marked him out from the other boys. 'I love comedy,' he says, 'because it is so satisfying. The laughter gives you a direct barometer of how you're doing with the audience, and that is a great sound. I don't have any special theory about comedy, other than that it must be believable. The fact that I'm offered a lot of comedy parts means simply that is what I'm best at. I also enjoy comedy because it's nice to be associated with something popular.'

Nicholas de Jongh questions Richard's commitment to bringing out the truth and authenticity when directing. 'Does this driving need to strip away and find the essence of truth, stem from the fact that in real life he finds that so difficult to do as an actor? How much does the real Richard Wilson hide behind the mask of comedy?' Susie Figgis, who often advises Richard on casting when he is directing, says, 'He is another person when he himself is directing; much more intelligent, and less closed off.'

Because he is not a protean actor like his friend Antony Sher, who is capable of re-creating himself with every role that he plays, and because he is so intensely private as an individual, it is indeed likely that Richard, as an actor, will continue to play safe, keeping to those roles which are best suited to his comic gifts, whilst being much more adventurous as a director. 'I would much rather direct a hard-hitting play about crack in Liverpool,' he says, 'than act in Shakespeare.'

The Return Journey

I have learned another lesson
When life's half done you must give quality
To the other half, else you lose both, lose all.
Select, select: make an anthology
Of what's been given you by bold casual time.
Revise, omit; keep what's significant.
Fill, fill deserted time. Oh there's no comfort
In the wastes of empty time. Provide for age.

Edwin Muir, *Soliloquy*

Although Richard's name above the title is no guarantee of success, as the fate of both *The Weekend* and *Under the Hammer* sharply reminded producers, none the less his career continues to ride high, so much so that close friends express concern at his increasingly pressured life. Being so immensely successful also means that he has less and less time to spend with them because there are so many more people wanting his time and attention. 'I think there comes a point,' remarks Dinah Stabb, 'when you think: am I just one more appointment for him to negotiate? No matter how much I'd like to discuss something with Richard, I'm always aware of that, and I think that's the only thing I worry about for him, that I would be one more worry.'

'His lover now is the public,' adds Susan Wooldridge, 'and he is the only person I know who fully embraces and honours that relationship.'

Antony Sher agrees. 'Leading, as he does, a solitary life, the love

215

that Richard receives from the public does substitute for the absence in his life of a permanent relationship which he has never known.'

But fame is ever fickle, none more so than that of a television star. 'It is the common lot of the TV personality,' writes Richard Ingrams in his biography of Malcolm Muggeridge, 'that if he fails to appear on screen for only a short time the public will forget him.' That was certainly the fate of Muggeridge whose 'vanity was such that he could not readily adjust to the new situation in which the world had begun to ignore him'.

The thought must often occur to Richard: is there life beyond the Grave? In contemplating his future he admits to a certain degree of paranoia. 'Victor is what I'm known for, and what I'm good at, because of David Renwick's writing, and it has given me my rise to fame. But it might never happen again. So I do worry about that to some extent and wonder what it will be like when all the excitement stops. Part of me would be quite pleased because life would be a bit more tranquil, but I would miss all the attention.'

Although there are times when the demands of fame crowd in too much upon him, as we have glimpsed during his Christmas in Kenya, Richard, who is not by nature introspective, does have a need always to be active. But behind the crowded diary there lies a profound restlessness. He is, as the author Monica Furlong once wrote of herself, 'a toe-tapper, a finger drummer, a watch glancer, a strider up and down of station platforms, a looker out of windows, a planner and list maker, a fanatically punctual person with the fear that if I stop chaos may come again'. As Dinah Stabb has observed, Richard likes everything to be done in an orderly fashion; 'he has an almost obsessive need to keep chaos at bay. Deep down I suspect he doesn't like himself.'

Part of Richard's relentless drive stems from the Presbyterian work ethic instilled into him by his father – as when Richard was tempted to give up medicine to become a travelling salesman, and his father wrote to him: 'My dear boy, maybe I'm old-fashioned but I still feel you're giving a service to the country in the job you are doing now which all the money in the world won't buy.' It is revealing that when Richard decided to go into medicine, part of his reason was that 'I might do some good.' The idea of service to others persists strongly, and explains why he does so much work for charities, for which he takes no fee. He is also very aware that he has been very lucky; others less so.

More than the Puritan work ethic, however, there is something else which explains his 'almost obsessive need to keep chaos at bay'. It is the wound that has never really healed, and which was inflicted on him as a youngster of thirteen, when he dared to reveal to his teacher, Mabel Irving, his secret ambition to be an actor, and was totally squashed by her response. In fairness to Miss Irving it must be said that there was no way that anyone, at that time, could have predicted that Richard would become not only an actor but a star. None the less, her remark deeply damaged his self-esteem, making him feel rejected, unwanted, and without talent.

When I started to write this book I commissioned the astrologer, Lee Donald, to draw up Richard's horoscope but without telling him who it was, giving instead a pseudonym, but the correct time and place of birth. Eventually there arrived an eighty-page document which I then put to one side and only read once the book was completed. I also lent it two of Richard's closest friends, inviting them to mark those passages which seemed to correspond with the Richard they know. Those passages are included at the end of the book. What is revealing, in the light of Dinah Stabb's comment above, is the following: 'Whatever your achievements, you may never believe you are good enough so you could drive yourself on and on in a relentless fashion ... you seem reluctant to reveal what is a complex inner self, even to your closest family. Feelings are easily hurt and engaged, so as protection you cover your vulnerability with secrecy.'

The degree and intensity of his subsequent ambition to succeed against the odds, and to prove himself, is perhaps best illustrated by the way he plays squash. John Michie, who is twenty-five years younger, is one of several friends who regularly partner Richard. 'Sometimes I beat him but, in general, even though I know I am a better player than he is, he nearly always wins. It's extraordinary because even now, when he's quite a bit older than when we started [they met in India when Michie had a small part in David Lean's film *Passage to India*], there is no question but that he beats me. It's because he lulls you into a false sense of security. You win an early game and you think: I'm just playing this old man, and *then*! This unbelievable concentration of energy and determination to win appears, and he just goes for it and beats you, and nothing can stop it.'

'It's clearly a way for him of releasing a great deal of suppressed energy, feeling and tension,' remarks Nicholas de Jongh who also plays squash with Richard at the RCA Club in London. 'And afterwards he loves swimming in the pool, it's a sort of cleansing process for him. He swims endlessly, as ardently as a goldfish around its bowl.'

Whatever the future holds, there will never be any shortage of work for Richard, whether as actor or as director. But now, in a wholly unexpected way, his life has taken on a new dimension, one which returns him to Scotland, and which could well have important and yet unseen consequences for him. In February 1996 he was elected Rector of Glasgow University, one of the oldest and largest in the country. In spite of, or perhaps because of, his celebrity status, he was not given an easy ride by the students during the election, and was keenly challenged as to his reasons for wanting to be Rector: was he simply standing as a celebrity? Did he intend to be a hands-on Rector; and how could he expect to carry out his responsibilities when he lived so far away?

The rectorship, which is honorary, is for three years and is a demanding position, which explains why the students were wary. In the university listings the Chancellor comes first, then the Rector, followed by the Principal. The Chancellor presides over the Senate which deals with all academic matters, and the Rector presides over the University Court, which deals with all matters relating to finance, administration, staff and buildings. The Rector is expected to chair eight meetings each year of the Court, and to be on campus at other times; whilst the paperwork relating to all the subcommittees, which the Rector has to read and report on to the Court, is in itself a formidable task.

Richard, however, is fully determined to honour his obligations. 'It is,' he acknowledges, 'quite a commitment to make, and in a sense it will change the work I do. It may mean I shall want to work more in Scotland so that I can be immediately on hand for the students. It could mean turning down certain jobs, and I may well have to fall back on after-dinner speeches.'

At his investiture as Rector on 24 April 1996, Richard emphasised in his speech his central belief that everyone should have the chance of further education and, with it, the possibilities that such education brings. More immediately he plans to fight for decent funding and to oppose any further erosion of student grants. He also proposes to question the closure of the Student Volunteer Service which was responsible for sending students out into schools in the community to work with backward children. 'This university, any university,' he declared in ringing tones, 'has a duty to serve not only the wider but the more immediate community.' It was this same belief which led him, as a student at RADA, to try and persuade John Fernald, the Principal, to send students out into the community. 'Universities,' he says, 'should be reaching out to kids who don't know about such places, encouraging them to want to go on for further education. A lot of youngsters never even get to smell that. They get kicked out of school not being able to read or write, which seems to me a terrible state of affairs. With so little work available, the more education you can get the better.'

If his views seem, at times, idealistic – perhaps fuelled by his own regret at not having been to university – he is realistic enough to acknowledge, 'Of course, I've got to find out how powerful I am, so clearly I am going to have to find my way.' But he does begin with considerable clout, simply by being who he is.

After the student elections Richard went alone one evening into one of the student bars, where a student offered to buy him a drink, saying, 'It's great to have a cult Rector!'

'Oh, God!' replied Richard, 'I didn't realise I was a cult.'

Increasingly, however, he will use that status, and the media attention that it ensures him, to effect change at a social and political level. He is deeply concerned about the degree of poverty, crime and drug-dependency in Glasgow, as he is about the state of education throughout the country. His ability to communicate at all levels and with people from varying backgrounds, coupled with his diplomatic skills and natural qualities as a leader, make him an ideal ambassador for greater social justice. It is almost as though his whole life has been moving towards such a responsibility. He is, as Monty Berman has written, 'a man of considerable integrity whose commitment is not only to his work but to the ideals of a more caring society'.

In reply to the students' questions as to why he wanted to be Rector, Richard said, 'because I want to give something back.' Richard is at an age when it is time to take stock: 'when life's half done you must give quality to the other half, else you lose both, lose all,' as the Scottish poet Edwin Muir wrote. At sixty, outward goals tend to recede in importance, while fame becomes relative. Richard no longer needs to prove himself to anyone. As he grows into an elder statesman his concern will always be with the young, especially those who are in any way disadvantaged, to listen to their needs, anxieties, and aspirations, so that he may use his influence to effect change.

Having achieved fame as an actor, far beyond the dreams of that boy in the hills above Greenock, he now hopes to make a worthwhile contribution to that city where he first learned to spread his wings, and to the country which nurtured him. He is returning to his roots and, like the speaker in Eliot's poem, *Little Gidding*, is about to arrive where he started and know the place for the first time'.

> If I could truly know that I do know
> This, and the foreshower of this show,
> Who is myself, for the plot and scene are mine,
> They say, and the world my sign,
> Man, earth and heaven, co-patterned so or so –
> If I could know.
>
> …

Make me to see and hear that I may know
This journey and the place towards which I go;
For a beginning and an end are mine
Surely, and have their sign
Which I and all in the earth and the heavens show.
Teach me to know.

Edwin Muir, *If I Could Know*

APPENDIX I

Extracts from a Horoscope by Lee Donald

Time of birth: 10.40 p.m.; 7 July 1936.
Place: Greenock
Name: Ian (aka Iain Carmichael Wilson)

This is a highly charged horoscope of great intensity. There is also a Stellium of four Planets and the Sun in Cancer. This emphasis in one sign indicates that you will be governed very largely by your emotional responses to everything that goes into making your life what it is. You will be actively involved in an ongoing search for greater meaning in life, approaching external affairs from a broad and philosophic point of view. From a subjective perspective you will be driven to question whether current attitudes are right, whether social morality has broken down, what has become of the principle of ethics, and whether there is any room for debate about religious orthodoxy.

There is an element of charismatic energy within, which you need to express in some way. You may, to all outward appearances, seem personally aggressive.

You will approach and understand life through your emotions. The profusion of differing feelings is sometimes almost overwhelming and so you build defences as a barrier to pain and hurt.

Normally your inner feelings are the ones to follow and so you should trust your hunches, not allowing your head to get in the way.

Perhaps the strongest characteristics are profound depth, seriousness and self-protectiveness throughout all your activities. You work hard, but you may not feel happy unless you are carrying some sort of burden. You have very strong survival and security needs and you somehow have to feel others rely to a great extent on your resources and sense of being the provider. Great energy goes into maintaining the safe haven, attachment to money and possessions.

You have to take great care that you do not let your feelings run out of control.

It is very difficult for others to understand you unless they realise and accept that you are chiefly motivated by deep yearnings and insecurities which you do experience some difficulty in identifying.

It is a sign which requires emotional security, a need to know that one's environment will support one's existence, that you will be nurtured by those around you. You will also want to nurture and nourish others by giving to them what you have already received.

Material possessions may become symbols of emotional security. You may even also surround yourself with things in order to derive from physical objects the emotional support you need.

You are extremely sensitive to the protocol which surrounds the manner in which you deal with unequal relationships. Much depends on how well you are able to conduct yourself when dealing with either superiors or inferiors in relation to fulfilment. You seem to prefer a strict and settled routine by which to live and work. Life without discipline would be almost impossible.

Above all else you want to be loved and to love. You will identify with the idea of being a loving and affectionate person. This is how you want to be seen, also to be recognised as someone who is amiable, popular and kind-hearted.

You are happy to give of yourself and to share what you have. There may be problems over identity and while you express a desire for recognition, you may fear putting yourself forward, but you do seem to need this kind of external reinforcement, but because you may not have been allowed to regard yourself as someone very special as a child you now tend to draw back from acknowledging this need to be seen. You want to be in a position of authority with responsibility so that others can recognise your worth in concrete terms. Whatever your achievements you may never believe you are good enough so you could drive yourself on and on in a relentless fashion.

By wanting to be recognised as someone special you run the danger of being unable to accept that which is ordinary about yourself.

You are able to stay close to everyone, yet at the same time remain distant, appearing quite disinterested in whatever you may be doing or talking about.

You seem reluctant to reveal what is a complex inner self, even to your closest family. Feelings are easily hurt and engaged, so as protection you cover your vulnerability with secrecy.

There is a suggestion of instability during your childhood. Perhaps you felt helpless and alone and even fearful, growing with an ever-increasing sense of insecurity which may still exist.

You are a sympathetic person who responds to others in broad, generous terms. But there may be a tendency to over-react, to make promises you will almost certainly find it impossible to keep, making wild gestures of generosity, simply because this is how you believe you should behave. The difficulty arises when you try so hard to be all things to all people, you manage to be very little help to anyone. There may be a distinct tendency to play 'God'. At best there is a strong feeling of a need to teach, even to preach, to instruct in your particular belief system [as in Richard's advocacy of minimalism, and his workshops].

I suspect you were aware quite early in your life that you had to become emotionally self-sufficient.

You will make every effort to behave in what is considered as socially acceptable a way as possible. You will develop a kind of conformity, being over-controlled, underplaying events or over-eager and flamboyant.

Your greatest need seems to be to find security and safety. Safe in the knowledge you are able to behave in the way you feel is appropriate. You need to feel secure enough to discover what you really do feel.

You will go to great lengths not to let anyone down. The danger arises when you take things too seriously, that you close up emotionally so that it becomes difficult to receive reciprocal emotional feedback.

There appears to be a need for space and freedom, particularly at the emotional and domestic level on a day to day basis. You certainly dislike being fenced in. You need to feel vibrant, believing that life could change at any time in the most exciting way. Restless and itchy for change.

There may have been some kind of shock or trauma as a child. You may have experienced some strong emotional amputation, like a sudden loss. Whatever the experience you will have learned something of the difficulties of emotional independence rather earlier than you should have.

I suspect you have spent a great deal of time trying to break away from the past and this may well have entailed rebelling against it in some way.

You can often change your mind a thousand times regarding any subject before you finally come to a decision [as before accepting *One Foot in the Grave*]. The heart rules the head over decisions and opinions and these are coloured by feeling and emotional attachment. You incline to remain subjective and so find it almost impossible to step outside your own needs in order to take an objective point of view. The larger canvases of life are not easy for you to comprehend and logical argument does not influence you to alter opinions or decisions.

Competition is exciting to you and you risk more verbally than in any other way.

You prefer your life to contain organisation. Regularity is something that you appreciate.

You are a good judge of people and it is likely you will gain through partnerships, business or older people.

Possibly a late starter! You are innately lonely and need a comforter of some kind to help overcome this. This in spite of being surrounded by family and friends.

Your Ego loves rising to the occasion.

Creativity is the cutting edge of your reason for living. When you create, you do more than simply express yourself. You plunge yourself totally into each creative event and so your 'Ego' becomes much more involved in creativity which makes you that much more vulnerable to failure. Fortunately rejection doesn't phase you for very long, returning to the fray as some new adventure or opportunity presents itself for your consideration. Use this creativity for self-renewal.

You appear a fierce competitor, yet an honourable adversary. There is something of the adolescent in your bravado, where challenges are personal and territorial. You love experimenting, for when you accept a risk, you are able to prove mastery and the validity of your life.

You dislike restraint of any kind and will proclaim that, 'This is what I am going to do and I don't care if you don't like it!'

The fields of Theatre, Medicine, Music, Literature are those where your talents can best be exploited to advantage.

Despite what others might think of you, you have a moral code to which you adhere no matter what. In other words, you will not deviate from your personal canon. This method of conduct has nothing to do with prudery; rather, it is your response to your private inner voice.

Your personal life may involve travel and you may also be involved with group activity. Your natural task is to work towards an operating network which connects people in a way which creates a whole.

You are seen as someone who is fortunate at the right moments.

It is possible you abandoned any formal religious belief some years ago, but the likelihood is that you will return to some structured belief system at some stage in your life. Saturn representing an inner image of the archetypal Father figure may suggest your Father did not represent what was considered to be the usual role model.

There is an underlying anxiety about being accepted and loved for who you really are and it is no comfort to you that there are many expressions of reassurance about your true worth and value. It is possible you will remain alone forever in the search for a perfect partner rather than compromise your ideals.

When someone tries to impose an ideology on you, you will react very strongly. You become perverse. You seem to have an innate fear of power.

While you may enjoy financial stability you will constantly fear sudden reversal of your fortunes. You were born at a time of great economic upheaval and change of every kind, and the probability is that you are coloured by the effects of that time.

Others may not be quite certain what to expect from you verbally. At the moment they have you in their sight, you will surprise them with some perverse twist in your style of delivery. Your speech pattern may be seen as a charmingly idiosyncratic affectation.

Inclined to obstinacy, but tenacious under pressure. You may suffer great inner tension, worrying over whether what you are trying to achieve is compatible with your basic aims.

Eccentric, individualistic, and excitable, you are capable of causing a stir wherever you go. Perhaps happiest when you keep others off balance, wondering what you will do next. There is an indication you like to shock ...

There is a quiet rebelliousness about your character and you promote a confidence that you are capable of going your own way. When there is disagreement with others you will unconcernedly travel your own path.

APPENDIX II

And Quietly Flows the Borishnolovoff

An Upper Slobvian Play in One Act with Subtitles

Draminski Personski

Dimitri	Smorsoska
Trinka	Smorsoska (his wife)
Linka	Smorsoska (his son)

The time is around 1925, just after the Slobvian Revolution. As the curtain opens Dimitri and Trinka are sitting in their humble cottage. It is evening. Trinka is knitting and Dimitri is reading the Financial Times. *Suddenly the door bursts open and Linka rushes in, obviously having run a great many miles.*

Enter Linka, gasping for breath, almost in a state of collapse.

Linka:	Matrouska …
SUBTITLE:	Mother …
Linka:	Matrouska …
SUBTITLE:	Mother …
Linka:	Matrouska …
SUBTITLE:	Mother …

At this stage the Subtitle carrier does not go back into the wings just in case another 'Mother' is to come.

Trinka:	(*Eventually looking up from her knitting*) Dra?
	(*Back to knitting*)
SUBTITLE:	Yes?
Linka:	(*still gasping for breath*) Matrouska …

228

SUBTITLE:	Mother …
Trinka:	Dra?
SUBTITLE:	Yes?
Linka:	Matrouska, niskolski broshno krina snotchicroff binos alska lobonoff nitch grallsnotbh. Borosk ni skolski scritchinok lotch aboka norilof kestricolokotch. Yada. Yada. Yada. Yadaka snorki bollifoffnok strobitch sholsko.
SUBTITLE:	They are after me.
Trinka:	*(Still knitting)* Oh, dra.
SUBTITLE:	Oh, yes.

The father has still not lifted his paper.

Linka:	Kisnotchka broffni yi scor?
SUBTITLE:	They are after me.

The Subtitle carrier realises his mistake and runs back for another board, which reads: What will I do?

Trinka:	Drobosno kitroch linka?
SUBTITLE:	What would you like to do?
Linka:	Matrouska, nisikolski … strobitch snolska … etc.
	As above, almost shouting.
SUBTITLE:	They are after me.
Trinka:	Sholoski mirnoff sholinska robrisnatch nitch golski braffolinka prolototch?
SUBTITLE:	Who?
Linka:	Tritch N.V.K.S.
SUBTITLE:	The N.V.K.S.
Trinka:	*(Still not concerned)* Oh.
SUBTITLE:	Oh.
Linka:	*(Shouting)* Tritch N.V.K.S.
SUBTITLE:	The N.V.K.S.

Trinka:	Oh, dra.
SUBTITLE:	Oh, yes *(The Subtitle bearer is now becoming distinctly exhausted)*
Linka:	Kisnotchka broffni yi scor?
SUBTITLE:	What will I do? *(Becoming hysterical)*

The Father is still impassive behind his paper and during the speeches the Mother continues knitting.

Pause. After which Linka shouts at the top of his voice ...

Linka:	Matrouska, niskolski ... etc. *(As before)*
SUBTITLE:	They are after me.
Trinka:	Polska?
SUBTITLE:	Why? *(The bearer yet more exhausted)*
Linka:	Kir ...
SUBTITLE:	I've ...

Long pause

Trinka:	Polska?
SUBTITLE:	Why?
Linka:	Kir ...
Trinka:	Dra?
SUBTITLE:	Yes?
Linka:	Kir snolski bornoff looksa rokatsa.
SUBTITLE:	I've been spying.

The Mother drops her knitting and stares at him. The Father's paper stiffens but he does not yet appear from behind it.

Trinka:	Looksa?
SUBTITLE:	Spying?
Linka:	Dra.
SUBTITLE:	Yes.
Trinka:	*(Louder)* Looksa?

Linka:	Dra.
SUBTITLE:	Yes. *(Subtitle bearer is now at a stage of collapse and is unable to keep up with the next part of the text and brings on subtitles such as:* They are after me. Who. Mother. No Smoking. Yes. Players Please. And – Gents.*)*
Trinka:	Youska?
Linka:	Dra Miska.
Trinka:	Looksa?
Linka:	Dra.
Trinka:	Bloodoska Hellski

The bearer has collapsed and the actors go to his aid, bring him round after babbbling in Upper Slobvian and the play continues ...

Trinka:	Kolski mogrov kit scornollitch na?
SUBTITLE:	Who ARE you spying for?

The Mother is extremely nervous as she awaits his answer and the Father's paper is quivering. Eventually after much stammering Linka answers:

Linka:	Uncloska Smalonska.
SUBTITLE:	Uncle Sam.

The Mother's face suddenly lights up and the Father jumps up with a shriek of joy. He is seen to be wearing an American Air Force cap, the Mother whips off the table cover and turns it round and it appears as the Stars and Stripes. The Father goes to some suitable spot and removes another Air Force cap and places it on his son's head, kisses him on both cheeks, and breaks into a long speech.

Dimitri:	Noskolska spirnoff ilska mootske by tatis nokiloff drosponshoff Ike, etc ... etc ...

The piano plays 'The Star Spangled Banner'.

	Loskinoroff spolska irnoff shilosko etc ... etc ...
SUBTITLE:	The End.

INDEX